D1190620

the insane chicago way

the insane chicago way

JOHN M. HAGEDORN

THE
DARING
PLAN BY
CHICAGO GANGS
TO CREATE
A SPANISH
MAFIA

THE UNIVERSITY OF CHICAGO PRESS

CHICAGO AND LONDON

John M. Hagedorn is professor of criminology, law, and justice at the University of Illinois at Chicago. He is the author of *People and Folks* and *A World of Gangs*, coeditor of *Female Gangs in America*, and editor of *Gangs in the Global City*.

The University of Chicago Press, Chicago 60637
The University of Chicago Press, Ltd., London
© 2015 by John M. Hagedorn
All rights reserved. Published 2015.
Printed in the United States of America

24 23 22 21 20 19 18 17 16 15   1 2 3 4 5

ISBN-13: 978-0-226-23293-5 (cloth)
ISBN-13: 978-0-226-23309-3 (e-book)
DOI: 10.7208/chicago/9780226233093.001.0001

Library of Congress Cataloging-in-Publication Data

Hagedorn, John, 1947– author.
    The in$ane Chicago way : the daring plan by Chicago gangs to create a Spanish mafia / John M. Hagedorn.
        pages cm
    Includes bibliographical references and index.
    ISBN 978-0-226-23293-5 (cloth : alkaline paper) — ISBN 978-0-226-23309-3 (ebook) 1. Hispanic American gangs—Illinois—Chicago—History—20th century. 2. Organized crime—Illinois—Chicago—History—20th century. I. Title. II. Title: Insane Chicago way.
    HV6439.U7C355 2015
    364.106'608968077311—dc23

2014047533

♾ This paper meets the requirements of ANSI/NISO Z39.48–1992 (Permanence of Paper).

Look over there: I'll tear away the cloud that curtains you . . .

Virgil, Aeneid

CONTENTS

ILLUSTRATIONS

PREFACE: THIS IS NOT A MOVIE

The following is slightly edited from the February 15, 1996, *Chicago Sun-Times*. It reports on seven people shot in less than three hours on Tuesday, February 13, and two more the next day. The shootings were not random violence, but coordinated attacks by Chicago's Maniac Latin Disciples (MLDs) and their allies, the "Maniac Family" against their rivals, the "Insane Family" of gangs. The hits were consciously modeled on the famous scene of multiple shootings at the end of the first *Godfather* movie and were in effect a preemptive strike. The Insane Family had scheduled a meeting for the very next day to plan their own coordinated assault on the Maniacs. These shootings marked the formal beginning of the 1990s "war of the families," which claimed hundreds of lives.[1]

- The first shooting was at 4:35 p.m. Tuesday (February 13) when Jose Munoz, 21, and Steven Wasilenski, 17, were shot by an assailant who walked up to them as they stood on the sidewalk in the 1800 block of N. Mozart Street. They were in fair condition at Illinois Masonic Medical Center Thursday.
- Twenty minutes later, at 4:57 p.m., Victor Sanchez, 16, was shot in the head, leg, and wrist as he left his home in the 2600 block of W. Evergreen Avenue. He remains in critical condition at Cook County Hospital.
- At 5 p.m. Tuesday, Theophil Encaldo, 18, was shot in the right thigh and right toe at 1545 W. LeMoyne St. by a passenger in a van who shouted a gang slogan and fired five times. Encaldo is in serious condition at St. Mary of Nazareth Hospital Center.
- At 6:11 p.m. Tuesday, Dawn Massas, 15, was shot in the back in her home in the 1400 block of N. Maplewood Avenue by two men on her front porch. She was treated and released from St. Mary of Nazareth Hospital. A 16-year-old boy was wounded in a shoulder that night at Cortez Street and Campbell Avenue.

- At 7:20 p.m. Tuesday, Jose Cartegena, 20, was shot in the neck at 2544 W. Cortez Street by two gunmen who shot from a gangway. He remains in serious condition at St. Mary of Nazareth Hospital.
- Just after 8 a.m. Wednesday (February 14), a 17-year-old youth was shot in an arm in the 1200 block of N. Rockwell Street, police said.
- 6 p.m. Wednesday. Eddie Ramos was an 18-year-old member of the Spanish Cobras. Grand Central Area Cmdr. Philip Cline said Ramos was sitting in his car at 2522 W. Shakespeare Ave. when a gunman approached and opened fire.

These shootings are part of a larger story of how gang warfare raged out of control in 1990s Chicago despite highly organized attempts by a secret coalition of Latino gangs to stop them. The "war of the families" began a chilling chain of events that explain why it has been so difficult to control gang violence in Chicago today. Most gang members are youths struggling for survival and identity, and given a chance can be productive members of society. At the same time, there have been covert efforts of a select group of power-hungry Chicago gang leaders to organize crime, regulate violence, and corrupt all-too-willing police and public officials. The hidden history of the rise and fall of the "Spanish mafia" calls into question some of the most strongly held beliefs about gangs by both social scientists and law enforcement.

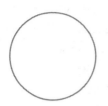

Introduction: Lifting the Veil

This is the story of a daring plan by Chicago gangs to create a Spanish mafia and why it failed. It is a story you have never heard before. The history of Spanish Growth and Development (SGD) is almost completely unknown to the public, the police, the professors, and even most gang members. It is basically a story about power, violence, and corruption.

As I learned about the history of SGD, I was forced to rethink much of what I had previously known about gangs. I was especially surprised to discover how Chicago gangs built complex, secret structures to regulate violence, organize crime, and buy off police and politicians. These multi-gang coalitions functioned like a mafia commission and are likely to have rough parallels in other cities. I decided to present what I learned as an institutional history, explaining why SGD was formed, how it functioned, and why it failed. I began writing this book determined to discover the reasons a ten-year-old SGD collapsed in a pool of blood on the steps of a 1999 "peace" conference.

I first learned about SGD in 2010 in remarkable way. I was at a meeting and a former student came up to me and told me of a man named Sal who could "tell you some things about gangs that will blow your mind." Now, I'd been doing gang research for almost thirty years. I doubted that anything some guy I'd never heard of could say was something I hadn't heard many times before. I was wrong.

I contacted him, doubts and all, and we arranged to meet at La Scarola, a popular restaurant on Grand Avenue in Chicago's storied mafia homeland called "The Patch." Sal got there first and had secured a window seat overlooking Grand Avenue. We sat beneath a wall of pictures, including the restaurant owners with Frank Sinatra and Johnny Depp. Sal looked like a stereotyped, if slightly overlarge Italian mobster. He was six feet tall, big-framed, and muscled, though age had begun to take its toll. He dressed plainly and not in the flashy style of what he would call "studio gangsters." He was about the same age as me—midsixties—and we exchanged stories, feeling each other out. He told me about the attempt of a set of Latino gangs to organize crime in Chicago and stop the violence. "Back then they were the most organized criminal gang in the country" he told me, with a hint of pride.

He explained how Spanish Growth and Development was formed by seventeen "Latin Folks" gangs in 1989 and was dedicated to curtailing violence and organizing the drug trade, as well as other illegal markets. As a soldier for the Outfit, Chicago's name for the mafia, Sal was a behind-the-scenes influence on one of the factions of SGD, the "Insane Family." He was the de facto "godfather" of the C-Note$, a gang which he called the Outfit's "minor league team," who were also members of SGD. I'll tell the story of the lives and deaths of the 1990s C-Note$ leaders concurrently with my main story of SGD's rise and fall.

Through his ties with the C-Note$ Sal had gathered official documents, including the SGD constitution, formal grievances of member gangs, minutes of meetings, and more. Sal proposed to do a book, and while he was convincing, I knew I needed to carefully check out what he told me. More to the point, I asked him: "Why do you want to do this? Isn't it sort of crazy? You might get killed." He laughed nervously. A verbatim transcript from our first recorded conversation follows:

SAL: *You're right about that. That's a chance that, you know, a risky chance that I'm taking by participating in something like this. Having been brought up the way that I've been brought up, uh, that you don't talk about what happens on the streets—what happens on the streets, you know. Uh, but the game has changed. The game has changed from when it started and when the rules were set down. And, uh, the geography has changed. The demographics has changed. Individuals that are involved in the game today are not holding up to the rules and laws of the street anymore. . . . And, you know, to me it's just, I don't know, it's just mind-boggling I guess at what has taken place over the last twenty, thirty years of . . .*

JMH: Well, what do you mean that it's changed? I've heard a lot of people talk about, "Well, it ain't like it used to be." But what do you mean by that?

SAL: *Well, it started out as turf gangs. You know, where you had the Irish on one side, the Italians on one side, Germans and the Puerto Ricans and the Mexicans and the blacks. And they basically fought, you know; you stay on your side of the street and we stay on our side of the street. And that was for years through the tumultuous sixties, through the seventies. But once the late seventies, early eighties came, uh, the game changed when narcotics were introduced at a high rate. And some of these organizations went from turf gangs and they evolved into more structured criminal enterprises.*

JMH: So is that the problem you have? I mean . . . you've been part of that as well.

SAL: *Yeah, and I have been a part of it. Uh, in more ways than one. I see people, you know, just turn in state's evidence for the most little . . . I mean, back in the day kids got caught for something like spray painting or assault and battery. You get caught, you sit and wait for an "I bond" [a no-cash bond] and then you're out, you know, in a few hours . . .*

But now these kids have no morals I guess. It's just the way I was brought up. You keep your mouth shut and that's the way it goes and you take your lumps and keep on going.

JMH: But you're not keeping your mouth shut. You're talking to me and to a recorder here. What makes you—

SAL: *You're right. You're right . . .*

JMH: So how does that make you any different from the rest of them?

SAL: *I don't know. I'm considered retired by now. I have a lot of my associates that are still heavily involved. I think I just want to tell the public there are people out there that are very naive. They don't have a clue about what is going on in the world today and who is really running things, whether it's inside the prison jail walls or outside in the community. And how entrenched organizations, or gangs, or clubs or whatever you wanna call them, are involved in the community. . . . And I guess I just wanted to let people know, you know, about the changes.*

Sal's motives to my mind were more complex than that. I think he really did want to "inform the public," and he was upset with all the naive misinformation out there on gangs. He thought the "rats" who tattled on the mafia and the first-person gang confessionals were simplistic, inaccurate, and poorly written. He could have produced a good exposé book or screenplay himself and made lots of money. But as a realist, Sal knew he needed to find someone more legitimate to tell this incredible tale—as well as to hide his identity.

Our interviews took place in hotels and public buildings where I could secure a private room. We had to be careful not to be seen together by anyone from the world of organized crime, gangs, the media, or law enforcement. Typically the interviews lasted two hours. I knew some of the Latin Folks figures Sal was talking about and many older gang leaders Sal did not know. I did not ask him for contact information on any of the still living gang chieftains he talked about, keeping his role completely confidential. Once Sal told me details about SGD, I independently interviewed several key Latin Folks leaders about it. While in the past they had never mentioned SGD to me at all, once I had knowledge of it they willingly discussed it. Sal is opinionated, and looked at SGD through the lens of the Outfit. But the rough outlines of what he described were corroborated by my own gang contacts.

To Sal, our interviews were not snitching. Sal was contemptuous of snitches and thought snitching was not only wrong but led to more violence as it sowed distrust within gangs. For Sal this tale is a lesson on how best to both organize crime and minimize violence. Sal's storyline is a familiar one of reason versus passion, with "reason" meaning the instrumental logic of organized crime. This is a theme that I will come back to, and understanding its importance has changed the way I look at gangs.

For me, Sal's previously untold story makes a fascinating history but also is a cautionary tale for youth. For kids on the corner, gangs are not always what they seem to be. I show how hundreds of youthful gang members lost their lives because of hidden decisions by manipulative leaders they didn't even know. As Sal said, "The purpose of this book is not to recruit America's youth into a life of crime but to let them know you can't always judge a book by its cover."

SAL AND ME

Sal is self-educated, widely read, and loves life. His laugh is infectious and he is very personable. I can see him mixing with politicians one night and street gang members the next. He describes himself like this: "Throughout the years, many people have approached me for assistance in resolving issues that normally could not be addressed or simply were neglected by the police. I made sure all issues were dealt with and resolved one way or another. Everyone, even many police, know how far my reach could go." This is a familiar portrait for anyone brought up on Tony Soprano and Michael Corleone. But this story is not Hollywood make-believe nor some tawdry true-crime novel. Sal Martino is a real character and his story, as told to me, is about his frustrations over how Latino gangs tried and failed to regulate violence and organize crime in Chicago. Everything you read in these pages actually occurred, and the characters found here are the real actors, though some names had to be disguised. The book is an insider's history but does not always accurately relay who did which specific criminal or violent act. This work is not intended to be, nor is it suitable as, grounds for new prosecutions.

I got to know Sal and his life story well. However, since keeping his true identity confidential is a life-and-death matter, I've taken "undisclosed measures" to conceal it.[1] This has caused me considerable anxiety, as I need to balance his safety with telling his story. He and I agreed that I would not say anything about him except what is written in this book. Sal can be very eloquent—his extended quotes appear in italic text, and I sometimes blended his colorful phrases into mine.

Sal had what I consider a healthy disdain for the "professors" who thought they knew what was going on, but who he said were "full of it." It was probably our common character flaw, an oppositional defiant disorder, that cemented our relationship.

The reason I chose to cooperate with you was because some dumb-ass know-it-all copper named Sparks was bad-mouthing you claiming that you didn't know your ass from a hole in the ground when it came to Chicago gangs. So I figured with me on your side you will know a lot more than they do, and then next time you can really stick it to them and make them look like the dumb asses that they are. Remember knowledge is power. I'm pretty sure that by now you have learned a thing or two that you were not aware off before. For instance the SGD concept, which is huge.

Also, as I mentioned, I was familiar with your book People and Folks. *One of my guys' sons was in one of your classes at UIC and he told me about you, that you were cool, so I took his word for it. I think if I would have met you thirty years ago with the work we are about to accomplish they would have made you a distinguished professor right off the bat. "The John Hagedorn Professor of Criminal Justice."*

Maybe Sal and I got along because I never fit well into the "professor" role. I only began studying gangs after I encountered them as an activist years ago in Milwaukee. My first book, *People and Folks*, was published before I decided to study for a PhD and was a plea for jobs, not jails, applying William Julius Wilson's underclass theory. Not wanting to live on Justice Department grants that defined gang kids as criminals, I accepted a tenure-track position at the University of Illinois–Chicago in 1996.

I started teaching and did not intend to study Chicago, but I was quickly seduced by Chicago gangs' fascinating history. I heard firsthand from Bobby Gore the amazing story of his 1960s Conservative Vice Lords (CVL) when they attempted to shed the label "gang" and work for the community. I traveled to Brazil and South Africa, among other countries, putting Chicago's gangs and the CVL experience into a global perspective. I advanced up the academic ladder, but have never been comfortable at my university.

One of the main insights of my research was that gangs and gang members are not one thing. In other words, gang members, like all of us, have many different sides or identities. In my last book, *A World of Gangs*, I argued that the best way to work with gangs was to figure out how to undermine what I called "gangsta" values and strengthen procommunity ones. I compared Bobby Gore's CVL to an old Irish gang, the Hamburgs, whose members had included the first Mayor Daley. I argued that gangs today could also take a conventional path.[2] Then I met Sal.

His story, as you will see, shows that the struggle over values is more complex than I thought. What I learned is that there is a hidden story of gangs in Chicago, of their attempts at criminal organization that reflect the experience of the mafia and other organized crime groups. One goal of organized crime has always been to exercise power and eventually assimilate into conventional society—to become respectable—and that was also a goal of SGD's Latino gang leaders. This book describes the Latin Folks' bloody path to that goal, a contemporary manifestation of what Daniel Bell called "crime as an American way of life."[3]

CHALLENGES TO CONVENTIONAL PERSPECTIVES

This story emphatically departs from traditional perspectives on gangs, particularly from the Chicago school of sociology. At the onset, though, I want to caution the reader not to mechanically generalize or see in these pages some new "power" theory of gangs. My method, ever since my first book, has been to test what I've found in my research against the traditional ways gangs are looked at by the media, law enforcement, and social scientists. This book continues that inductive method, and what I've learned questions many of our most deeply held beliefs on gangs.[4] These lessons go well beyond Chicago, but I think how they are applied depends on a careful study of the history of gangs in each city.

First, the book dispels any idea that gangs are always "disorganized crime." As Sal says, he wanted "to make the world aware" of the existence of Spanish Growth and Development (SGD), Chicago's Latino successor to the Italian Outfit. This book represents his desire to give the public a "rude awakening." SGD's existence was a carefully kept secret, even to many gang members.

The leaders need to protect themselves from these kids. I mean, they're doing knucklehead stuff so I'm not gonna bring you into the top levels of the organization if I don't trust you. Trust has to be earned. Respect is earned, not given. So, as you prove yourself to me, as we grow into the organization and you're being referred to by some well-established individuals, then you start bringing these individuals in. A lot of them don't know anything about the concept—Spanish

Growth and Development. They never heard of this, a lot of them. Even some higher ranking people don't know this!

Chicago is undoubtedly unique and my tale may seem strange, even bizarre, to those familiar with gangs in other cities. The reader will learn that there have always been relationships between the Outfit (Chicago's mafia) and street gangs. Throughout the book, I'll relate the exploits of the C-Note$, who functioned as a liaison between the Outfit and the street gang world. While the attempt of Latino gangs in 1990s Chicago to organize crime and control violence failed, I suspect some form of these organizational dynamics occur elsewhere but remain uninvestigated. I need to remind the reader most gang kids have always been desperate youth, and most of their gangs are indeed "disorganized crime." But not all. This is a history of the puppeteers, not the puppets.

Second, while most research on gangs centers on neighborhood, this history is more about networks of power. Historically, I'll show how from the Irish Hamburgs to the Italian Outfit to the Gangster Disciples and Latin Kings, the will to power has been a prime motive force in Chicago gang evolution. I'll explain how Chicago's gangs since the 1960s have built impressive cross-neighborhood alliances that foreshadowed the even broader People and Folks coalitions and later SGD. I'll tell how 1960s black, white, and Latino gangs at first were organized on race, then by the end of the 1970s on profits through seizing control of drug markets from the Outfit. Throughout the book I'll show how organized crime—both its reality and its instrumental "business first" values—is a much more potent influence to gangs than I had imagined.[5]

Power manifests itself in the use of violence. Sal believed violence should be used only when necessary, for profit or power.

In the old days killing was a tool used to maintain power and control. If a person broke the rules it would be used as a form of discipline to maintain order. Taking somebody out to earn your stripes was not a prerequisite for membership in the Outfit.... Those who couldn't hack it simply got their jackets and went on their way, never to be heard from again. That's a concept the members of the SGD board failed to implement among their ranks.

In Sal's world, more organized crime meant less violence, and in my global studies I found considerable support for his views. As he said, there is so much money in the drug game—worldwide estimates range from roughly $300 million to $1 billion annually—why fight over corners?[6] For Sal and SGD, gangs were mainly about power and money, more than neighborhood.

A third challenge raised by this book explores the variable nature of gang violence. Our main story revolves around the 1990s, when murders in Chicago hit dizzying heights, twice the number of their highly publicized 2012 spike. Police, the press, and the public all saw the carnage as irrational and basically about turf, revenge, or drugs. Traditional researchers argue that violence can be explained by the characteristics of neighborhoods, but I will tell how the 1990s surge of violence on Chicago's North Side directly related to the maneuvering of Latino gang families for control of SGD's ruling board, called La Tabla.

The story of 1990s violence is mainly a story of organizational contests for power, not a lack or decline of "collective efficacy" in a neighborhood. The destructiveness of the 1990s war eventually undermined gang leaders' authority and they lost their capacity to either call hits or stop them. I situate the 1990 wars within international studies that find overall rates of violence related to desperation of unemployed young men, but the highest levels of violence are the result of formal gang warfare.[7]

A fourth challenge introduces the literature on organizations and institutions to the study of gangs. While gangs are often seen as disorganized and explained by "group processes," I tell the natural history of an institution, Spanish Growth and Development. SGD was formed directly out of the needs of gang leaders to keep themselves safe in prison. It took on a life of its own and developed into a formal bureaucratic organization with economic and political goals. I'll reprint excerpts from their constitution and many key documents, but I'll also explain how the lofty rhetoric of these documents was undermined by factional power plays and inertia in its prime task of mediating disputes.

To understand SGD, we will have to journey in a popular manner through theories of how institutions form and the reasons for their dissolution.[8] The inability of gang leaders to keep SGD from eroding and collapsing has helped to spawn unprecedented conditions in Chicago to-day. Rather than the controlled violence of hits called from prison cells in the 1990s, we have uncontrolled violence more responsive to rappers than gang leaders.[9]

Finally, for most gang research, police and the political order are treated only as instruments of social control.[10] I'll show how in Chicago, gangs and politicians are often more part of the problem than the solution. Chicago's political machine has always run on the oil of greasy palms, and today's gangs continue a long gang tradition of "the Chicago way." Sal will tell inside stories of how some of the most corrupt police officers in Chicago's history, including Joseph Miedzianowski and the infamous SOS unit, had ties to Latin Folks gangs, including Sal's beloved C-Note$. I'll argue that Latino gangs—more so than black gangs—are climbing a crooked ladder in politics and are the latest examples of the utility of crime in "ethnic succession." Sal says: "Spanish Growth and Development was an attempt to try to get everybody on the same page. To try to get power and become a part of the Machine."

My intention in discussing police and political corruption is to force this issue onto the gang research agenda. Too many studies of gangs treat the police and politicians as the "good guys" or just ignore their more complex role. While other researchers may want to dismiss my stories of corruption as if they could only happen in Chicago, I challenge them to investigate the police in their own cities, not just the gangs. They might be surprised.[11]

TRYING TO TELL A DIFFICULT STORY

My own work has always aimed at promoting "research, not stereotypes," painting portraits of gang members as human beings. This book compli-cates my mission but does not change it. On the one hand, to tell the public the story of how street gangs worked together to build a Spanish mafia is sure to give credence to right-wing and media demonization and stereo-types of gangs. On the other hand, Sal's evidence of widespread police corruption and how gangs work with Chicago's political machine will be no comfort to the law-and-order crowd. While SGD was organized crime, at the same time it represented gang leaders' desires for less violence and understandable aspirations for a conventional life. Gangs are more than one thing.

Weighing all this, I decided to write a natural history of SGD as an antidote to both liberal and conservative stereotyping. Studying the history of gangs, I discovered, sheds light on issues typically neglected in the mainly ahistorical accounts of gangs by police, media, and academics.

Research to me has always required building relationships, not relying on formal methodologies that require distancing of the researcher from those interviewed. Over the course of three years the twists and turns of my relationship with Sal produced the remarkable disclosures you will read in this book. For Sal, our relationship may have been mainly instrumental to his financial success and for him to gain some self-satisfaction. For me, I needed to be able to speak truths, even if they might endanger that relationship—in this case Sal's and my agreement to write this book. My solution was to balance my quest to understand Sal's perspective with periodic statements of my own values. This book is an uneasy mix of two perspectives.[12]

I interviewed Sal on and off for over two years and carefully confirmed what he was telling me. Documentation is always crucial. When I researched the drug business in Milwaukee many years ago the funder was so amazed at what I found he asked if I made the story up in my garage![13] What Sal was telling me was even more shocking: a level of organization of gangs that contradicted both the naive texts of the professors and the "good versus evil" fairy tales of the cops.

This kind of "data" meant that I had to eschew the traditional style of criminological writing and the format of my prior books. I decided not to write the book as a series of anecdotes, like Sanyika Shakur's *Monster* or the semifictionalized *My Bloody Life* by Reymundo Sanchez. It is not ethnography, like Sudhir Venkatesh's *Gang Leader for a Day* nor a tale of lower-level corner boys, like Felix Padilla's *The Gang as an American Enterprise*. It is not a gripping day-to-day depiction of street life like David Simon and Ed Burns's *The Corner*. But it does tell a story similar in some ways to the citywide Baltimore gang coalition fictionalized in *The Wire*.

I showed Sal a clip from *The Wire*, where Stringer convenes a "commission-like" gang meeting. Stringer extols to Prop Joe and the other gang leaders the benefits of a formal, citywide coalition over individual gangs and takes a vote on changing drug suppliers to get a better price. As the meeting ends, Stringer asks a youngster sitting in the corner what he is doing. The kid answers, "Robert's Rules say we have to have minutes of the meeting right? These are the minutes." Stringer stares and says incredulously: "You taking notes on a criminal fucking conspiracy?" Sal watched the clip and chuckled. "They did in Chicago," he said. I'll use some of those documents to demonstrate how SGD worked. Sal's and my stories, like *The Wire*, build to a violent crescendo where SGD loses control through factionalism, personal greed, and an almost unchecked culture of snitching.

In the *Aeneid*, Aphrodite "lifted the veil" from Aeneas so he could see that the bloody violence at Troy was being manipulated by the gods. This story intends to lift the veil on the 1990s spike in homicide among Latino gangs, but the gods in my tale are not impersonal economic forces or the structural violence of poverty. The gods behind the curtain are gang leaders ordering young men to kill and die for hidden motives of power and greed. These leaders who think themselves gods also rely on corrupt police and city officials who share responsibility for our current gang problem. While I reintroduce agency into the study of gangs, I also argue that policy needs to include a much stronger emphasis on police misconduct and official corruption.

To reiterate, this book is not meant to be a new theory of how to understand gangs. Rather it is a story that by its very telling is meant to encourage others to ask new questions and to look at familiar forms in different ways.

part
one

1 The Hit

January 27, 1995

Joey Bags didn't like giving me bad news. He seemed nervous as he walked into the Aberdeen Club. This was my favorite joint in "Little Italy" and I hung out there with my crew. I sat at my regular table by the window listening to the trains rumbling a block away. I was killing time, staring out at Hubbard Street hoping some pretty gal would walk by.

I liked Joey but wondered if he was ready for bigger and better things. I was always on the lookout for C-Note$ who might move up to be a made guy or an associate. Joey had what it took, though as a Puerto Rican, he could never be one of us. His Spanish background, I had realized long ago, made him useful in dealing with the Latino gangs, but I questioned his temperament.

Joey was a leader of the C-Note$, which had been around since I was a kid. If you were associated with them all sorts of people looked up to you, and the kids in the neighborhood envied you. Joey was tall for a Hispanic, say six foot, and slender. He said his dad was a founder of the Spanish Lords, a nearby gang, who had died in his early forties from liver disease.

Joey was a man of his word, though he had both a woman and a drinking problem. I always said he brushed his teeth every morning with Miller Lite. His girlfriends brought him and the Note$ nothin' but trouble. On the streets he flaunted his connections to us and got respect from his soldiers. He was street smart and had a temper, but then again so did I. For me the bottom line was he was a good earner.

On this day he told me about a hit. So, no big deal, these things happen all the time and are part of the business. But this one was on a member of the Maniac Latin Disciples, one of the crazier gangs out there and one of the richest.

Joey said this guy Robert Detres, a MLD soldier, was walking down an alley last night on Maplewood. A punk, who Joey knew to be a Latin Lover but also a snitch—"Baby Face" Nelson Padilla—jumped out from behind a garage and popped Detres in the head. It was payback for a MLD killing of a Lover last year.

Joey was afraid that this time things were going to get out of control. I felt a twitch in my neck that always acted up when something was wrong. I sensed trouble, but I also thought that Joey was showing more stress than usual. You know you gotta learn to control your emotions to be one of us.

Sal Martino described these events to me as part of our nearly three years of interviews which revealed the story behind the origins and collapse of Spanish Growth and Development (SGD), Chicago's Latino successor to the mafia. The events I describe are complicated, and you will see as the chapter progresses how the threads weave together to produce the cloth of the overall story. This chapter intends to give you a glimpse of what was at stake in what appeared to outsiders as just one more gangland murder, and it previews the story to follow.

Baby Face Nelson Padilla, the shooter, had been a member of the Latin Lovers. The Lovers had been one of the Maniac Family of gangs, a grouping of what are called Latin Folks gangs, whom you will hear much about. The murder of one of the Lovers, "Cook Dog," the year before by the Maniac Latin Disciples (MLDs), had never been settled. The MLDs had first agreed to turn over Cook Dog's shooter to the Lovers for punishment but reneged. Instead the MLDs shot at the houses of several Latin Lovers, and that broke the rules. Tensions between the two gangs had been rising ever since. Joey and Sal both thought Padilla's hit would bring an inevitable war that would interrupt drug sales, costing everyone lots of money.[1]

On the surface, the problems caused by Baby Face's hit were because of the power and arrogance of the MLDs. In the 1990s this Humboldt Park gang was riding high partly due to their superior drug connections. One of their members, Hugo "Juice" Herrera, had family ties to a Mexican drug cartel, and the MLDs exacted a street tax on smaller gangs buying their product. Their drug monopoly and the profits that flowed from it made them popular on the streets as young kids flocked to the biggest and baddest gang in the hood. Everyone knew the Detres hit by Padilla was overdue retaliation by the Lovers. That didn't matter. The MLDs were determined to be the lords of the streets, were bound by no honor, and flaunted their power while violating even their own rules.[2]

A POLICE-GANG DRUG CONSORTIUM

For Sal and Joey Bags the problems with MLD arrogance were only the beginning. The hit threatened to unravel gang dealings with a Chicago cop, Joseph Miedzianowski. The Outfit had long relied on dirty cops to protect their vice businesses. So for Sal, buying drugs from Miedzianowski, a decorated gang-squad cop, was in some ways business as usual. Cheaper is almost always better, and buying from a cop meant the C-Note$ could avoid the MLDs' onerous street tax and have a degree of protection.[3]

Baby Face Nelson Padilla, the shooter of the MLDs' Detres, had long worked as a snitch for Miedzianowski. Padilla, five foot eight inches and an unimposing 125 pounds, struck up a friendship with Joe the cop in the 1980s when he was sixteen years old. The first time Padilla got arrested, Joe helped him beat the rap and one thing led to another. By the end of the eighties, Baby Face had become a "prince" in the Latin Lovers and was making big money covertly working as Joe's business partner.

Joseph Miedzianowski was a tough cop and was publicly praised by Chicago police brass for how many guns he turned in and how many drug dealers he busted. He received fifty-nine CPD citations for valor and arrests. He would ride into a neighborhood and do his Dirty Harry act, intimidating young gangbangers. He was "the Man" and he lived and loved his role in the drama of the streets. Baby Face said Joe was definitely not a "Dunkin' Donut cop" or "one of those fat asses." But Joe the cop was no Dirty Harry. He was just plain dirty.

Joe went into business with Baby Face and with Juan "Casper" Martir, second in command of the Imperial Gangsters, another Latin Folks gang. To the CPD high command, Miedzianowski's many drug busts were an impressive score, but they also had the calculated effect of eliminating Baby Face and Casper's competition. Some of the drugs Joe confiscated in raids were recycled by selling at a discount back to Baby Face, Casper, and other allied gangs, like the C-Note$. We will hear more later about Mied-

Table 1.1. Dramatis personae in the Latin Folks drama

Joey Bags	Puerto Rican leader of the C-Note$. Outfit Associate and for a while Sal's main guy
Sal Martino	Outfit figure; godfather to the C-Note$
Robert Detres	MLD soldier shot by Baby Face, sparking war
"Baby Face" Nelson Padilla	Shooter of Detres; business associate of CPD gang squad officer Joseph Miedzianowski
"Cook Dog"	Latin Lover killed by MLDs
Hugo "Juice" Herrera	MLD drug supplier from Herrera family central to the Durango Connection drug network
Joseph Miedzianowski	Highly decorated and corrupt CPD gang squad officer; later convicted as a "drug kingpin"
Juan "Casper" Martir	Imperial Gangster leader; later major drug distributor from Miami for Miedzianowski
Alina "Ala" Lis	Drug dealer; lover to Miedzianowski and Joey Bags
John Galligan	Miedzianowski's corrupt CPD gang squad partner
David Ayala	Leader of 2-6ers; SGD leader in Stateville
Fernie Zayas	Leader of MLDs; SGD leader in Stateville
"Rambo" and "Godfather"	Leaders of Latin Lovers; filed grievance with SGD against the MLDs

zianowski's main intermediary, his girlfriend, Alina Lis, who was also sleeping with the C-Note$ Joey Bags. Just like in the movies, sex screws everything up.

Joe the cop and Baby Face brazenly collaborated in over a dozen *guisos*. A *guiso* is Spanish for "stew," and on the streets it means "a straight-up robbery of drug dealers"—in this case, Sal said, by "a mixture of low-lifes like Joe and his friends." Miedzianowski would sometimes stage fake arrests of his snitches to give his allies cover. The upshot of all this was that Joe got decorated, Baby Face and Casper got protected, and they all got rich.

When Baby Face killed Robert Detres he asked the guy he called his "mentor" and "guardian angel," Joseph Miedzianowski, to hide him from police and the MLD. Joe and his partner, John Galligan, made twice-a-week visits to Baby Face's hideout in Casper's apartment. They brought him a gun for protection, food, updates on the investigation, and even lists of witnesses. Joe was one ambitious, if greedy, bastard, but he wanted to protect his investment in Baby Face.

Joe's "bite" for the eight or so participating gangs in his operation was $10,000 per month over and above the price of the drugs. That amount alone should tell you how much money was being made on the streets. Neither Sal nor Joey Bags realized it then, but Joe's drug business would expand enormously before it came crashing down. If this story is a familiar tale of cops and robbers, you will see that sometimes the cops—and not just Joseph Miedzianowski—were also the robbers.

SPANISH GROWTH AND DEVELOPMENT

But the plot is thicker, and the hit exposed even deeper, more serious problems. Joey and Sal were most worried that the hit threatened the stability of Spanish Growth and Development (SGD), a mafia-style commission that Sal had enthusiastically, if quietly, encouraged. SGD was a closely kept secret from police and even from the rank and file of the gangs. The conceptual origins of SGD lie in the lessons the Outfit had learned about how best to organize crime and the proper uses of violence. Here is how Sal first told me about SGD:

SAL: *It started as a prison thing for protection because a lot of these organizations were not big, so strength comes in numbers: "You got my back, I got your back." And a lot of these people, even though they belonged to different gangs, came from the same neighborhood—grew up in the same neighborhoods, attended the same schools, whether it was elementary or high school, they were both from the same neighborhood—some of them were even related. So, by putting their resources together—strength, as I mentioned, comes in numbers. In the late seventies, the Folks coalition came into play. There was still some infighting going on amongst the Folks coalition, which still exists behind the walls today.*

JMH: Didn't it start as mainly black groups? Wasn't it Hoover [Larry Hoover, head of the Gangster Disciples] that was the key person to push that when he was in Stateville penitentiary?

SAL: *That's what is allegedly said—that it was Hoover who brought the concept of Folks together. What I was told was that they were the main leaders of it and they brought the Hispanics into the fold. And the whites, at that time the Simon City Royals from Logan Square were the main group. In turn, the Royals* brought in the Insane Popes—another white gang—and they later joined under the Latin Folks umbrella.

In 1989, as I mentioned, a call went out from the White House—Stateville—to all families that deemed themselves to be Folks, that they needed to register. So, there was over forty gangs that were out there that were affiliated with the Folks coalition. And out of those organizations, only seventeen became registered, at the time.

JMH: And what does that mean, to register?

SAL: That means that they were voted on, they submitted their paperwork—part of their paperwork they had to submit was to have a structure. When you saw the OCG concept—"Our Continuous Growth and Development"—in order to be a part of it, your house had to be cleaned. You had to have a leadership structure with prayers, laws, by-laws, all of the above. You couldn't have no infighting going on; all these things. Because if there was, you weren't accepted. So, seventeen got registered in the beginning . . .

The leaders of individual gangs sat on La Tabla, the SGD executive body that met behind the walls. They made decisions to regulate disputes and facilitate drug sales. The idea was to stop the killing, both because no one wants to be killed, and because it also is not good for business. But there was trouble almost from the start. Rather than working together for profits, the two largest gangs, the MLDs and the Insane Spanish Cobras (ISC), were recruiting fellow gangs to join their factions, called "families," and engaged in a violent power struggle. The C-Note$ eventually joined the Insane Family and in 1995 applied to register with SGD. In a nutshell, the Padilla hit threatened to rip apart the Latin Folks Alliance. And it eventually did.

SEEDS OF DESTRUCTION

Sal, from his Outfit perch, had a long-term perspective. The Padilla hit had been very bad news, and Sal told me it was then he first began fearing the worst for SGD.

The worst is what happened. What the hit had done was give the MLDs an excuse to "eradicate" the Latin Lovers, meaning to "unregister" them

Table 1.2. Spanish Growth and Development (SGD) Latin Folks gangs

Insane Family	Maniac Family	Almighty Family
Spanish Cobras (ISC)	Latin Disciples (MLD)	Simon City Royals
Insane Deuces	Milwaukee Kings	Harrison Gents
Ashland Vikings	Campbell Boys	Imperial Gangsters
C-Note$	Latin Jivers	Latin Eagles
Dragons	YLO-Disciples	
Orchestra Albany		
Latin Lovers		

Major Latin Folks gangs outside the families: 2-6ers, Ambrose, La Raza, Satan Disciples
Major African American Folks gangs: Gangster Disciples, Black Disciples
Major Latino and white People gangs: Latin Kings, Latin Counts, Spanish Lords, Gaylords
Major African American People gangs: Vice Lords, Blackstone Rangers (for a time named El Rukn)

from SGD. While on the streets it looked like simple revenge, what was at stake was votes and influence on the SGD board. The Latin Lovers had broken away from the Maniac Family and the MLDs wanted to deny them a vote. Sal, who followed SGD developments closely from Joey's reports, explained it like this:

> The Latin Lovers at one time were under the Maniac umbrella—now they broke away and they want to be sponsored by the Spanish Cobras under the Insane coalition to be a registered organization. Well, the Maniacs are upset because they used to pay taxes to them, so they're losing money. So they influence other registered families by giving them narcotics and weapons and whatever they needed to vote their way . . . They bought David Ayala's [2-6 leader and a top dog on SGD] vote. Because, "What can you do for me?"—just like the politicians do out here!

Gang warfare in 1990s Chicago was about politics as much as revenge or economics. Boiled down, the MLDs wanted the majority vote on La Tabla, and keeping the Latin Lovers out got them closer.

After the hit by Padilla, things began to unravel quickly as members of the Insane and Maniac Families became victims of gunfire. The top leadership of SGD were incarcerated at Stateville penitentiary, known as the "White House" because that is where major decisions were made. Stateville royalty Prince Fernie Zayas of the MLDs and Jefe David Ayala of the 2-6ers called a "junta," or a meeting of gang representatives, to stop the violence. Agreements were made to call a temporary ceasefire, but eventually those agreements were broken and the war raged on.

SGD had created a formal process for mediation. Accordingly, the MLDs filed formal charges with SGD against the Latin Lovers, claiming they had allowed a known confidential informant—our shooter Nelson Padilla—to be a member. It is a direct violation of SGD rules to talk to law enforcement, and the MLDs wanted the Latin Lovers punished. Rambo, the Lovers' leader, said everyone knew that they had already expelled Padilla for being Miedzianowski's snitch. In a formal written grievance to the SGD board, the Lovers objected to the MLD power play. Document 1.1 is taken verbatim from the Lovers' grievance and the MLD response.[4]

To Sal, listening carefully to Joey's words, the whole scene foretold nothing but disaster. The Padilla hit revealed the deeper meaning of what seemed to outsiders like senseless violence. Control of SGD was what was behind the 1990s war of the families and for Sal, this kind of power struggle was pointless. SGD had been founded, Sal believed, in order to make money and gain power in the city. He told me that when the gangs decided to move from fighting over turf to becoming more criminal enterprises they should have put their organizations in order, like the Outfit did after the beer wars of the 1920s.

> Killing people and doing drive-by shootings is bad for business. All it does is bring the attention of law enforcement. When law enforcement has all eyes on you, no one can make any money. You get state's attorneys involved and all these different task forces that come in, from the FBI on down, from local authorities and they come in from all angles—and nobody's making money. And there is billions and billions of dollars out there to be made. If you're into the narcotics end of the business, why are you fighting for a street corner when you can just walk down a block and make just as much if not more? But if you start killing each other over a corner, it makes no sense.

Indeed Padilla's hit proved to be the beginning of the end for the ambitious attempts of Latino gangs, with the covert blessings of the Outfit, to orga-

3-05-95

First of all they knocked one of our boys, he is R.I.P. He got knocked for no reason. Later they shot three more of our boy's. BabyFace which is no longer a part of this familia~knocked one of there boys. This is not R concern. Baby face has been radicated by Godfather & Myself. We forwarded his informant papers months ago. The trick ass bitch is not a LL [Latin Lover—jmh]. And as far as the war going on in the calle [street—jmh] we didn't start that the LD [Latin Disciples—jmh] did. My familia is just counter reacting to there moves mentally and if necessary physically.

Respectfully,

Rambo, Chairman (LLN)

Godfather Co-Chairman

MLD Response one week later:

3-12-95

Well my brothers, the only reason that we Maniac Latin Disciples are pursuant in the issues to totally annunciate the fact that the Maniac Latin Lovers have been, and are unequivocal with our leadership is because they and everybody knows they are having a serious problem identifying their true leadership. Their igno-ramus Board Member Rambo, has been illusive and despotic about their sincerity with regards to our denoument!

. . . If any B.M. [board member—jmh] is dcnounced also we will not talk to any L.L.s to arrange no agreement because all them brothers were supporting a stool pigeon and we are not implicating ourselves so that's not possible. Rambo himself said that out of his own mouth. So my brothers of the Union we finish this letter with plenty much love, and respect. They are the one's that treated this perverse referendum asking for total denouement and denudation of the Maniac Latin Lovers and from our Union and the latin folks SGD concept mind, body, and soul. Thank you brothers and wish you all the best

Sincerely Yours,

#333 Maniac Latin Disciples

nize crime in Chicago. Sal understood that the Italians had had their day and he saw SGD as potentially the seeds of a new Outfit. He and I discussed the increasing number of Hispanics in Chicago.

SAL: *Well, with numbers comes power, but it takes money to make money, and you gotta get everyone together and on the same bandwagon to sell them the dream. You have individuals that are like, "Look, we've been killing each other over colors for thirty years and nobody's winning." But there's money to be made here, whether you make it illegally, and you take those illegal funds and now take them and convert it over, just like the Kennedys. And the Hispanics are doing that. They're opening up restaurants; they're opening up grocery stores. They're taking their money and turning it over. So sooner or later, they no longer have to do the illegal stuff and the legit stuff is taking them over.*

JMH: Like the Italians.

SAL: *Absolutely, just like the Italians, just like the Greeks. The Greeks, they come in from the old country, they bring in relatives, they work at the little hot dog stand, they save enough money and buy their own greasy spoon and then Greek lightning [arson] hits it and boom they get a fully rehabbed restaurant, then they bring more relatives over and the cycle starts all over again. The Orientals are doing the same thing—you come in, and you work and work, and go to the next one, now you sponsor somebody else.*

That's what these people are starting to realize. You have to start somewhere. So let's say I'm gonna be out on the corner. I start by selling two-dollar joints, or five-dollar nickel bags or even ten-dollar dime bags. My goal is to work my way up so that I no longer have to be on the street. My goal is to have somebody else doing it for me. And with time, once I get established, I no longer have to be tied to that; somebody else takes over. Some of these people don't see the big picture. They want everything today, forget about tomorrow. And that's the problem.

The Padilla hit threatened the ambitious goals of Latino gang leaders to organize crime, control violence, gain power, and enter the halls of respectability like their Italian predecessors. The C-Note$ and the Outfit were ultimately helpless in influencing events. The Padilla hit was the first major step down the road to destruction of SGD. Violence, we'll see, got out of control not because of how organized the gangs were, but because the "legitimate" authority of SGD itself was fatally undermined by its warring families. The hit revealed that Chicago's key Latin Folks gang leaders failed to see Sal's "big picture."

 **The Old Man and the C-Note$**

The big picture for Sal was how to fit SGD into the Outfit sphere of influence, to nudge volatile street gangs to more rationally organize crime. This differs from traditional perspectives that see the world of gangs and organized crime as entirely separate spheres. This chapter explains the importance of the C-Note$ as intermediaries between the Outfit and Latin Folks gangs. It introduces some of the key players in a relatively unknown gang who played a crucial behind-the-scenes role in SGD.

The internal state of the Outfit in the 1990s had implications for the struggle to shape the direction of SGD. Sal explained to me that the Outfit at that time was adjusting to the death of Tony Accardo and the ascension of Joey "the Clown" Lombardo as their new leader. Sal reports:

> In May of 1992, after having battled various illnesses, Accardo called it a day at the age of eighty-six. At the same time, Joe Lombardo, after having served most of his sentence for allegedly plotting to skim $2 million from a Las Vegas casino, was granted parole. Shortly after his release he actually took out classified ads in local newspapers to let all the readers know that "I am not part of the Outfit!"
>
> The boys in the neighborhood were ecstatic with his return. He had done it all and at this point of his career was deemed by many to be headed straight to the top. With many of his cohorts locked up or actively fighting cases, it was a no brainer that everyone thought of him as being the next boss of the Chicago Outfit. This meant good financial news for everyone in the hood.[1]

As soon-to-be-chief of the Outfit, Lombardo was interested in new money-making ideas. Sal followed events in the street gang world closely, and the formation of SGD gave Sal an idea. But he had concerns about his main guy, Joey Bags, and needed to figure out a way to solve it. Sal was always thinking ahead.

> Joey Bags at the time was running his own burglary crew for me. Lucky had gone to jail, and in his absence Joey, as the oldest guy around, had taken the reins of the Ohio and Leavitt C-Note$. Joey Bags was sometimes out of control and even his crew was afraid of him. He always had a broad around him and that got him into trouble more than once. But he was a good earner and everyone knew he was an associate with our protection. He got off on being seen as our guy, and he was.
>
> I had been taught that our thing was better off smaller and surrounded by non-Italians. We called them associates who ran rackets and paid street tax. We usually got a 10 percent "bite." Really, we got protected in that way. They were the ones who got caught, while we got paid. You never see that many of us behind bars.

The problem for Sal was that Joey Bags was not really somebody he could trust to even covertly represent the Outfit to Latin Folks gangs. While he was Puerto Rican and "had that Latin hot blood," he wasn't really leadership material since "he was hardly ever sober."

> I heard from Joey about SGD, and later he told me about the Insane Family. We already did some quiet business with some of them Insane gangs. I thought SGD was a brilliant idea and the way to move past all that drive-by nonsense and get on to making money. But to reach out to them, we needed a Hispanic, one of them. They wouldn't fully trust one of us. The problem was how to do it.

For Sal, gangbangers generally presented a self-image that unnecessarily and dangerously called attention to themselves. Sal wanted his associates to promote a persona that was not so flashy, but inspired both fear and respect. Joey Bags had the fear part down, but more "moxie" was needed to deal with the Latin Folks group. Sal also needed to convince his superiors, particularly Joey the Clown, that Latino gang members could fit into their plans.

There was a frame of mind among Outfit guys like the Grand Avenue Crew and the Old Man: bangers and Outfit don't necessarily mix. The problem with Joey was that while he worked for us and ran his own crew, he wasn't stable and wasn't no model for his troops. His drinking and his women added up to a situation we couldn't stomach. To me he wasn't really who we wanted representing us to SGD.

The other main leaders of the C-Note$ at the time weren't Latino and few were Italian.

Big Wally was a good earner, but he really wasn't interested in politics. He wasn't Italian, but his partner Luigi was. Wally was making too much money collecting a city paycheck and doing robberies. I loved Wally. He had told me of the heist his boys pulled on Daley's house in Sauganash. Not the mayor—his brother Bill, who was at his confirmation hearing for commerce secretary in Washington when they cleaned out his house. I laughed long and hard at that, but I knew they would get in trouble for it. I thought since they were gonna go down, they shoulda hit the mayor's house and taught the fucker a lesson that nobody is untouchable. But we had our own understandings with that guy.

There were other candidates to be the Outfit representative to SGD but none of them really fit.

I didn't respect Lucky. He was a hillbilly and terrorized everybody, even his crew. I didn't want anything to do with him. He had been born into the C-Note$, but his brawn ruled his brains. Besides he was locked up then, and that was what gave Joey his chance to run things on the street.

I really liked Sammy. He had our blood in him and was brutal to his enemies. Everyone was afraid of him, but his crew loved him. He threw those X-rated parties for his guys out of his own cut and he had their total respect. But he was one of us, not them. Too bad.

Dominic had the same problem. He was born in Italy and had gone up the ranks through burglary. He was locked up then, though. He would work out better for us as our guy behind the bars dealing with the SGD leaders. Because he was one of us, he couldn't be touched there.

Table 2.1. Dramatis personae in the C-Note$ and Outfit

Joey Bags	Puerto Rican leader of Ohio and Leavitt section; Outfit Associate; Earlier Lucky's #2 and Sal's main guy
Sal Martino	Outfit figure; godfather to the C-Note$
Tony Accardo	Outfit boss for many years; died in 1992
Joey "the Clown" Lombardo	Outfit top boss after Accardo's death; called by Sal "the Old Man"
Sammy	Italian Jefferson Park section leader
Dominic	Ohio and Leavitt Italian leader; Outfit Associate; deported to Italy
Lucky	Ohio and Leavitt leader, aka "Hillbilly"; mentor to Joey Bags
Mo Mo	Jefferson Park leader; Puerto Rican Outfit Associate liaison to SGD; chair of Insane Family
Big Wally	1980's Ohio and Leavitt leader; burglar who cleaned out Bill Daley's house
Mickey "the Pancake"	Jefferson Park soldier; mentor to Mo Mo

In the spring of 1993, Joey Bags found out that Mo Mo was back. Mo Mo had a fearsome reputation in the eighties as a hot-tempered soldier and smart tactician. He had left Chicago for a few years to avoid some serious problems. Mo Mo wanted back in and at the time was apprenticing with one of the guys, Mickey, who was called "the Pancake" because he flipped several times between different crews. Mo Mo was Puerto Rican, but he idolized the Outfit. One Hispanic gang leader told me he was a "wannabe Italian."

Mo Mo had grown up in a stable two-parent family in Jefferson Park and chose a life of crime. He was one of those guys who could do well in the straight business world, but his deepest dreams were to be like Al Capone. Joey told Sal that Mo Mo was already a young man when he realized that he could never be a made guy.

So Joey tells me about Mo Mo being back and I get to thinking maybe this is our guy. I tell Joey to bring him to me. I didn't talk to too many of the guys and except for Joey Bags, none of the non-Italians. But I knew we needed to find someone who could be our face to SGD, who could represent our interests without having to say it.

Joey told me Mo Mo was nervous. He didn't know why I'd be interested in him. Besides he wasn't from the Patch, but out west. Dominic had good words about him and I trusted what Dominic said. Mo Mo didn't see it yet, but he would get it pretty quick. I chose well.

So Joey brings him to the Aberdeen Club—well, that was its name back then. One of our guys bought it and changed its name to the Peek-a-Boo Club and now it's a yuppie place, the Aberdeen Tap. I don't go there no more.

Mo Mo comes in and seems uncomfortable. The club was full of us, and though a couple of guys call out to him, he seemed wary. I liked that. I had Joey Bags lay out a proposition to Mo Mo. To start, he would work for us and make half a stack a week. Then he could work his way up to serious money.

"Look here," Mo Mo said, "before we go any further, I want to make sure I don't get in over my head. I want to be clear we are all on the same page. I need to know who is in on this. I want to make sure that I don't step on any toes. Next thing I know I'm getting a bullet in the back of the head." Mo Mo was the cautious type.

I told him with a little edge in my voice. "I'm running this thing here. You report directly to me. I got this thing on lock and the Old Man gave me his blessing, so there's no worries." But the kid had a head on his shoulders and asks, "What if I get pinched?" I explained to him that for all the associates we had a lawyer on retainer. That was the least of his worries. I didn't say anything then about SGD. I needed to see how he worked out, and it wasn't really my call.

Mo Mo "worked out" both as the leader of the Jefferson Park C-Note$ faction and as an associate of the Outfit, like Joey Bags. As time went on it became clearer to Sal that Joey Bags was unsuitable to be the Outfit's voice to SGD or the Insane Family. So he made the next step.

Joey brought Mo Mo over to the Aberdeen and I got one of my guys to drive us over to the Bella Notte. The place was real popular with made guys and associates. The Old Man himself held meetings there, though they were more like a king's audience. You didn't talk but listened to what he had to say.

Mo Mo was awestruck. He had never met the Old Man and was shocked when Lombardo called him by name. "We want you to become a liaison between us and the Latin Folk clubs—particularly the ones in the Insane Coalition—

and for that you will be taken care of," he said. That was it. To outsiders, the Old Man didn't talk much about our business.

We walked out and I let Mo Mo know he and I would talk soon. I had told Joey the Note$ should cast their lot with the Insane Family and Mo Mo could help that happen. Both Joey Bags and Mo Mo hated the Maniacs, and I was reading the situation carefully. "Just make sure that you are available when I call you." Mo Mo nodded and said respectfully, "I'll be waiting for the call."

Before I go into depth as to how SGD was founded and how it operated, I need to supply some crucial historical context. I'll begin with a brief overview of the transitions that black, white, and Latino gangs made from being concerned mainly with protecting their neighborhoods to mainly making money. The Outfit influenced that transition, at first, by giving up the retail sales of drugs to the more aggressive street gangs. The 1970s saw a sharp escalation of violence, as well as gang efforts to organize the drug trade. It was mainly these two factors that set the context for the formation of the People and Folks coalitions and then SGD.

3 The Transition from Turf to Profits

The history of Chicago gangs in the 1960s is a contested narrative. While law enforcement argues that the black and Latino gangs of the 1960s were nothing more than hoodlums, others have pointed out how the Conservative Vice Lords, Blackstone Rangers, and Young Lords were deeply immersed in the civil rights movements of the day. I told some of that story in my last book, *A World of Gangs*. I also described how the Conservative Vice Lords had responded to the loss of their leader, Bobby Gore, by turning away from a social agenda and systematically taking control of Lawndale's drug markets.

Useni Perkins, who wrote the definitive book about the period, *The Explosion of Chicago's Black Street Gangs,* vividly describes some of the tensions within the gangs between street life and liberation politics. Perkins had personally taken part in negotiations between black gang leaders and the Black Panthers, who were trying to move the gangs onto a revolutionary path.[1]

While the short-lived involvement of black and Latino gangs with revolutionary movements is an important story to tell, it is only part of the story. Street gangs all over Chicago were simultaneously moving to take over the retail distribution of drugs and control other vice businesses long dominated by the Outfit. The romantic narrative of 1960s gangs as "protorevolutionary" and the law enforcement conviction that gangs were *mainly* criminal organizations are both one-sided. Nationalist politics, activism, gang rivalry, and criminal processes were occurring at the same time in every gang and often in conflict. Gangs and their members, I've long said, have multiple, conflicting identities.

The increase in African American and Puerto Rican population in the 1960s shook Chicago politically. It also racialized gang identity, as whites defended their turf against nonwhites, as well as blacks, and Latinos affirmed their own racial and ethnic identity in the face of racist violence. This violence coincided with deindustrialization that in turn led to unprecedented increases in concentrated poverty, particularly among African Americans. These desperate conditions led inevitably to the expansion of the illegal economy. Hypersegregated neighborhoods of the black poor, which had shaken loose the control of black politics by the white Daley machine, made it impossible for the Italian Outfit to keep control of retail drug sales and vice markets from the new street gangs.[2]

This chapter explains how black, Latino, and white gangs adapted to both the loss of jobs in the 1970s and sharply increased gang rivalry. Economics and violence were the two principal factors that pressured gangs to organize into nations, build coalitions, and go beyond neighborhood peer groups. What marks Chicago gangs since the 1960s has been the will to power of their leaders and their drive to organize across neighborhoods. The classic notion of Frederic Thrasher and other Chicago school figures that gangs were mainly defined by their neighborhood was going out of date as early as 1970.

The transition of gangs from turf to profits is closely related to the Outfit, and 1960s events foreshadow the creation of SGD. While I interviewed older gang leaders about the 1960s, I also turned to the Outfit to get their side of the story.

THE DON

It was shortly before I met Sal that I interviewed another mafia elder. I'll call him the Don. He was the grandfather of a young man I had gone out of my way to help in a court case as an expert witness. The Don was long retired, but had been a much more important figure in the Outfit than Sal. The Don was Sicilian, from a family with a mafia pedigree going back to the early twentieth century. He had been friends with Outfit heavyweight Paul "the Waiter" Ricca and had been close to the longtime boss of the Outfit, Tony Accardo, whom he affectionately called "Joe Batters."

He had heard all about me from his grandson. To demonstrate his gratitude, he had agreed to answer questions about the Outfit and street gangs in the 1960s. My question for him was how it came to be that the Outfit lost control of the street vice markets to the gangs? The Don had direct experience with the events I wanted to learn about. The Outfit, he explained, has had a long, tangled relationship with Chicago's street gangs.

The Don came into my office on a Saturday when no one was around and we talked nonstop for nearly two hours. He was dressed formally, with suit, vest, and bright red tie, looking like a man of distinction. The Don had asked that his grandson not be present for our discussion, and we began with a brief, awkward silence. He spoke first and said he wasn't sure what we were going to cover, and that his grandson had said I was interested in how street gangs in the 1960s were connected to the Outfit.

I laid out my interests quickly. The Don was sitting between two bookshelves, one filled with books on the Outfit and mafia, the other on street gangs. This is my problem, I said. I think these two literatures belong together, although no one has figured out how they fit. Further, the space between the two shelves, linking them, I thought, was the police and city machine. The Don laughed easily and readily agreed. "Without the cops, none of this stuff could happen."

I told him I wasn't interested in names or fingering anyone for any crime; I just wanted to understand. In fact, the Don had no problem naming names and discussing hits and drug distribution. He made me feel like we were old friends, and he was reminiscing about his life as a businessman. Only the businesses he talked about included gambling, drugs, murder, and prostitution. He showed little or no emotion in his discussion of any of these topics, even when people close to him had been victims of hits.

It was hard for me to read this lack of emotion. I would see it later in Sal, though more as his ideal than reality. Sal was impatient and often displayed anger, particularly at snitches, and disgust over the lost opportunity of SGD. The Don, on the other hand, appeared detached and more self-conscious. His life had been filled with personal tragedy as well as financial success. Perhaps, I thought, the Don, as an important Outfit elder, had a firm grip over what stories he was ready to tell and which ones he would withhold. Thinking back, I realized I was witnessing a grand performance. Still, acting is not the same thing as lying. I came away with more than I expected.

The Outfit had controlled vice markets in the black community only since the 1950s after their violent takeover of Policy, a black-run forerunner of the lottery. The concerted effort by Outfit boss Sam Giancana to wrest control of Policy is best told in Nathan Thompson's brilliant book, *Kings*. Big Ed Jones, one of the main black Policy kings, bragged to Giancana when they briefly shared a prison cell that Policy was bringing in $50,000 a day. There were approximately sixteen major wheels, or places where black folks could bet as little as five cents in hopes of making a few dollars. At its height in the thirties and forties Policy employed more than 5,000 black people, many of whom were "runners," performing low-skill service jobs. One Policy wheel alone reported a profit of $3,656,968, even after reported "overhead." Policy overall grossed tens of millions annually. Congressman Bill Dawson, the boss of the black machine, was a recipient of regular contributions, as were hundreds of policemen. Estimates of the overall payoff "downtown" in the 1940s was $30,000 a week. Giancana couldn't wait to get out of prison to snatch this plum for the Outfit.[3]

According to Thompson, the unwritten code of the Policy kings was "never associate with Italian gangsters." Policy was a black "community institution,"[4] and legend had it that the black Policy kings had cut a deal with Al Capone in the 1920s: they would not get into bootlegging, and he would leave Policy in black hands. This all changed with Giancana's power play. One 1970s Vice Lord leader told me his mother had run a Policy wheel in the 1950s. "One night," she had told him, "a group of Italians came in and said from that day on she paid them, not her regular. She was afraid to ask questions."

The Outfit also controlled heroin in the black community, especially after World War II as Lucky Luciano's French Connection vastly increased heroin trafficking to the US. Heroin was never meant as a drug for whites. According to Sam Giancana, the word was: "Not in our neighborhood . . . but shines [African Americans] want it and somebody's gotta supply it. It may as well be us." As with Policy, by the 1950s retail heroin sales were handled by blacks, but only as employees or contractors. Italians were still the main suppliers and made the big bucks.[5]

The Don said that drugs were the best example he knew of Outfit hypocrisy. The top leaders didn't want to be tied to it directly, but loved the money. The Italians directly dealing in heroin were all bit players, but the Outfit bosses got a substantial bite. Drugs were therefore off the books to mobsters—ironically in contrast with what the Outfit bosses saw as "acceptable" income from gambling, skimming from Vegas, and extortion.

The Don strongly disapproved of drug use. He told me once he had walked in on a distant relative and an Outfit guy doing crack. The Don showed only the slightest hint of emotion as he told me that he was offered a pipe but angrily turned it down. He told his relative to never do that again or have his friend, an addict and notorious hit man, around him. Drugs were like prostitution, he said. You could make money at it, "but Joe Batters had forbidden anyone into drugs or whores to become one of us." The old world morality of the "Mustache Petes" of *Godfather* movies was a natural fit for the Don.

Sal confirmed the Don's take. "We couldn't get involved with narcotics because of our laws. But depending on who you were and how much was in the envelope, the bosses were willing to turn a blind eye. People violate rules and you see it, but you can't say anything because you'll end up in the trunk."

Heroin had run through Corsica, the Don told me, and the mafia there were middlemen for distribution networks from Turkey and the Chinese Triads. The Corsicans were widely feared. Even the Mexican cartels, the Don said, with their extreme violence, were no match for the brutality of the Corsicans. In the 1960s, the Outfit was making crazy money in Hollywood and Las Vegas and through the Teamsters pension fund, so Chicago's retail drug markets may have been relatively neglected. In the 1970s, the Outfit renewed their local focus by violently taking over Chicago's stolen car business in the chop-shop wars and eliminating most independent gamblers.

BLACK POWER

I told the Don of an interview I had with "Iron Mike," one of the founders of the Blackstone Rangers. Mike had been one of the Main 21, the coalition of gangs whose leaders formed the initial ruling group for the Rangers. Mike explained to me how the Rangers took control of drug markets in

Woodlawn in the 1960s. He took part in what he called "serious beefs" among gang leaders about how to deal with drugs.

There were two points of view, Mike told me. Bull Hairston, the Rangers' senior leader, was opposed to drugs in the community. He favored the use of violence against Italian-paid runners who supplied black retailers with dope. Jeff Fort, on the other hand, wanted black control of drug sales. The influx of heroin into the community meant a lot more money could be made on drugs than on protection rackets or robbery. Mike told me that Bull was arrested for ordering the hit of a heroin runner. It was only after Bull was jailed, that "Jeff met with them [the Outfit] and negotiated a deal."

The Don listened to me tell this story and confirmed the essentials. "The black gangs were rough," he said. With whites leaving black communities and black gangs growing in strength, something had to change. "The business model was broken," he told me laconically. "We didn't have the muscle to hold on to the business, and our guys could make as much money or more as suppliers anyway. It was just good business."

Good business also meant understanding Chicago's largest gang at the time, the Blackstone Rangers. Charles Lapaglia, one of the whites who prominently worked with the Rangers along with the Reverend John Fry, was listed in the Congressional Record as a low-level mafia heroin distributor. At first I wondered if it was just someone with the same name, but in Henry Harris's chilling personal history of the Rangers, he describes a meeting with Milwaukee mafia chief Frank Balistreri, set up by Lapaglia.

That meeting between Fort and Balistreri is legendary. Fort gives a $10,000 fur coat to the Milwaukee mafia chief only to find it lying outside in the mud as a foot mat as Fort nervously scurries out. Lapaglia is described in Harris's book as a gun runner and low-level mafioso, consistent with the Congressional Record report. The Outfit had infiltrated the Stones and were sizing things up.[6]

What is important is that the control by black gangs of drug markets was a conscious process, an ethnic succession of organized crime.[7] What Giancana's statement that "shines want it" shows is that the black nationalist idea that drug distribution is a conspiracy of whites to sell to the black community is historically accurate. But the "whites" are organized crime in cahoots with paid-off law enforcement officials who together flooded the black community with drugs.

All Chicago's black gangs have their own urban legends of how drugs came to dominate the black community, and how the Outfit passed on drug sales to them. Some border on the fantastic: a Vice Lord told me of how the Italians opened up a railroad car filled with drugs for the gangs to sell to black kids.

A Gangster Disciple leader described to me how white Outfit mobsters told black gang members that since social program funding was ending, the only way they would be able to make money was to sell dope. In this telling, the railroad car was downsized into a closet full of cocaine. The Blackstone Rangers were already selling dope, this "OG" went on, and while there was opposition to drugs within the Disciples, realism set in. "Uh, and then as time went on a lot of what the Stones was putting out there filtered over into Disciple territory, and you have people, a lot of them using. And it was at that point that the Disciples decided then that, 'shit they gonna use it. They gonna buy it from somewhere. The Stones getting money. We ain't getting nothing so we might as well, you know, sell it."

The notion of a "black mafia," popularized in the 1970s by movies such as *Superfly* and anthropologist Francis Ianni, represented the idea that black gangs would inevitably replace the Italians as organized crime.[8] Things would prove more complicated, as we'll see later. But in Chicago during that time, black gangs evolved from single-neighborhood peer groups into multineighborhood "supergangs." Some of the new super- gang leaders were drawn into nationalist and revolutionary politics and rejected drugs as poison to their community. The historical record reports that these leaders did not last long.

Most of the black gangs at the time took over vice markets that had been formerly run by the Outfit. For example, replacing the white man as the "lords of all vice" was the reason, one gang leader said, that his gang adopted the name Vice Lords. From the Outfit's perspective, faced with black gangs' determination to exercise "community control" over drug sales, they made a business decision, adapted, and looked to other paths to profit and power. From the black gangs' perspective, a "black mafia" and control of illegal markets would be their contribution to "black power."

The city's response to black and Latino gangs was a "war on gangs"[9] that was widely viewed by nonwhites as racist in implementation, if not design. Mayor Richard J. Daley referred to street gangs as "the new organized crime" and concentrated the new Chicago Police Gang Intelligence Unit on waging war against them, particularly against the Blackstone Rangers. It should be noted that Daley's actions conveniently diverted public attention from the Outfit, which was then at the height of its international power and on cozy terms with the Chicago machine. The Outfit was able to hand off retail vice markets to the gangs, exposing them to the most risk, while concentrating on more profitable businesses that were less vulnerable to law enforcement. While drug sales continued as before, the black gangs would not get the protection of the Outfit's corrupt connections with police. The CPD would launch a war on drugs and gangs while giving less priority to crackdowns on Outfit-controlled gambling.

The police response to gangs also reflected deep racism within white ethnic communities faced with growing numbers of blacks and Latinos and threatened by the loss of industrial jobs. The Don said simply that police hated black gangs because so many cops were racist. "We got along with the cops because we were both white," he said. It was partly the strength of this racism that drove white and Latino gangs to organize across neighborhoods. For Latinos, this cross-neighborhood racial organization laid the groundwork for much more grandiose ambitions, Spanish Growth and Development. For the C-Note$, quietly one of the city's most influential white gangs, organized crime and white racism gave them direction and meaning.

THE C-NOTE$ AND WHITE POWER

Gangs in Chicago have always started as neighborhood peer groups, but in the 1960s things changed as local gangs either expanded or got devoured by others. The dynamics were mainly racial, aimed at projecting power against racial rivals, and later, for some, making money. Black, white, and Latino gangs in the sixties all expanded across neighborhoods, forming new sections by assimilating or conquering existing local groups.

The C-Note$ began in 1952 in the Patch or Little Sicily, not far from the Cabrini-Green housing project. A World War II tank loomed over the corner of Grand and Western until it was moved to Smith Park in the 1980s. The moving of the tank in some ways represented changes in the neighborhood as Latinos and other ethnic groups mingled with Italians. But the sense of order remained, along with places such as the Bella Notte Restaurant or private clubs like the Huron SAC, where Outfit leaders like Joey "the Clown" Lombardo hung out until his conviction in the Family Secrets trial in 2005.

Sal told me proudly that some of the Outfit's most notable members came from this neighborhood "with names like Accardo, Lombardo, Spilotro, and DiFronzo. These guys mentored many C-Note$." Sal compared the C-Note$ favorably to the more notorious 42 Gang located a few miles south of the Patch on Taylor Street. The Outfit leader Sam Giancana and hit man Sam Destafano were members of the 42 Gang.[10]

For white "greaser" gangs like the C-Note$, "white power" was the name of the game, as any look at graffiti or the "compliment cards" from those gangs of that time will show.[11]

The C-Note$ were one of a dying breed of white gangs, but the origins of this originally Italian gang were entwined with the Outfit.

JMH: Do you know how the C-Note$ started?

SAL: *The C-Note$ started in the early fifties. Allegedly, it was made up of sons of organized crime figures. Look at some of the names out there today, last names like Cozzo, Lacoco, and Calabrese. I mean, these are lots of families whose kids grew up together. Some of them have gone on to become soldiers in the organization. Even those that were not of Italian heritage—Chicago is one of the only ones that has non-Italians in the fold, like Big Wally, one of Chicago's most successful burglars, and "the slot machine king"—both made their bones on Ohio Street.[12]*

Little has been written about the C-Note$. They are unmentioned in the scholarly literature on gangs, and they hardly ever appear in the mass media. The Chicago Crime Commission's Gang Book has only a short paragraph on them. Sal was pleased with the C-Note$' lack of notoriety. The C-Note$ indeed functioned like a junior mafia and produced many

FIG. 3.1. Huron Social Athletic Club. Photograph by author.

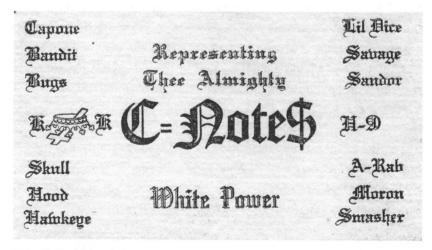

FIG. 3.2. C-Note$ compliment card

members of the Grand Avenue Crew and filled the ranks of their associates. Sal stressed to Joey Bags and the other C-Note leaders over the years the importance of keeping a low profile:

> One of the first lessons you learn is not to live beyond your means but to live modestly. Some of the biggest Outfit guys lived in the same house and neighborhood most of their lives. The worst thing you want to do is to be thought of as a big spacone [blowhard or "flashy fool"]. The older guys always told the Note$ to stay out of sight, out of mind. In other words, stay under the radar. It took them a while to comprehend this, coming from a gang member mentality where you wanted to be known as the biggest and the baddest. Let's just say that the transition took some time.

The C-Note$ are not mechanical products of poverty or racism, like most gangs described by social scientists. The C-Note$ grew up in working-class neighborhoods and their criminality was the result of careful organization and family traditions. While some of their leaders had backgrounds filled with serious family troubles, many were raised in solid two-parent families, and their choice of organized crime was conscious, if strongly influenced by peers. While most of the gang members I've studied from poor black and Latino neighborhoods were driven by desperation and hopelessness, this description did not fit most of the C-Note$.[13] In their home turf of the Patch in the sixties and seventies the C-Note$ were known as fiercely racist, and resisted encroachments by "invading" Puerto Ricans. They were never a very large gang.[14]

The sheer numbers of "invading" Latinos led the C-Note$ to find common cause with other white gangs. In 1968 they helped form a "GCG" coalition of Gaylords, C-Note$, and Lazy Gents. In 1972 they joined the United Fighting (later changed to Five) Organization (UFO), an even larger racist coalition with the Gaylords, Playboys, and Ventures.

The UFO members attacked black and particularly Latino gangs, adding muscle and numbers to white gangs, which were now on the defensive. At times UFO gangs would target specific Latino gangs for retaliation, and sometimes large numbers of them, clothed with white armbands, would swoop down on Humboldt or Kosciuszko Park looking for nonwhite enemies.

UFO
Gaylords Whiteknights
Riceboys C-Notes Playboys

FIG. 3.3. UFO II compliment card, circa 1976

The UFO reflected the strength of racial identity as neighborhoods were changing. "At one time," says Sal, "whites were the overwhelmingly majority of this city. Hispanics and blacks were not. The whites picked on the blacks and Hispanics for years. And as these ethnic groups began to come in more and more, they started to band together for protection against the whites." White gangs also banded together and backed one another up in confrontations with Puerto Rican gangs, who were steadily growing on the West Side of Chicago. UFO was strictly about racial identity. I asked Sal if at the time money making entered into the rationale for the UFO. "No, No, it was race, it was race. It wasn't money, it was race. It was 'You stayed on your side of the tracks, we stay on our side'—they were trying to protect their neighborhood from the growing influx of Hispanics moving in and blacks moving in. And you know who won that war . . ."

The self-congratulatory books written by the Gaylord writing as "Michael Scott" and the Simon City Royal "Mark Watson" tell race-based war stories of that era, as whites and their gangs gradually were ousted from their neighborhoods by Puerto Ricans.[15] The Gaylords today hold an annual picnic reunion, and their newly adopted name, Gray Lords, describes their fate and ultimate defeat. Sal, reflecting his disdain over gang life that was not about money, sums up the Gaylord experience from his perspective: "When you look at some of these other guys, all they wanted to do was get drunk, get high, and go kick some spics' asses. Where are they today? Nowhere to be found. Oh yeah, you might find 'em in the corner bar, in a dive, reminiscing about what they did in 1974!"

The UFO was a desperate attempt to keep the Latinos out of what we might call the white "Ft. Hood." UFO went through three different iterations, the UFO III forming in 1978 as a coalition of Playboys, Ventures, Rice Boys, C-Note$, Gaylords, Hells Devils, and Jousters. UFO III broke up in 1982, and later most of the UFO gangs joined the People coalition, with the C-Note$ staying independent before becoming Folks in 1995.

For most of the white gangs, like the Gaylords, the traditional image of gangs as wild peer groups and "disorganized crime" apply quite well. But such descriptions are incomplete. The Gaylords and other white gangs were also hell-bent on expanding their own power, linking with and assimilating sections or clubs throughout the North Side. Their website lists fifty-eight sets or local gangs at one time part of the Gaylord nation. Their expansion was, in a way, about making money, but more importantly, to project power against Latinos and other rivals as the number of white ethnics declined on the West Side. Above all, the expansion of gangs into many neighborhoods meant that violence in one neighborhood inevitably led to retaliation across the city, increasing death and destruction.[16]

The largest of the white gangs at the time, the Simon City Royals,[17] was among the first to expand by accepting Latinos into membership. The C-Note$ also shed their racist image, and by the 1990s, some of their most capable leaders, like Joey Bags and Mo Mo, were Puerto Rican. Both of these chiefs looked up to the Outfit and modeled their leadership on what they learned from Sal and others. Sal points out that even earlier, not all C-Note$ were Italian. "You look at Little Joe and Bandit from the C-Note$ or the Hobo brothers from the C-Note$ that were members in the seventies. They all have Hispanic blood in 'em."

For the Outfit, non-Italians were absolutely barred from becoming "made men." But they also believed ethnicity should not get in the way of making money, and in the final chapter I'll explore the importance of the category of associate. By the 1970s most street gangs were beginning to move from being fixated on race and turf to making money. The C-Note$

Table 3.1. Dramatis personae in the 1960s and 1970s

Bobby Gore	Vice Lord leader who led them on a prosocial turn
Useni Perkins	Author of *Explosion of Chicago's Black Street Gangs* and mediator between Panthers and gangs
The "Don"	Retired Outfit figure involved with 1960s dealings with street gangs
Sam Giancana	Outfit leader who organized takeover of black Policy gambling operations
Big Ed Jones	African American Policy king
Tony Accardo	Top Outfit boss; called "Joe Batters"
"Iron Mike"	Blackstone Ranger leader; one of the "Main 21" or original leadership group from 21 gangs
Bull Hairston	Original Blackstone Ranger top leader
Jeff Fort	Top Blackstone Ranger leader; made deal with Outfit after Bull Hairston was jailed
Charles Lapaglia	Blackstone Rangers sympathizer; named as Outfit heroin runner by a congressional committee
Frank Balestreri	Milwaukee mafia boss; met with Jeff Fort
Mayor Richard Daley	Mayor and former gang member; led "war on gangs"
Mike James	Organizer of white revolutionary group Rising Up Angry
Cha Cha Jimenez	Leader of Puerto Rican Young Lords, a gang turned revolutionary organization
Aracelis Cruz	Puerto Rican youth shot by police, setting off 1966 Division Street riots
Albert "Hitler" Hernandez	Original leader of the Maniac Latin Disciples
Richard "KC" Medina	Cobra leader murdered by Insane Unknowns
Anibal "Tuffy C" Santiago	Cobra leader; top figure in SGD's La Tabla
"Indigo"	Cobra founder of I-Team; mentored by Tuffy C
Lord Gino Colon	Top leader of the Latin Kings
David Ayala	Leader of 2-6ers and La Tabla
Prince Fernie Zayas	Leader of Maniac Latin Disciples and La Tabla

were already there, and when they joined the Latin Folks they did their best to keep SGD's eyes on the prize of "business first."

C-Note$ wanted nothing to do with white groups with a political agenda. The main one at the time, Rising Up Angry (RUA), was organized by former Harvard student turned community organizer Mike James. RUA started a newspaper and allied with the Panthers and Young Lords. RUA's attempts to recruit white gang youth, like Gaylords, were largely unsuccessful. Crime, drugs, and racism were all stronger for white gangs at the time than any appeals to class solidarity. RUA faded away even before the Gaylords and lives on in pictures on the walls of the Heartland Cafe.[18]

White gangs in the 1960s were largely shaped by the racial and spatial dynamics of ethnic succession. They were confronted by what they called a Latino invasion and even uniting in coalitions like UFO, they didn't have the power to stop them.

CROSS-NEIGHBORHOOD ORGANIZATION OF LATINO GANGS

There are no good histories of Latino street gangs in Chicago.[19] Their story is much richer than I can do justice to here. For the mainly Puerto Rican gangs of the sixties, the key issues were (1) racism, manifested by lack of jobs, poor education, and violence from police and white gangs; (2) power, as they expanded from neighborhood gangs into cross-neighborhood "nations"; (3) rampant intergang violence and concerns of how to control it; and finally, (4) a growing interest in making money, following in the footsteps of black gangs. Chicago's Latino gangs, like their black and white counterparts, have always been about more than neighborhood.

A substantial Puerto Rican migration began in Chicago after World War II, and gangs formed with the second generation. Cha Cha Jimenez, who would become the leader of the Young Lords, explained how many gangs were simply groups of kids from the same town in Puerto Rico who were together displaced to Chicago. The Puerto Rican experience in Chicago is also one of displacement, as Puerto Ricans were pushed from areas around my campus, UIC, to Lincoln Park, which became upscale and unfriendly to Puerto Ricans, to Humboldt Park, where the community finally made a successful stand against the gentrifiers.

The Young Lords began as a gang and then in the spirit of the sixties tried to fashion themselves after the Black Panthers. Cha Cha Jimenez was a redheaded, skinny white kid who looked more Irish than Puerto Rican. He led a transformation of the Lords from street gang to the revolutionary Young Lords Organization. Among other struggles, the YLO staged an occupation of DePaul's McCormick Theological Seminary. This was the beginning of a community-wide resistance to gentrification, and it publicized the YLO as more of a community organization than gang.[20]

Another major factor facing Puerto Ricans in the 1960s was police brutality and racial hatred. There are many stories of police collaborating with white gangs like the Gaylords and C-Note$ to harass Puerto Ricans. The first race riots in Chicago since 1919 took place on Division Street on June 12, 1966, when police shot a Puerto Rican youth, Aracelis Cruz. Puerto Rican youth responded with anger against the police, and the riots helped shape the future Puerto Rican political agenda. The Young Lords put themselves forth as a vanguard for the Puerto Rican community, with stated goals of ending poverty and racism.[21]

The political path of the Young Lords, though, had few followers among gangs. The Lords themselves did not create "junior" groups nor absorb other gangs. They died out in the 1970s and did not experience a rebirth even as Cha Cha garnered substantial support in his 1974 run for alderman. One Latin King leader told me that while the Kings were friendly with the Lords, they never did more than provide security for them. At that point the Latin Kings did not have a political vision, and were expanding mainly to increase their power and status.

At the same time in Chicago, the Puerto Rican independence movement was surging and the FALN (Fuerzas Armadas de Liberación Nacional) took root among activist Puerto Ricans, many of whom went on to become prominent politicians. The Latin Kings ran a safe house for the FALN at Leavitt and Schiller, where the FALN reportedly made explosives that were used in a bombing of the Schubert Theatre in 1979. This incident, I was told by one of the LK leaders, led the Kings to back away from the FALN and radical politics.[22]

Like black gangs, Puerto Rican youth at the time first formed from neighborhood peer groups and then began expanding and absorbing nearby gangs. The Latin Kings, which is still the largest Latino gang in Chicago, formed its first section at Kedzie and Ohio and quickly formed a second chapter on Schiller and Leavitt. Their main turf was to be at Beach and Spaulding on the west side of Humboldt Park. The Kings fought with white gangs amid growing tensions with other Latino gangs on the east side of the park.

One night at a party, they ran into a South Side Mexican gang called the Coulter Kings, and the two gangs agreed to unite. Thus the Latin Kings became the first Latino gang combining Puerto Ricans and Mexicans, North and South Sides. For many years the Kings had de facto dual leaders, or Coronas, North Side and South Side, Puerto Rican and Mexican. The LKs were following the cross-neighborhood path that had been initiated by black gangs, and they grew into having thousands of members in Chicago and later formed chapters across the country and even the world.

Their main rivals, the Latin Disciples and Spanish Cobras, also took the path of expansion and absorption. The Latin Disciples were formed from many neighborhood gangs, including the Latin Scorpions, who had earlier tried to recruit the Young Lords' Cha Cha Jimenez. Their first corner was at Hirsch and Rockwell. Later, they would open up shop on Potomac and Rockwell, a set that would be dubbed the "Twilight Zone." In 1966, Albert "Hitler" Hernandez would become their leader and aggressively build their strength across neighborhoods and in battles with white gangs.[23]

In 1970 the MLD leader Albert "Hitler" Hernandez was murdered as he demanded that Latin Kings passing through Disciple turf had to remove their colors. This killing began a violent feud between Kings and Disciples that intensified in the late seventies and eighties and morphed into blood rivalries between People and Folks. As the bodies piled up, so did incarceration of both Kings and Disciples. Both gangs recruited heavily in prisons, establishing themselves as the two major Latino gangs in both Chicago's Latino community and in Illinois' black-dominated correctional facilities. Out-of-control violence and the incarceration of nearly all of the most important gang leaders, along with the profit motive, became the principal factors in the eventual formation of SGD.

INSANE SPANISH COBRAS (ISC)

For our story the Spanish Cobras are surely the most important Latino gang, and the least is known about them. No *Gangland* specials tell their story, and their history is largely kept secret. One governor, or leader of a neighborhood section, told me that when he was young, if he even mentioned the name of their leader at the time, "Tuffy C," he got a "mouth shot." The Cobras from the beginning were more multifaceted than other

Latino gangs, and took organization more seriously. The Cobras initiated the I-Team, as the Insane Family was called, and become "cousins" or sponsors of the C-Note$.

Like other gangs, the Cobras started out from several local gangs, but the main one was Culebra Loco, or "Crazy Snakes." One leader said that in the 1960s the Cobras hated the Young Lords and Kings because they were "sellouts" and "doing dirt for the white man." The Cobras always saw themselves as representing the salt of the earth, the alienated and rejected, and resented the higher status of the Kings and Young Lords.

Like other Puerto Rican gangs, Cobra members had two flags: the blue, red, and white of Puerto Rico, and their gang colors, green and black. Indigo, a Cobra who was one of founders of the I-Team, proudly told me of his support for Puerto Rican independence. The nationalist and racial identity of gang members, I argued in *A World of Gangs*, is a potentially powerful tool to persuade gangs to reduce violence in their communities.

The Cobras consolidated in turf adjacent to the MLDs, who in the beginning were their allies against the Kings and the Insane Unknowns. They studied how the Outfit did business and kept their organization relatively small and tight. They saw the benefit of business and aspired to be "plugged in like the Dagos." In the 1960s, like the Kings and Disciples, they began to expand and absorb gangs in other neighborhoods, but proceeded more carefully than the other major gangs and initially stayed smaller in size, though they would grow rapidly in the next decades.

In the 1970s, Richard "KC" (King Cobra) Medina took control of the organization. The leaders of the Cobras, similar in some ways to those of the C-Note$, early on began the serious study of organized crime. One Cobra *veterano* called the 1970s the "Capone" era, when the nation began to emulate the Outfit and focus on how best to do business.[24]

But in those years violence from the white gangs needed a response, and KC Medina in 1976 joined with the Latin Disciples to form a coalition, the Young Latin Organization (YLO). This alliance aimed at countering the UFO coalition of white gangs, meeting violence with violence across the city. In 1978, another alliance was built, called United Latin Organization (ULO), which expanded to include the Imperial Gangsters and Latin Eagles. But the battles with white gangs were becoming a thing of the past simply because Puerto Ricans had won the war, and white gangs were either fading away or becoming mixed-race.

The 1970s became the most violent decade in Chicago's history. Among black gangs, the Rangers and Disciples killed each other at gruesome levels even as each were consolidating their hold over illegal markets. The MLDs organized countless hits against Latin Kings, who had killed their leader, Hitler Hernandez. The 1977 Puerto Rican Day Parade erupted into Latin King/Cobra violence. Rather than targeting the police or the oppression of Puerto Ricans, the gangs were targeting one another.

The violence stepped up considerably when in 1979 the Latin King–allied Insane Unknowns gunned down the Cobra's KC Medina.[25] This began an extremely bloody war dubbed by the media as the "war of the Insanes" as Insane Spanish Cobras members hunted down Insane Unknowns and vice versa. The Unknowns would be hit with a tsunami of violence. In 1976 the Simon City Royals had lured the Unknown's leader, Capone, to his death in a phony peace conference. Later, Fernie Zayas, the prince of the MLDs, was fingered for allegedly killing three Unknown soldiers and was sentenced to spend the rest of his life in jail. The Insane Unknowns of Schiller and Leavitt did not survive the onslaught and the Unknowns ceased to be a major force in Chicago's gangland.

Under their new leader Anibal Santiago, whose street name was Tuffy C, the Cobras looked to expand as well as streamline their organization. Tuffy was a new type of leader, very intelligent and able to operate in many worlds. He stressed education to Cobra youth and was for a time enrolled in college. He often appeared in the neighborhood in a three-piece suit and added a sense of purpose to the organization.

Indigo, the street leader of the Cobras in the 1990s, insisted to me that Tuffy had been set up by the cops and framed on a murder charge. Once in prison, Tuffy's leadership was even more threatening to law enforcement, and he was transferred to New Jersey to keep him away from direct contact with his organization. One gang leader who was locked up with Tuffy said of him,

One guy I knew from behind the walls was Tuffy from the Cobras. This guy took advantage of his situation and went and got education while he was behind the wall. So he educated himself so he could be able to deal—psychology and all this other stuff—to be able to deal with his people and his issues, better. A lot of these other guys, they're stuck on stupid—and it's a shame.

Tuffy's orders to expand Cobra territory, however, prompted a second major war, this time with the Simon City Royals, over control of Kosciuszko Park. I'll tell later how the Cobras won that war by the late 1980s, though at the cost of many lives.

The most important events in Latino gang history in the seventies and eighties were unanticipated and the result of the almost unchecked violence of the times. During these years, gang leadership was moved by the police and courts from the streets to the prisons. In 1972, the dominant leader of the Latin Kings, Gustavo "Lord Gino" Colon, was sentenced to life in prison for murder, and he would be joined by the MLDs' Fernie Zayas, the Cobra's Santiago, and David Ayala of the 2-6ers. Their incarceration had the unintended effect of vastly strengthening gang organization and bringing leaders of diverse gangs into regular contact. While Lord Gino presided over the People coalition in Stateville, Ayala, Zayas, and Tuffy became the major forces on the Tabla or board of SGD. Gang dynamics from the 1970s to the mid-1990s were controlled by incarcerated leadership.

THE MEXICAN SOUTH SIDE

While the Puerto Rican gangs on the North Side were making alliances with one another, anticipating the People and Folks coalitions, Mexican gangs on Chicago's South Side also began expanding, fighting with one another, and choosing sides. In 1983 David Ayala, the leader of the South Side Mexican 2-6ers, was sent to jail for life for organizing a shooting of Latin Kings that went wrong and killed two bystanders. The 2-6ers whose turf was on the west side of Little Village had a bloody rivalry with the Latin Kings, whose turf was on the east side. Like other gangs, the 2-6ers went from being a softball club to being a gang, and violently responded after the Kings killed one of their members. David Ayala, whose father I was told was a hit man for Chicago's version of the Mexican mafia, had taken control of the 2-6ers and embarked on a rapid expansion, warring with the Kings at every turn.[26]

Another major South Side gang, La Raza—meaning the People or the Race—formed due to tensions with black and white gangs in the schools. They grew out of an earlier gang, Los Braseros, and then united with other crews to increase their size and capacity to fight rival gangs. They became part of the Party People nation, a large coalition of Mexican gangs, but fell out with them, and later they became deadly rivals.

As on the North Side, racial hostility was a major element in the organization of Mexican gangs. As Mexican students increased in number, the black gangs who ruled South Side schools by violence were challenged. Mexican gangs quickly became the strongest force in schools in Little Village, Pilsen, and Back of the Yards, all South Side communities with quickly growing Mexican populations. Like the Cobras, whose colors were both those of Puerto Rico and their gang, La Raza adopted the colors of the Mexican flag. Both the 2-6ers and La Raza would become key members of SGD.

But while the future lies with the Mexican gangs who now dominate Latino gang life throughout the city, it is the Puerto Rican North Side gangs that played the dominant role in the 1990s. As one Insane Family leader told me, "North Side controlled all the politics. North Side controlled everything on the street. OK, we're Insane, this is the way we're going. South Side just followed. Because the Mexicans on the South Side back then were just fighting gangs, gangbanging, gangbanging, you know what I mean. That age is gone."

The Cobras at the time were perhaps more advanced than other Latino gangs in their understanding of the need to transition from turf to profits. The dark clouds of violence that draped over Chicago gangs in the 1970s might best be summarized by the words of one older Cobra leader, who told me they were taught as young kids the three M's: "Money, Mack, and Murder." While these terms are often sensationally bandied about by law enforcement, this is an aspect of gang culture that should sober any young person thinking of joining a gang.

"Money," of course, is the gangs' commitment to illegal businesses, something the Cobras did quietly as well as by dominating street sales in certain areas. The money, this Cobra told me, went to support their leaders, like Tuffy and Rabbit, who were incarcerated, as well as to buy guns. "Mack" meant loyalty to the gang and a rational structure based on firm, if violent, discipline. "Murder," he coldly said, was "the price of opposing the nation." This ethos reflects a central element of 1970s and 1980s gang culture. The failure to implement this code of the streets in the 1990s, Sal coldly argues, is why violence got out of control.

With so many gang members locked up, survival in prison became a very serious issue. While the white gangs had been defeated, there were now racial fears by Latinos of the much larger number of black prisoners. At the same time many powerful and very intelligent gang leaders found themselves in prison together with no chance of release. They began meeting, and those sit-downs were directly the result of the need to protect gang members in prison, but also began to explore how to moderate violence on the outside. Less violence on the streets, as Sal says, is a prerequisite for making money, and money means power. The result of these four factors: prison, violence, profits, and power is what led to the formation of the People and Folks coalition and later to SGD.

part
two

ORGANIZAT

Document 4.1. Introduction to the Constitution of Spanish Growth and Development

Introduction of O.C.G.

Irregardless of where we come from or where we originate from, "We are together." We as a Union have put personal feelings to the side in order to remain
together as one. We must work hard in our togetherness to reach our goals that
are outlined in the unions Preamble. We must not only exist to survive against
opposing forces, but harmony must also exist among the personnel of this union.

We all originate from different factions and each of our factions have lost many
who now rest in peace. Many of the brothers of all factions are now imprisoned
living in another world that does not belong to us and therefor, we have created
this union by principles. These guiding principles unite us closer and bonds us as
one. (see S.G.D.Insignia)

Brothers of individual beliefs who lie only concerned with their nation, must
put aside the personal shields built up around themselves as walls and we all have
to realize that we must work together.

"Our Continuous Growth"

4 Spanish Growth and Development

The introduction to the SGD constitution is reproduced in document 4.1 word for word from the original that was secretly circulated to Latin Folks in 1989.[1] Sal told me that when he first heard about SGD from Joey Bags he was impressed.

> Yes, when I heard about the Table, and that was what they were trying to create—just like the commission—that's what the registered families were trying to create, or emulate—trying to copy.
>
> We didn't organize it. We probably inspired it. But it was always a Spanish thing. It showed me they had vision. I was at the Aberdeen Club and Joey Bags comes in and tells me he's got news. Now Joey is an action guy. He goes out and makes things happen and he don't care that much about anything else. But he knew that this SGD thing was a big deal.

A big deal indeed. Sal told me that SGD as it began was the most structured criminal organization in the country, outside of the mafia.

JMH: Why was this the most structured?

SAL: *I think they were the most structured because they have more rules. They met more regularly.... In order to become registered into the Latin Folks ... they looked over your rules to make sure there was a structure, a leadership established to make sure you're not one of these knucklehead organizations, four or five guys that will fly off the handle or shoot from the hip.... They say, "Look, these guys are established, they got structure, they got literature, nation laws, by-laws—all this stuff, it's there."*

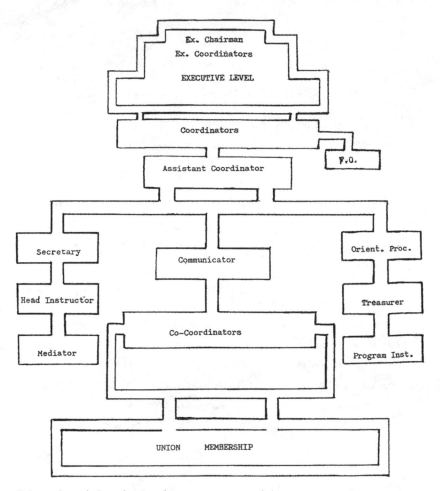

FIG. 4.1. Spanish Growth & Development organizational chart

For Sal, SGD was important for another reason. By the end of the 1980s, the Outfit had completed wars on independent gamblers and stolen car operatives. Led by a spree of violence by Jimmy "the Bomber" Catuara, they had rubbed out anyone who refused to pay them street tax for stolen cars and the sale of car parts. Stolen cars at the time, Sal said, was a $40 million-a-year business.[2]

The consolidation of the Outfit's local businesses would be briefly interrupted in 1992 when longtime Outfit leader "Joe Batters" Accardo passed away. On the one hand, in the Outfit's ranks there was uncertainty. On the other, Accardo's death would mean opportunities for the made guys in the Grand Avenue Crew and the C-Note$.

For Sal a new Patch-led Outfit regime meant money-making opportunities for him. In my interviews Sal clearly saw the potential of SGD as a mafia commission-style organization that could be informally guided by the Outfit and perhaps someday replace it. It was Sal's disappointment with the collapse of SGD, and probably his losing some face in the Outfit, that led to our interviews.

SGD AS A SOCIAL INSTITUTION

From the point of view of its Latino leadership, SGD was more complex than just a business organization or a simple coalition of gangs. It was a powerful myth of unity and hopes for peace and profits, both in prison and on the streets. To understand the birth, growth, and death of SGD we have to put aside the traditional theories of how to understand gangs and look more carefully at how social institutions rise and fall.[3]

An institution—for example, a school, church, or the Boy Scouts—Philip Selznick tells us, forms as a "natural product of social needs." It becomes more than a "bare bones organization" or "expendable tool" and evolves into "a responsive, adaptive organism." Institutions persist over time despite changes in leadership and in external conditions. To understand an institution, organizational theorists explain, we need a historical perspective on changes in the environment and how the institution adapts to those changes. The "aleatory processes" of conventional gang literature are ill suited to explain the conscious emergence of a social institution like SGD.[4]

The origins of SGD, this chapter will explain, can best be seen as a natural, adaptive response to increasing violence of 1970s gangs, persisting poverty, police repression, and mass incarceration. SGD also stemmed from prior Latino gang attempts at cross-neighborhood organization, and it was a stepson to the People and Folks coalitions set up by black gangs. SGD was also likely modeled on the mafia's commission, a mimetic process much noted by observers of more conventional organizations. Above all, SGD was the conscious creation of Latino gang leaders, and it transcended neighborhood.

IMMEDIATE ORIGINS OF SGD: OUT-OF-CONTROL VIOLENCE

The expansion of neighborhood-based gangs in the 1960s into multineighborhood gangs and multigang nations focused on power led to increased violence between them in the 1970s. As the gangs expanded to all corners of Chicago, there were more and more opportunities for conflict. A death in one part of the city could lead to war in dozens of neighborhoods. The murder rate tripled from 1965 to 1974, as bodies fell at a pace even exceeding the worst year of Prohibition's beer wars. Adding to street gang violence, the Outfit during this time was also engaged in consolidation efforts in the chop-shop wars and the violent elimination of independent gambling operations. In 1977 sixteen unsolved murders were attributed to the Outfit. In 1978, at least a half dozen professional burglars died after Outfit boss Tony Accardo's home was foolishly burglarized.[5]

The increase in violence can be seen very clearly in Humboldt Park, where homicides, mainly between the Latin Kings on the one side and the MLDs and Cobras on the other, more than doubled in the early 1970s and doubled again by the early 1980s. As we saw in the last chapter, the killing in 1979 of Richard "KC" Medina of the Cobras by Insane Unknowns set off a hyperviolent spate of killing called the "war of the Insanes." You'll note the jump in Humboldt Park killings starting in 1979. The 1981 rate of 40/100,000 means that more than fifty people were murdered in Humboldt Park in that year alone.

While criminologists correlate violence with neighborhood characteristics, such analyses do not typically take into account gang wars, which account for the sharpest increases and can later explain sudden declines. To make sense of variations in violence it is necessary to understand the history of gangs and their war and peacemaking efforts, as I'll spell out more clearly in my chapter on the war of the families. Gangs are more than reflections of neighborhoods; they are also independent actors whose history is crucial to understanding violence.[6]

In the black community, the 1970–80s war was even more horrific. Blackstone Rangers and Black Gangster Disciples were killing each other at even higher rates than Puerto Ricans in Humboldt Park. Police pressure and violence toward gangs was most intense on Chicago's South Side,

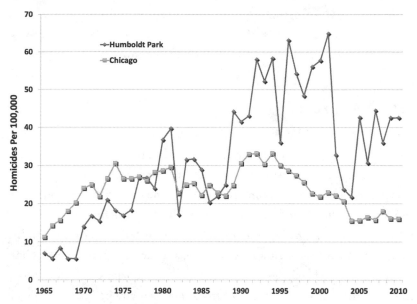

FIG. 4.2. Homicides in Chicago and Humboldt Park, 1965–2010

where Jon Burge, Chicago's most notorious cop, began a two-decade-long unchecked spree of physical torture of black gang members. Burge brought his Vietnam War experience as an interrogator to Chicago's ghetto streets, which in truth were beginning to resemble a war zone. Ironically, the worst excesses of Burge's torturing of more than 100 black gang members occurred during African American mayor Harold Washington's regime. No Chicago police officer reported Burge's criminal acts at the time, and his superiors, who were well aware of his violations of human rights, gave him commendations and promotions.[7]

The war-like conditions and the high-profile 1984 gang killing of high school basketball star Ben Wilson prompted Mayor Washington to experiment with conflict mediation programs employing former gang members.[8] The YMCA outreach program led by Ray Vazquez was expanded by the City of Chicago, emulating the Crisis Intervention Network of Philadelphia. Their efforts touched the lives of thousands of people, and homicides slightly declined in the Washington years. But with Washington's death, a conflict mediation approach was discarded by new mayor Richard M. Daley in favor of an aggressive gang suppression strategy. Homicides increased.

But to see Washington's approach as working and Daley's not is too simplistic. What is left out of such analyses are the actions of the gangs themselves to control violence . . . or to set it spinning out of control.

PEOPLE AND FOLKS

SGD was preceded by the organization of the formal People and Folks coalitions. Larry Hoover, the leader of the Gangster Disciples, organized the Folks coalition of gangs in 1978 in Stateville prison. The original idea was that what happens on the streets stays in the streets, and prison should be its own world. Thus blood feuds out in the neighborhoods, which were then at all-time highs, would not be allowed to carry over to prison life. But Larry Hoover added a twist and took a racialized principle of survival to a higher level. Sal explains: "When you look at California, people in other states, it's a black and white issue when you go behind the wall. Illinois' prison system is not like that. . . . People that were enemies on the street are now behind the wall saying, 'Well we gotta cover each other.'"

Larry Hoover brought fellow Stateville residents Tuffy from the Cobras, David Ayala from the 2-6ers, and the MLDs' prince Fernie Zayas into the Folks coalition. Rather than organizing prison alliances on strictly racial lines as they were elsewhere, Illinois prison gangs at that time divided into multiracial coalitions of People and Folks. Protection for their members in prison, for example, is what prompted the Gaylords and their fellow white gangs to become People and the mainly white Simon City Royals to turn Folks.

One young rank-and-file La Raza member told me that when he entered prison being Folks was the difference between "being treated like royalty and being treated like a peasant." Once his Folks credentials were accepted he was given a tour of what areas of the prison the Folks gangs controlled and introduced to "cool" Folks gang leaders.

Black, white, and Latino gangs chose to be in either the People or Folks coalition for protection in prison. This was indeed different from the crude racial divisions in prisons in other states at the time. But racial tolerance was only on the surface. As the Insane Deuces' leader, Blade, pointed out, racism was strong among Latinos in a prison environment where an overwhelming majority of the prisoners were black. One Latino Folks gang leader of that time said to me pointedly, "Blacks are ignorant, lack education, especially moral education. They got numbers, lack human rights stuff, they are their own worst enemies. They have numbers in prisons and in the streets but can't stay organized." While SGD was a "Latino thing," its stepfather was Larry Hoover's "New Concept" and his Gangster Disciples dominated the Folks coalition. I asked Sal to explain how SGD worked along with Hoover's Black Gangster Disciple's board. As usual, Sal saw the relationship primarily in business terms.

It's separate but it's collaborative. Because, you know, you don't cross this line and I don't cross this line and then you continue a business relationship. Hoover's crew—they're not flying the planes, they're not driving the vehicles. The major importers of narcotics in the city of Chicago are Hispanics. For example, the Herrera Family, who are part of the Maniac Latin Disciples. You have 'em coming in and out. The Insane Deuces had a big part of the bringing in narcotics to Aurora and into the city of Chicago. So, because they aren't the ones that are bringing it in, the African Americans gotta have you on their side or they're not gonna be making no money.

IN THE BEGINNING

The formation of the 1970s Latino gang coalitions of the YLO and ULO to fight racist white gangs established a precedent for more collaborative gang organization. It was the incarceration of nearly all the major gang leaders in the 1970s, added to the example of prior Latino gang organization, plus racial animosity to the black-led Folks coalition that precipitated SGD. Blade explained to me how SGD began: "Spanish Growth and Development started in the joint. The concept was just like the blacks. The whole concept, the Spanish cross. Rules and Regulations. . . . The Latinos and blacks, they get along, but they don't really like each other. What happened is they made up their own concept of SGD . . . that was 'we are all together to protect us from the blacks.'"

The SGD Tabla, consisting of the key Latin Folks leaders in Stateville, put out the 1989 call for all Folks gangs to register. This meant they had to formally submit their organizational request to join SGD and be voted on by existing members. Sal saw things mainly as a question of power, with his own economic twist.[9]

JMH: OK, what was the SGD agenda?

SAL: *It depends. The agenda was power. Money. All of the above. When you're united, there's money to be made. When you're divided, nobody's making money. If you're fighting and killing each other it brings too much attention to what you are trying to do. So what they were trying to do was get everybody on the same page in order to build a stronger community. Their perception was we've been excluded from a lot of things—government—they're trying to get a piece of the pie. They figured the only way to do it was, through the sale of narcotics, to build a war chest, to build money, a bank, to utilize that money to bring it back to the community so that you can start buying your politicians, buying your stores. That is what it was all about. By bringing these people together to the same table, conflicts would be kept to a minimum . . . because one of the lessons of the Outfit . . . Here it is different than New York. We don't have five families here, just one structure. We had crews and all that, but they all responded to one structure.*

Latin Folks gangs first had to register, and to do that, they needed to have formal lists of members both behind bars and on the streets. The historic pattern of informal membership, of being "jumped in" or "blessed in" had to add a bureaucratic component. This was important, since so many people were being locked up at the time. Gang leaders and cell block coordinators in prison needed to know who was actually a member in order to distinguish between friends and enemies and provide security.

The formal application for membership in the 2–6 Nation in document 4.2 is reprinted below. Each gang had to present its by-laws and constitution to La Tabla with wording added to them to reflect Folks doctrine, symbols, and metaphors. Registration and enrollment was the first step, and the leaders in Stateville realized that even among Folks gangs, many of whom bordered one another, territorial disputes could unravel SGD. Indigo, from the Cobras, explains: "So they decided to make maps of all the gang areas. They made like a survey and they had surveyors go

Document 4.2. Membership Application for 2-6 Nation

Application for The Two Six Nation

Name: _____

Address: _____

City: _____ State: _____ Zip: _____

Birthdate: _____ Age: _____ Sex: _____

School: _____ Year: _____ Grad Yr. _____

Address: _____

City: _____ State: _____ Zip: _____

Employer: _____

Address: _____

City: _____ State: _____ Zip: _____

Nickname: _____

Branch: _____

Tattoos (Y/N) If Yes, What Of: _____

Location: _____

Have you ever been arrested? (Y/N)

Have You Done Time? _____ If So How Long? _____

I understand that all the information on here is true. I give you permission to investigate on anything that might leave a doubt. If there is any false information I will be violated.

Signature: _____ Date: _____

out there and draw actual maps. Then they brought the maps back to the joint and the Tabla approved them."

Another of the principal Folks leaders described the early plans of SGD and the importance of boundaries.

> The main objective of all the families was to prosper together. Contracts were established and signed by everyone. Border lines started to be respected and money began to flow in from all the various business arrangements that each individual family had established for themselves. Also established was a line of communication along with secret codes that only members could understand. Most professional linguists would consider it jargon. By doing so, it gave them a better opportunity to settle issues before they escalated into bloodshed. In

most cases many issues were settled peacefully, and then again others were
settled in a more violent way, depending on the seriousness of the problem.

The work of SGD quickly became concentrated on dealing with the
violent disputes between Folks gangs. La Tabla would meet at Stateville
and other prisons and hear formal complaints of gangs against one another. Then they would deliberate and were supposed to render a decision.
Intense lobbying and bribery took place among factions or families to influence the votes on La Tabla.

CONTAINING VIOLENCE

The prime motivation for the formation of SGD was the need to control
bloodshed on the streets. This concept is embedded in their constitution
(document 4.3). It would be a mistake to read these passionate words as
merely rhetoric, or as a front for SGD's "real" function as a single-minded
tool to better organize crime. Make no mistake, I agree with Sal that SGD
surely was a framework for criminal organization. In my discussions with
Folks gang leaders they were careful to minimize the criminal nature of
SGD with a sensible fear of federal criminal conspiracy indictments under
the RICO Act.

But SGD was more complex than a simple criminal conspiracy. The
levels of violence at the time and the gang rivalries were independent factors that pushed Latin Folks gangs to unite and influenced the way gang
leaders saw themselves. This peacemaking tendency can be seen in efforts
by gangs in Central America over the past years to negotiate truces. The
need to control violence caused SGD itself to be infused with value beyond
the specific criminal tasks of its members. The documents reproduced here
show how SGD intended to give meaning to gang membership that transcended day-to-day business issues.

THE SPANISH CROSS

If the need to contain violence was one leg of the newly born SGD, racial
and ethnic consciousness was the other. Following the solidarity of the

Document 4.3 "Loving Memories," from the SGD Constitution

Loving Memories of Our Brothers and Sisters

Please. With a powerful, unseen faith, with meaningful trust, and for the sake of the loving memory, let us combine our hearts in a true moment of silence for our Sisters and Brothers who have lost their lives in being part of our unions struggle.

A mere moment is vaguely enough to show tribute for the feeling we have. With this dedicated thought to you of our deceased, we will carry you in our hearts for the peace that we had in our daily lives.

We feel you through the music we hear, we feel you through the things we see, and most of all we have a hold on each others hearts.

At times we have a picture in our hands, at times we have a vision in our minds, and at times we pray that you be Rested in Your Peace.

1960s social movements, discrimination and police brutality reinforced Latino ethnic consciousness. Racial animosity behind bars to black gang members also built on this consciousness. Despite Sal's idea that SGD should basically be a rational, criminal-minded conspiracy, from the start the Latin Folks concept was also rooted in Latino cultures. Its myths and ceremonies would reflect the influence of the African American Gangster Disciples, but they were more strongly guided by the Latino experience and the need for unity and peace among Latino gangs.

The SGD constitution spells out the ritual significance of their symbol, the Spanish cross. Rather than merely provide a means to better organize crime, as Sal often implies, SGD's primary goal was to create an identity for its members that could rise above, not replace, the specific identities of the various gangs. SGD was birthed to become a living organism, not just a single-purpose criminal tool.[10]

To understand this, Sal could have looked at the history of Chicago's Outfit. Italian gangsters in the 1920s had allegiance to various street crews, but with Capone's elimination of rivals in the beer wars, Frank Nitti institutionalized the Outfit as more than a sum of its parts. To be a "made man" from then on was to be part of "Our Thing"—Cosa Nostra or the Outfit—not just a specific street crew.

Business was a central part of SGD but also existed separate from it.

Document 4.4. Insignia of the Spanish Cross

FIG. 4.3. Spanish cross

Insignia

The Spanish Cross derives from our heretic ways, the first word in our Union's name. in which we find our Race, our Creed, our Essential Beliefs, and our Faith

***

These guiding principles unite us closer and bonds us as one. The Circular Disc behind the Cross represents the highest degree of Unity, Unity being the reason for which we have constructed the Union coordinating the structure of all of our affiliate branches under one foundation . . . One Union.

The Disc behind the Cross is to be carved on edge with Wreath type circles for our Loving Memories of our deceased.

Each stone on the Cross will represent the color of our original branch. The middle stone is to be the color of your original branch. All colors on the Insignia are there to show respect and tribute to each of our affiliate branches which secures Peace, Praise, and Credit to the foundation of our Union.

The Insignia is to be worn proudly and with constant loyalty being shown to the personnel of the Union. The New Concept of 1987 added the Six-Pointed Star in the center of the Cross on behalf of the unique Union that represents the Star. The Star although, will be optional to the brothers who wish to wear our Insignia in the form of jewelry.

Even the bitter-rival People and Folks alliances didn't always get in the way of gangs making money. Both Cobras and Latin Kings told me about the "Snake Pit," an actual hangout on neutral turf near Humboldt Park, where rival People and Folks gangs have met for many years to transact drug sales and other business matters. But these rational business dealings were of a different order than SGD, which, I became convinced, was intended to be more than just a front for business.

Indigo, who ran the Cobras street side in the 1990s, insists that SGD was above all a "concept," an idea that gang members could live in peace. Indigo himself still has longtime street cred but has been a successful legitimate businessman for nearly twenty years. He still identifies strongly as a Cobra and advises them as what some people would call an OG. Reflecting on his past leadership, Indigo told me he believed gang members needed to get educated, both "academically and morally," and SGD was an attempt to accomplish this.[11]

I listened noncommittally to Indigo's point that the Cobras and other gangs needed more "moral education" for their youth. Moral education for him included working with community agencies and churches, participating in elections, and above all trying to prevent and control violence. Yet for Latin Folks leaders like Indigo, running a criminal enterprise created some unique ethical problems. Street gangs were involved with the drug game, and as we've seen, murders of rivals or even their own members, were part of the business. As one leader told me, once members "knew things, they couldn't be allowed to loosen their tongues." Chief among what could turn out to be a lethal sin was snitching. Given values of solidarity and the need to protect the organization, violence against snitches was seen as rational, even moral. I see the values of SGD gang leaders as self-contradictory.[12]

The SGD constitution states the hopes of many Latin Folks gang leaders and infuses it with value. But it also hints at the catastrophe to come. What Indigo and others bemoaned was that the "concept" did not really take hold. As we will see, what could have been a loftier identity supplementing and elevating individual gang street loyalties eventually fell facedown into a pool of blood. We need to recall that it was pools of blood in the first place that compelled Latin Folks gang members to create SGD.

To reduce SGD to only a criminal conspiracy means seeing gang members as one-dimensional. It should be clear that there were more than one set of values embodied in Latin Folks' ideology, documents, and rhetoric. Rationality didn't always mean the same thing. I found SGD gang leaders at various times reflected one of the identities or roles listed in table 4.1. These are not mutually exclusive roles; they are ideal-typical examples of what I've called multiple conflicting identities of gang members. Each

Document 4.5. From the SGD Constitution

DEFINITION: The S.G.D. Union does not imply, nor does it mean for anyone to abandon their original Faction. We as Hispanics are merged in that we can accomplish COMMON COLLECTIVE OBJECTIVES set forth by our delegated committees, and ideas given to our leadership by all our personnel who are able to propose and manifest said ideas. The leadership cannot do anything without the aid of its membership.

[See appendix 5 for the SGD provision on independence of gangs within SGD—jmh]

Table 4.1. Typology of SGD leaders

Businessmen	Maximized profits to secure influence; violence was instrumental, not expressive of revenge, retaliation, or factional interests
Statesmen	Those who worked to end or limit the violence through the People and Folks concept or applying principles of SGD; often ended up involved in city politics, licit business, or community organizations
Gunmen	Those who were motivated by revenge and factional identity more than the goals of peace and stability of SGD
Dopeheads	Those whose substance use interfered with their duties in the gang; these leaders were either purged in one way or another or just dropped out and faded away
Snitches	Those who put their own survival ahead of the group; snitching often led to violence, and snitches were universally, if sometimes hypocritically, despised

Latin Folks leader I interviewed adhered to one role more than another, depending on how I put my question or depending on the kind of situation they were describing to me.[13]

Law enforcement was largely unaware of SGD and pursued a single-minded goal of minimizing the influence of gang leaders. For example, they transferred the Cobra's leader Tuffy C to a New Jersey prison to weaken his ties to the streets, not knowing—or caring—of Tuffy's "statesman" role as a proponent of the violence-reducing role of SGD. Tuffy C, like other Latin Folks leaders, including one faction within the Maniac Latin Disciples, was among those most intent on using drug money to influence politicians, buy off police, and move their gangs into the mainstream.

One approach to policy, it seems to me, is to strengthen the values of the statesmen and isolate those of the gunmen while being wary of the businessmen, dopeheads, and snitches. The most effective tactics in gang intervention, I've long argued, consist in a cultural struggle with gang youth over values instead of the law enforcement approach, which tends to lump all gang members together into one enemy.

FROM PEOPLE TO FOLKS

SGD was the conscious creation of Latin Folks leaders, and their primary opponent was the People coalition. There were many similarities between the two, but one of the main differences was that the Folks created an actual between-gang organization, SGD, with sets of laws, rules, dispute-mediating mechanisms, and explicit ideology. One way to look at these differences is to listen to Blade, whose Insane Deuces (ID) had been members of the People alliance for years. Their internecine war with the main People gang, the Latin Kings, coincided with the creation of SGD. They changed their allegiance during that time, and thus Blade is in a position to compare the two.

As far as the Deuces, we were People. We hated Disciples. We were People. We ran with the Latin Kings in the projects, over there [Lathrop Homes housing project].

And what happened was there was a couple of Deuces that their brothers were Kings and Kings that their brothers were Deuces. We were all family. But then it started getting crazy because the Kings started taking control of the drug market, saying you can't hang here, this is our hood. That is when the war started. Back and forth, this and that. This is the 1980s: 1986, 1987. The war started.

Basically everyone picked sides, this side or that side. You're Deuces or Kings. But you're still People. Every time you go to the County [Cook County jail] you getting stabbed up, getting whacked. We had a meeting with the Unknowns, PR Stones, GBO, YBOs [all People gangs at the time] We had a meeting with them by the lake. Look, we're getting tired of being pushed around by the Latin Kings. We're People, you're People. Let's stop the shit. Everyone agreed, "Yah. You go to war—we all go to war."

But that didn't work very well, and the Insane Deuces had a dilemma on their hands. Folks gangs, particularly the MLDs, were anathema to Deuces. But in the jail and prisons Insane Deuces members were now being attacked both by Folks gangs and the Latin Kings. It was fight or switch, and they eventually switched. But it wasn't easy.

> We were about to transform from People to Folks. We had guys in the joint who were talking to the Cobras who said, "We got your back—don't worry about it. We'll help you. You ride with us, we'll be first cousins, da da da." So we transformed into that. And it worked. The guys in jail said, "We wanna switch to this." So I say OK let's try, and we had a vote and it was 25-1. I was the only one who voted yes. The others said "Fuck them Folks."

But Blade didn't give up, and he eventually prevailed.

> So we went through a transformation. I told them "Damn we want to be Folks, but we don't like them." So we had to change all our rules and regulations. Supposedly. It's just junk. "Don't steal, don't . . ." People make it up—I don't know why. They have to feel a feeling of something. They need ingredients. So they make up these rules. Now we have to change the rules, now we're Folks. It was a big vote. They all voted us in except the Maniacs and the Royals. They voted against. We never liked them anyway [The Deuces in 1974 had killed "Arab," an SCR leader, and the Royals never got over it].[14] Now we're Folks, we have to go through the SGD concept. You have to understand all this, all the paperwork and crosses and this and that . . .'[15]

Now an elder statesman, Blade sees the roots of violence as greed and "hot blood" but also realizes that gang members "have to feel a feeling of something." In order to bind Folks gangs together, SGD provided "ingredients" in the form of laws, prayers, and a guiding ideology to create a new culture that would encourage unity and an end to factional violence.

I have spent considerable time with leaders of the Latin Kings, Vice Lords, and Blackstone Rangers over the past years trying to determine if the People coalition ever produced an organization like SGD or the more inclusive Our Continuous Growth and Development coalition. While there have always been meetings between gangs to deal with common issues or problems, I think the People coalition remained mainly an unwritten concept and that alliances were mostly informal, situational, and temporary.[16]

One reason for the absence of multiorganizational forms among People gangs was the large size and strength of the main groups, Latin Kings, Vice Lords, and Blackstone Rangers. These groups' individual constitutions, laws, and prayers played the same role within those gangs that SGD did for the Folks Alliance. All Chicago gangs and coalitions moved beyond merely "unwritten laws," or rules of conduct, and codified these rules in actual written documents that bound them together as street institutions, beyond being "bare boned" organizations.[17]

LATIN KING CONSTITUTION

One example of such codification, the Latin Kings Manifesto, was written by Lord Gino in Stateville in the 1970s. Along with Mexican leader Baby, or BK, the manifesto provided a religious ideology for Latin King members that infused the Almighty Latin King and Queen nation with values beyond the daily tasks of members.

The Latin Kings were by far the largest Latino gang in Chicago, with thousands of members, quite a bit larger than the runner-up, the Maniac Latin Disciples. Thus the MLDs at first sought out the Cobras and allied with the largest black gang, the Gangster Disciples, to offset the citywide strength of the Kings. Power, as I've written again and again, trumps neighborhood if we are to understand the evolution of Chicago's gangs.

Lord Gino for years exercised control over the Kings on the streets. The LK "empire" was in fact a coalition of neighborhood gangs, and there was a need to bind them together beyond the mechanics of drug sales. Thus the manifesto and constitution were among the first gang documents and served as a model for other gangs. One longtime Latin King leader reported to me on an incident in Stateville penitentiary: "Tuffy [leader of the Cobras] was in the library all by himself copying our Constitution. A bunch of Kings tried to get in and the guards told them you can't go in

Document 4.6. The Latin Kings Manifesto

Almighty Latin King Nation

The Almighty Latin King Nation is a religion which gives us faith in ourselves, a national self-respect, power to educate the poor and relieve the misery around us.

It is the Brotherhood of man, blending like the waves of one ocean, shining as the Sun, one soul in many bodies bearing fruit of the same tree.

It creates in us a thirst like the heat of the earth on fire, a thirst for knowledge, wisdom, strength, unity and freedom.

It is the Sun glowing in the essence of our being, the brightness in our eyes that cast reflections of its rays spitting fire in all directions.

It is the unshakeable spirit and the nobleness of our hearts, the limitless power of the mind the unrelentless will to be free.

It is pride, ambition, love, sacrifice, honor, obedience and righteousness, all our powers and destinies thrown into the mission of human service and united into one Single Gold Sun.

If you want to find Yahweh, serve the Almighty Latin King Nation. Put on the Gold Sun—Black and Gold colors, place your right fist upon your heart and pledge devotion to the Almighty Latin King Nation, to Yahweh and all oppressed people. This is the Nation of Kingism . . .

Behold King Love!

there, there's Cobras. The brothers pushed them out of the way and came in and there was Tuffy copying our laws by hand. The Cobra laws are really copied from us."

This is perhaps a Latin King "Folks" tale. But what is similar is the prime function of the SGD and LK constitutions to bind members together on a set of supraneighborhood values that go beyond loyalty to a local faction. One section of the LK constitution states: "For Nation Men there are no horizons between clicks and branches for they identify only with the Nation, not a particular click, branch, or section—natural allies together in one nucleus, one Nation, the Almighty Latin King Nation."

The final stage of a Latin King's life, according to their laws, is called the "New King" where a King evolves out of a street-fighting identity and embraces values of community and being an advocate for oppressed people. While the Latin Kings have always been a criminal enterprise, they also have always been much more.

HOPE AND GLIMPSES OF CATASTROPHE

The lack of multigang People organization underscores the almost breathtaking scope of SGD. I agree with Sal: At first, SGD was the most organized gang structure in Chicago and perhaps the country. At the onset, its principal leaders set forth a daring plan to transform Latino gang life in Chicago into a more rational, violence-mediating, and consciously criminal structure.

Many of those I interviewed referred to SGD as a contract. For them SGD was a rational concept, and problems arose when individual gangs failed to implement it.[18] While SGD was in a narrow way a contract, it was more complicated than that. Sal explained it in more down-to-earth terms:

> One of the main goals of the SGD concept was for families to "bury the hatchet" on past incidents and let the past be the past. The objective was to start fresh with new directives to better govern themselves. For some that was easier said than done. A lot of blood had been spilled throughout the previous years and a lot of mistakes were made that had led to such bloodshed. In order to move forward, time was needed to help some of these individuals heal from their wounds and losses.

Burying the hatchet was not so easy. In fact La Tabla became preoccupied with grievances between gangs, now taken to a higher level. But instead of the Table resolving disputes, individual Folks gangs engaged in fierce lobbying to settle scores, placing the SGD leaders in a bind.

As an example, consider the formal grievance shown in document 4.7 from the leadership of one original Folks gang, the Almighty Ambrose, to SGD. La Tabla heard this grievance and, as far as I could tell, never came to a decision. Losing a valued and numerically large member like La Raza was not a simple matter, nor was it in the long-term interests of the union. While SGD was intent on developing a rational bureaucracy that

TO: THEE S-G.D. EX. BOARD
FROM: THEE ALMIGHTY AMBROSE LEADERSHIP.
DATE: MARCH 14TH. 1995
SUBJECT: ERADICATION OF THE RAZA FAMILIA
RESPECTFUL S-G.D. BOARD, AND MEMBERS,
We, THEE ALMIGHTY AMBROSE LEADERSHIP, would like to respectfully address the following issue to the entire S.G.D. Board and it's appointed members. We feel that it is time for us to present complaint respectfully to the Board in order to continue our AMBRO Growth and Developement. Our conflict with the Raza Familia has been a serious problem that has been gradually escalating throughout the past few years. This escalation has become a major disruption of the Growth and Developement of our AMBRO—FAMILIA, causing many unecessary and costly losses that can and will never be retrieved.

Upon registration into our Great S.G.D. Union, the Raza Familia beforehand were notified of specific conditions, and for the record, all of the conditions stipulated to the Raza Familia in order for them to register and become a part of our S.G.D. Union were agreed upon by the Raza's. It has been almost six (6) years now that the Raza Familia became a part of this Union, and till this day they have failed to comply with certain stipulations and conditions handed down to them by our respectful S.G.D. Ex. Board.

At this time we, THEE AMBROSE LEADERSHIP ask that the Raza Familia be eradicated from this Union. Our case and complaint against the Raza Familia is authentic and genuine. I'm certain that the S.G.D. Board will find that we do have merits in our respectful request for eradication of the Raza Familia.

We submit the following charges that hold true substance and facts in our charges. The charges will be attached-in the following page of this complaint. The Raza Familia had ample time to at the very least make efforts to show resolvement to the various issues and complaints regarding our two (2) Familias, but things have still been the same. Therefore we feel that we must take these measurements and avenues in order to maintain the Domestic Tranquility that is stipulated in our S.G.D. Concept. We are optimistic that the S.G.D. Ex. Board will rule in what is right in this case, and vote appropriately in the only way fit. After reviewing the charges and facts, and evaluating all aspects, along with all of our losses stemming from these conflicts with the Raza Familia, we are certain that the S.G.D. Board will have no other choice but to respect our request for eradication of the Raza Familia.

We will gladly debate any issues regarding this matter. We will also present all facts and evidence in our case.

Note: See appendix 3 for factual charges.

could serve as a referee for warring gangs, its delegate members all were dissatisfied by how slowly it moved. What was rational to one family was irrational to another, which led to paralysis. Leadership regularly failed to resolve intergang disputes.

An underlying theme of this book is the tragic conflict between rationality and emotion, and you will watch how that drama was played out within SGD's politics. More accurately, I look at the different chains of logic practiced by families within SGD and see how reason itself was driven by passion and ultimately led to catastrophe. Procommunity values were drowned out by a wave of violence unleashed by leaders primarily driven and overcome by revenge and greed. The leaders of the Latin Folks gangs were unable to unify SGD as the Outfit had done after the beer wars of the 1920s. While SGD had been born with the promise of succeeding the Outfit as a social institution organizing crime and controlling violence, its factional, family-based structure proved its undoing.

Rather than efforts to settle disputes, too often grievances brought to SGD were nothing more than bald power plays, like the Ambrose petition in this chapter or our earlier story of MLD demands to eradicate the Latin Lovers. Conflicts between powerful members or families produced inaction by SGD leaders. Ultimately, La Tabla's "entropy" led to frustration that in turn undermined SGD's authority, which then led to more bloodshed. Born in the need to minimize violence, SGD ultimately was helpless to prevent it.[19]

But the accomplishment of SGD should not be minimized. It was indeed a farsighted and potentially game-changing organization for Latin Folks gangs. They had succeeded for a time where all other Chicago gangs had failed. They had created a mafia-style commission that had potential to bring order on the streets, a sense of purpose to its soldiers, and a path to respectability. To do this, SGD aspired to produce stable conditions for carrying out the gangs' various illegal businesses, something Daniel Bell called a "queer ladder of mobility." No other gangs or groups of gangs since the original mafia had accomplished so much.

Before I go on to describe the origins of SGD's violent family squabbles, I want to return to Sal's C-Note$. The story of the C-Note$ cautiously

turning Folks and joining the Insane Family underscores the conflict between Sal's and the Outfit's instrumental plans and the avarice of factional rivals within SGD. Greed and raw emotions were not the property
of Latino gang leaders alone, but were also displayed in varying degrees by
the 1990s C-Note$ leadership: Joey Bags, Mo Mo, Dominic, Sammy, and
Lucky. Their lives and deaths put a human face on how difficult it was to
control basic human passions, even with the benefit of the time-tested and
finely honed criminal rationality of their Outfit godfathers.

5 "Two Dagos, Two Spics, and a Hillbilly"

Most descriptions of street gangs describe them as bare-bones neighborhood-based peer groups with little formal organization. Suggestions that street gangs might be connected to organized crime are almost completely absent if not outright dismissed by scholars. We have already seen the role of C-Note$ in organizing multineighborhood white resistance to the Latino "invasion" of their turf. But the C-Note$ evolved, while other white gangs like the Gaylords did not. Their ties to the Outfit made them different from most other gangs, and they represented Outfit interests in joining SGD. The C-Note$ and their largely working-class backgrounds challenge conventional notions about what a gang looks like. This chapter describes this remarkable gang and how individual leaders helped shape broader historical events.

The C-Note$ and the Outfit played no formal role in the initial formation of SGD. The Outfit and the mafia commission may have been a model for SGD, but Sal first learned about the call to register Latin Folks gangs from Joey Bags. Sal immediately saw the value and potential of SGD and steered the C-Note$ into position to bring SGD under Outfit influence.

As I interviewed Latino gang leaders about SGD, most saw the C-Note$ as minor players in their world. Some of those I interviewed believed that the C-Note$' reputation for being "mobbed up" was probably more braggadocio than real. Others saw them as good earners and were eager to take advantage of their rackets. But from Sal's point of view, even the smallest fear among street gangs that the C-Note$ might be Outfit "connected" served them well on the street.

The possibility of the Note$ having strong ties to organized crime assisted them holding onto their stronghold even through the worst times. In truth, fear was what kept their rivals at bay. Between the violence, secrecy, and the traditions of organized crime, the community knows little about the C-Note$ and their ways. But the exaggerated media images of organized crime let the Note$ capitalize on them and intimidate their opposition. I enjoyed watching the show.

The C-Note$ had their own destructive wars against the Latin Kings, Satan Disciples, and others. Still, those battles paled in numerical significance to the Humboldt Park killing fields of the Cobras and Disciples. While the Chicago police kept a crude roster of C-Note$ members, this Patch-based gang has to this day been largely ignored by law enforcement. Organized-crime penetration of the Chicago Police Department has likely encouraged this oversight of the Outfit's principal minor league team. There are no academic studies of them.

Sal describes the C-Note$ and Outfit position from the 1980s up to the Latin Folks era.

The eighties were a tough time for both Outfit crews as well as the C-Note$. For us, the chop-shop wars had just ended and we were cleaning up. At the same time we suffered some heavy casualties. Several individuals got rubbed out— may they rest in peace: William "Butch" Petrocelli and William "Billy" Dauber (1980), Nick D'Andrea (1981), Jasper "Jay" Campise, Johnny Gattuso, Allen Dorfman (1983), Charles "Chuckie" English (1985), Michael Spilotro and Tony "Ant" Spilotro, John "Big John" Fecarotta (1986).

For the C-Note$ some guys we knew, William "Red" Brock and Tommy "Lil Pasta" Positano (1988) were taken out by gangbanging. Michael "Jake" Marrone lost his life as well (1989).

For the Note$ at that time it was them against the world, having not become part of either the Folks or People alliances. What I learned from Joey Bags was that this go-it-alone attitude probably wasn't going to cut it for long in the street gang world. To my way of thinking, and probably sooner rather than later, the C-Note$ had to do something or they'd be history.

In the 1980s when the other white gangs in the UFO joined the People alliance, the C-Note$ decided to stay independent. Sal describes the C-Note$' principal leaders in the 1990s when our story largely takes place.

You had two Dagos, two Spics, and a Hillbilly. That was their core. Throughout the late eighties and nineties that was who led them. . . . So here you have a predominately Italian organization who went on to be led by two Hispanics. And the Hispanics had more respect from us than some of the Italians from the crews. Because of what they did and what they accomplished. And we knew they could carry themselves with no problem.

Through Sal's eyes, this chapter tells the story of these five leaders—Sammy and Dominic, Joey Bags and Mo Mo, and Lucky. I'll also tell you of a major Outfit-connected female drug dealer, Tina, whose life intersects with Joey Bags in predictably gendered ways. This chapter explains why and how the C-Note$ decided to join the Insane Family en route to full membership in SGD. This was not a straight road, and the drama within the C-Note$ parallels in many ways internal conflicts within other Chicago gangs. The failure of all the Latin Folks gangs to control substance use and emotions of revenge, greed, and a thirst for power were major causes of SGD's downfall.

THE C-NOTE$' TURF

The main branch of the C-Note$, run in the mid-1990s by Lucky and then Joey Bags, was around the corners of Ohio and Leavitt, just east of tiny Smith Park. Grand Avenue, the namesake of the Outfit's Grand Avenue Crew, lies just to the south of Ohio Street in Chicago's historic "Patch." Humboldt Park, the combat zone for the nineties war of the families, lies less than a mile away to the northwest. The C-Note$' Jefferson Park section, six miles north of the Patch, was founded in 1976 by the Hobo brothers (recall Sal saying in chapter 3 that the Hobos had some "Hispanic blood" in them). Dominic, who was an Ohio and Leavitt leader, formed a C-Note$ branch in Elmwood Park, popularly called "Spaghetti Hill."

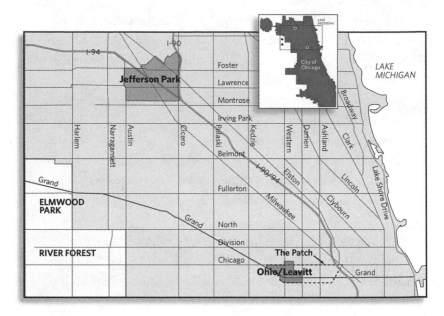

FIG. 5.1. C-Note$ and Outfit territories on Chicago's West Side. Map created by Tamada Brown & Associates

Elmwood Park, as well as nearby River Forest, is home to many Outfit bosses. In the nineties Mo Mo ran the Jefferson Park organization and for a time was Joey Bags's number 2 in the C-Note$ hierarchy before rising to the top spot.

In the 1980s, Big Wally had graduated from the C-Note$ to running his Outfit burglary crew full-time. Among the Ohio and Leavitt members at that time were "Crusher" and "Legs," blood relatives of noted Family Secrets trial figure Frank Calabrese. In the 1970s, Joey "the Clown" Lombardo was touted as the youngest and most promising of the Outfit leaders, running the Grand Avenue Crew before his stint in federal prison for the attempted bribery of US senator Howard Cannon. He was admired by the Outfit guys and worshipped by young C-Note$.

Joey Bags learned the business from Big Wally and was being introduced to the ins and outs of being an Outfit associate and taught how to run a crew. The day-to-day workings of the C-Note$ were being led then by Lucky, a rough and exceptionally brutal leader. Sal describes Lucky with disdain:

Table 5.1. Dramatis personae in the C-Note$

Joey Bags	Puerto Rican leader of Ohio and Leavitt section; Outfit Associate; earlier Lucky's number 2 and Sal's main guy
Sal Martino	Outfit figure; godfather to the C-Note$
Sam Giancana	Outfit boss in 1970s disliked for flamboyant style
Sammy	Italian Jefferson Park section leader
Dominic	Ohio and Leavitt Italian leader; Outfit Associate; deported to Italy
Lucky	Ohio and Leavitt leader; "Hillbilly" mentor to Joey Bags
Mo Mo	Jefferson Park leader, Puerto Rican Outfit Associate liaison to SGD; chair of In$ane Family
Tina	Outfit blood-related drug dealer from Ohio and Leavitt
Fiend	Ohio and Leavitt soldier; husband of Tina
Alina "Ala" Lis	Drug dealer, lover of both Miedzianowski and Joey Bags
Joey "the Clown" Lombardo	Outfit top boss after Accardo's death
Frank Calabrese	Outfit figure and target of Family Secrets organized-crime trial
Big Wally	1980s Ohio and Leavitt leader
Hobo Brothers	Jefferson Park leaders
Mickey "the Pancake"	Jefferson Park soldier; mentor to Mo Mo
Salas Brothers	C-Note$ who "flipped" and turned Latin Kings and led a King branch at Huron and Hoyne
"Chuckie" English	Outfit figure, loyal to Sam Giancana; sponsor of Salas Brothers
Suzie Shelton	Lady Insane Deuce, related to C-Note$ and girlfriend to Joey Bags and other gang leaders
Francisco "Pimp Daddy" Garcia	Brother to MLD leader "Rick Dog" Garcia; represented MLDs in prison; cellmate to Dominic

For Lucky there were no rules, other than the ones he liked or made up along the way. Those who dared defy his rules ended up being violated or worse. In my memory he was the C-Note$' most unstable leader. I heard his behavior was because of the loss of a younger brother "Red" to a rival gang when he was a teenager. Regardless of the reason, at the end, he had to be cut off. We always demanded respect for all rules and regulations that hold our organization together, and those who chose to defy them were dealt with accordingly.

Lucky was born in Chicago into the gang life, with C-Note$ tattoos adorning his mother's arm. Sal said he never stood a chance at being anything but a gangster. Not being Italian, Lucky made good use of a violent, nasty disposition to demand unquestioned respect. Sal explained to me that for C-Note$, if you were Italian, your life's ambition was to be a made man. If you were not, the "best of them" like Big Wally, Joey Bags, or Mo Mo, aspired to be an associate. Outfit guys like Sal watched C-Note$ mature and made judgments on whether or not they could cut it in the life.[1]

By the late 1980s Lucky, who was a plumber by profession, had accumulated a minor police record and he began to move up the ranks. Lucky took over much of the drug trade in part of the West Town area of Chicago. His brother's death led to his own increasingly brutal and irrational actions. He seemed unable to control his emotional outbursts. This volatility, on the other hand, gave him the daring to pull off ambitious money-making schemes. What it boiled down to, Sal said, was "he simply had more balls" than anyone else around. In any event it was Lucky who aggressively moved on independent operators on the West Side in the 1980s and with relentless violence turned them all into his underlings. Not even his own crew liked or respected Lucky, but they certainly did fear him.

Guys in the Grand Avenue Crew looked down on Lucky. This was probably due to the way he carried himself. Classified by popular culture as a hillbilly, he acted and dressed like one, even though at the time he probably had several hundred thousand dollars at his disposal. Sal admired his focus on profits. "One thing you did not want to do was mess with his money. You could kick his dog and you could poke fun of him, but don't dare come up short. If you did, Lord help you!"

Lucky was quick to use violence against those who didn't pay up and sometimes against those who just irritated him. Sal wasn't upset by Lucky's violent way as much as how he carried it out. Sal explained that for violence to be effective it needs to be controlled, or instrumental to some purpose. Lucky's violent rages also alienated him from his own crew. In the early nineties Lucky was arrested for angrily ordering the murder of a Latin King. He spent several months in jail, and when he made bond, none of the Ohio and Leavitt C-Note$ really wanted things to go back to the way they were. Joey Bags was effectively in charge then, and while Joey was no one to mess with, he ran things in a more controlled fashion.

Eventually Lucky got convicted for conspiracy to commit murder and sentenced to a term in prison. Lucky hadn't thought or cared much about gang politics prior to his imminent sentencing. But suddenly he started pressuring the C-Note$ to turn Folks, thinking about spending time up close and personal with lots of friends and foes he had screwed over.[2]

Sal didn't care much what happened to Lucky behind bars, but Lucky's panic emphasized the advantages of the C-Note$ members having allies when locked up. This got Sal to thinking about the growing strength of Latino street gangs and the shape of the future. Sal realized that on one level the issue for the C-Note$ was that they needed to decide whether to turn People or Folks.

The Outfit had some dealings with People, notably the Latin Kings, but these interactions had left a bad taste in Sal's mouth. Adam and Omar Salas had been Hispanic C-Note$, but they never got along with the other soldiers. Racial hostility and tension between Hispanics and Italians did not disappear just because they were all out for money. The Salas brothers had been friends of Lucky's brother Red and knew the extent of C-Note$ ties to the Outfit. In the early 1980s they had "flipped," meaning they quit the C-Note$, and formed a Latin Kings branch at Huron and Hoyne, adjacent to the C-Note$ Ohio and Leavitt home turf. Their defection made the two brothers a danger to C-Note$ security. But they became untouchable, since they were allegedly selling dope for Charles "Chuckie" English, a midlevel Outfit figure Sal disliked. For the C-Note$, as long as the Salas brothers were under Chuckie's protection, they and their turf were off limits. Resentment swelled among C-Note$ like Joey Bags.

Sal didn't like Chuckie English because he had been sponsored by Sam Giancana, a flashy mob boss who had not done things the under-the-covers Outfit way. After Giancana met his fate on his kitchen floor in 1975, English split to Florida and tried to go low-profile. But on February 13, 1985, English was back in Chicago dining at the old Horwath's restaurant in Elmwood Park. As he was leaving he was summarily executed, likely on orders of then Outfit boss Johnny DiFronzo and longtime Outfit heavy Jackie Cerone. Sal shed no tears.[3]

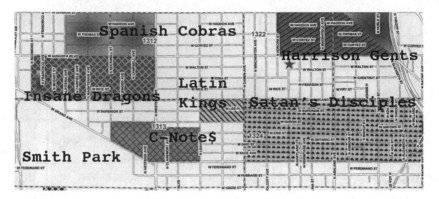

FIG. 5.2. C-Note$ and nearby gangs. Source: Chicago Crime Commission

English's hit also marked open season on Latin King turf on Huron and Hoyne, called "Heaven and Hell" by the Kings. For the next ten years it was tit for tat, and eventually the Kings were driven off and the C-Note$ took over the area. The Chicago Crime Commission's gang maps, from which figure 5.2 is taken, still showed a Latin King chapter at Huron and Hoyne in 2012, although the King chapter had been eradicated years before.[4]

Feelings against the Latin Kings ran high in the C-Note$, and for Sal, any friend of Chuckie's was no friend of his. Joey's reports of the formation of SGD convinced Sal that the Folks Alliance was the best bet for the C-Note$. He began to see that big things might be possible, including his sponsorship of a full-blown Spanish mafia with all the credit and profits that could mean for him. Lucky's imminent incarceration, as well as the sentencing at about the same time of Sammy and an Outfit-connected C-Note$ drug dealer, Fiend, made alignment with Folks a more urgent matter.

JOEY BAGS TAKES CENTER STAGE

Sal had always liked Joey Bags. The kid had spunk, if not always the best sense in fooling around with women. And then there was his drinking problem. But Sal admired Joey's ruthless streak in extending the C-Note$ rackets on the West Side and striking fear into deadbeats and any others who thought they didn't have to pay every penny they owed . . . and promptly.

Sal told me, with what I'd call a fond look, this story of Joey Bags letting everyone who owed him a dollar know what's up.

> There was this time when Bags walked into Peabody's Pub with a claw hammer and stuck it in this kids' head for having an outstanding debt. Now Joey had grown up with this kid since elementary school, and here they were in their twenties and one was going after the other, no questions asked. Needless to say, the debt was paid in full shortly after this incident and the kid was never late again.

Joey was Lucky's number 2 guy for years. Together they ran their show with more ruthlessness than brains. Joey's violent reactions like the one above were modeled on Lucky's all-too-frequent sudden acts of violence. They also stemmed from his father's own alcoholism and Joey's need to constantly prove himself as a Puerto Rican in an Italian world. But Joey had much more empathy for the guys who worked for him. Joey's demeanor was a welcome change for C-Note$ members who had been constantly in fear of being violated for nothing more than an odd look when Lucky walked in. Lucky's erratic behavior also caused friction with other C-Note$ branches and kept the organization divided even as they were faced with enemies on all sides. Bad leadership can undo even a very profitable operation.

Joey also began to be cultivated by Sal as someone who could be a good earner. He became an Outfit associate at the same time that he had risen to number 2 under Lucky in Ohio and Leavitt. While Lucky was nominally the boss, Joey extended the C-Note$ criminal activities to areas like arms trafficking, and he made use of the skills he learned from Big Wally in burglary. It was because of these skills, and the recommendation of Big Wally, that Sal began to mentor Joey and give him assignments as an associate. These activities were separate from his C-Note$ operations and Joey had to kick back a "bite" of 10 percent of everything he made to Sal. As a Puerto Rican he flaunted his associate status and was both feared and respected in the West Side underworld.

Joey hated the cops. Sal told me about an incident in the eighties when three of Joey's buddies were in a car pulled over by a squad car. The officers asked them why they were in Latin Disciples' hood, snatched the keys and locked them in the trunk. Joey's guys would have to walk home through hostile turf. Soon after the cops drove off, Ds came out of hiding, surrounded the car, and opened fire. Jake, one of Joey's friends, was hit by a single gunshot to the head and died. Joey went on a drinking binge after that and railed on and on about his anger toward the CPD. Joey's attitude toward cops would contribute later to his untimely end.

Sal understood how Joey felt, but he put more importance on how to manipulate the police. For the Outfit, figuring out how to work with cops was the key to longevity. Cops loved money just like anyone else. Sal encouraged several local men and women to become police officers, and they saved the day more than once for C-Note$.

Joey had served as an apprentice to Big Wally and was one of the older guys in the current crop of C-Note$ leaders. Big Wally, like so many Outfit associates, was a burglary guy, and Joey learned how to case a target and go in and out without getting caught. But Joey's nickname came from his fascination with the riches of the drug game—both "bags" of dope and the "bags" of money that it produced.

While Lucky did his business mainly with the Harrison Gents, Joey found willing buyers of "weight" in the Insane Dragons, a gang just north of his Ohio and Leavitt section. These ties would prove useful when tensions with the Harrison Gents stalled C-Note$ overtures to joining SGD. By the early 1990s, Joey was "rolling" and his reputation growing, but his drinking and eye for the ladies constantly landed him in trouble.

TINA'S STORY

"You'd never guess Joey was a ladies man," said Sal. "He didn't look like no Clark Gable. But he had the gift of gab." When he got older, Joey even talked himself into local political circles, and Sal wondered "what babes he was chasing there." Whatever he had, he attracted fast women and more than one at a time.

An example of his penchant for woman trouble was the wild and pretty

"Lil Suzie" Shelton. She had unsuccessfully testified for the defense in the murder of a Spanish Cobra, Jacobo Lozada, by her former boyfriend, Simon City Royal soldier "Sammy" Sotirios Georgakapoulos. Suzie was a Lady Insane Deuce but was related by blood to Cobras as well as to a high-ranking C-Note. Later, she was riding in the car when two Insane Deuces committed a murder, and she testified against both of them to save her own hide. "She was working all sides," said Sal disgustedly. She was one of many women who were drawn to Joey, but after she testified in court, he dropped her like bad debt. Sal said, "He was just really lucky that she didn't turn around and rat him to the authorities on the type of business he was conducting."[5]

Joey's fling with Tina, an Outfit-tied drug dealer, brought even more headaches. Since there were so few descriptions of the role of women in the C-Note$, I asked Sal to tell me Tina's story. Sal's description was so vivid, not only of Joey and Tina, but of conditions in early-nineties Chicago, that I thought it best to present Sal's words at length and only slightly edited.

During the 1980s and 1990s, the spread of cocaine meant prices quickly dropped and coke became the drug of choice for most of the users in the Chicago metropolitan area. This led to a massive increase in drug profits, and its impact on the city of Chicago is surely underestimated. You'd never guess how many real estate and economic booms that took place during this time period were financed from the overflow of money as drug dealers poured their money into various legitimate businesses. One of the best of these entrepreneurs was a woman, who I'll call Tina.

By the 1990s entire building projects were built in and around Chicago financed with dope money. Local businesses boomed and the nightlife seemed to be roaring. Whereas a typical dealer would make $1,000 in profits per day, Tina and her crew were making close to $5,000 each day. Tina was now profiting more from this explosion than your average dealer, and it was all due to her many connects built by her and Fiend, her other half.

Tina was born to a middle-class family in the early seventies in Chicago. She suffered much abuse at the hands of her alcoholic and drug-addicted father, and by the age of fifteen was out on the block learning the ropes. By her teenage years, this 5'4" dirty blond had already been rumored to have been dealing and wheeling all over the hood.

She was the daughter of an Outfit associate whose bloodlines were tied to a long line of Outfit members, including Frank "the Enforcer" Nitti. Tina began transforming herself into the Cocaine Queen of West Town. She entered the West Town-based cocaine drug trade and underworld when her husband, who also had Outfit blood, went to jail for the distribution of narcotics and armed violence. This Bonnie and Clyde couple moved millions of dollars' worth of drugs and swag in the streets of Chicago throughout their criminal careers.

Tina met her husband, Fiend—you can guess why he was called that—in the late eighties, and they soon began their love-and-hate relationship. Together they had two children. Fiend introduced Tina to Joey Bags, something that they both would live to regret. Fiend eagerly taught Tina how the drug trafficking business worked, and together they built a thriving drug and fencing business in Chicago and the surrounding suburbs. By the midnineties, with Fiend serving time, Tina was pretty much free to do as she pleased.

Her new business partner was Joey Bags, and by the midnineties, Tina started to expand her trafficking network in Chicago. Always trying to stay one step in front of the law, she now found herself constantly on the move, jumping from one apartment to another every few months. As far as I was concerned, Tina was no more than a cunning sexual deviant with a taste for violence. I stayed away from her.

Her business philosophy was simple—she exploited her family ties to organized crime and informed all business associates that if they failed to pay back monies owed, they would have to answer to the Outfit. The thought of having to answer to the Outfit made everybody pay in a timely manner or they would have to be prepared to suffer the consequences. Knowing the Outfit's history of violence, all transactions most often went off without a hitch, but there were some that needed extra attention and she gave it to them with a sadistic smile. By the midnineties, Joey told me her drug empire was netting over $50,000 a month. She was living high off the hog.

Tina used several shrewd business methods to operate her empire. She moved from the Patch to North Mayfair Park, and there she quickly surrounded herself with nearby Jefferson Park soldiers. The guys operated as paid muscle and were put together with the help of her husband, having himself been a

Note since his teens. Tina used single mothers as mules to carry her drugs. To the average Joe, the single mothers looked unsuspecting, and they would go undetected about their business across the city and suburbs.

One of her favorite mules we called "the Hag." In the early 1990s the Hag's boyfriend, a C-Note$ soldier, was gunned down on the corners of Grand and Oakley by rival gang members, and the Hag was left to fend for herself and her three small children. The Hag was not the best-looking thing in the world. As a matter of fact she reminded me of Broomhilda. Joey used to say that she had fallen off of the ugly tree and hit every branch on the way down. Even so, she managed to lure some of the young unsuspecting bucks in the hood into her web—a trick she had probably learned from hanging out with good ol' Tina. One such unsuspecting young buck would later go on to say that he was going to file a law suit against Miller Lite for letting him get so drunk off of their product that it led to him and the Hag ending up in the sack together.

Tina had orchestrated a master plan with Joey Bags, who had been living in her apartment prior to her husband's incarceration. Fiend's cousin, a C-Note, moved into the apartment downstairs in order to keep some additional muscle close.

It was during this time period that Tina began to have sexual relationships not only with Joey Bags but with other members of her network. Joey himself was beginning to get involved with Alina Lis, who everyone called Ala, one of his many connects. That relationship eventually caused Tina to become jealous and she ordered Joey to move out. The fact of the matter is that the guy was single and he was planting his seed everywhere that he got the opportunity to do so. To me, you should never mix business with pleasure. His situation with Tina was a perfect example of what not to do.

Tina was angered that Ala was fucking Joey Bags behind her back, and even though she ordered him to move out he didn't go far. He moved less than a thousand feet away into a twelve-unit building directly behind Tina's. There he kept on dealing with Ala and Tina, both in drugs and sex. Joey would get his from Ala later, as she dumped him for that dirty cop Joseph Miedzianowski.

Another person that moved into the twelve-unit building was Tina's brother Tiny, who had become Joey Bags' flunky. Tiny was a big boy but his elevator did not stop on all floors. Thus, Joey Bags used him as his own personal errand boy. It wasn't long before Joey Bags added some additional muscle, as another recently released soldier moved in with him. This brother was "no nonsense" and handled business at the drop of a dime, thus making him the ideal roommate to protect their empire.

It was in this same building that Chicago's finest tried to serve a search warrant on Joey Bags. Unfortunately for them, Joey Bags had been tipped off by our guys in the CPD and moved days prior to the warrant being served, across the hall and into Tiny's apartment. When the cops came to the door and announced that they had a warrant to search the premises they found there was no Joey Bags living at that address. Tough shit.

Taking full advantage of the current street war that was brewing, assassins were being dispatched across the city as the war of the families had kicked into high gear. When the opportunity arose, bodies began to drop left and right as these assassins opened fire on unsuspecting victims. For Tina, as well as Joey and the C-Note$, this was a perfect cover to wage war on opposing dealers and rivals. The public and enemies both simply believed that the victims were just casualties of the Maniac vs. Insane war. While law enforcement looked for who they believed to be the obvious culprits, the C-Note$ would sneak in and out after pulling burns without the worries of being suspected as the attackers.

"Ghost," one of the hit men who participated in this campaign, said in a sworn affidavit that Tina had wanted rivals dealt with because she had a master plan to take over the drug business that was left behind by guys who were now incarcerated. Even she knew that she would not have stood a chance at making a move if those individuals were still out on the block. Having them out of the way was a perfect opportunity and she began to capitalize on it. She was one tough cookie.

Nearly a year after her hostile takeover began Tina was seen out partying more and more into the wee hours of the morning. It was suspected that she might have also begun to sample some of her own product. She began to really let herself go, as her complexion suffered along with her weight. Individuals began to notice that some of her dealings had become more and more erratic. So erratic, that her business began to suffer. While out all night she was known to have sex with both unknown men as well as some known ones. Her rep around the hood started to get questioned, and with her man soon to be released, she began to look for property outside of the city so that her other half would not be exposed to her behavior for the past years while he was locked up.

Tina's story reminds us that women sometimes play major, though typically unreported, roles in the gang and drug game. Her tale ends badly, but at this writing she is still alive, while Joey Bags is not. In the mid-1990s Joey moved on, though his open affair with Tina prompted the C-Note$ to amend their laws to prohibit relationships with other members' girlfriends or wives. It was Joey's flings with Suzie, Tina, and Ala, as well as his drinking, that led Sal to question his capacity to lead the C-Note$, especially in dealings with SGD.

JOEY, DOMINIC, AND SAMMY

Joey Bags became quite the fence and was able to make huge profits with stolen merchandise acquired from his crew. He established a partnership with Fat Charlie from the Orchestra Albany gang who owned a dollar store near the corner of Division and Rockwell. Charlie then began to move the stolen goods just below wholesale prices. Everyone made a profit, and soon newly acquired merchandise was being moved at local flea markets across the city and in the biggest pawnshops of them all, local taverns. Since the late 1980s the C-Note$ have appropriated millions of dollars' worth of goods from homes throughout Cook County, as well as from the rich suburban counties of DuPage, Lake, and Will.

For years the C-Note$ were moving swag at the old Maxwell Street Market on Halsted and Maxwell. In 1994 the city moved the market to its new location at Polk Street, due to the expansion of the place where I teach, the University of Illinois–Chicago. The city then forced sellers to get vendor's licenses. Sal said: "All this meant was that the city wanted to get a bigger piece of the pie. Any way the city tried to slice it, the C-Note$ adapted and still made a profit. Tens of millions of dollars' worth of clothing, electronics, and other stolen goods are still moved through that market every year without them skipping a beat."

Joey began to extend his Ohio and Leavitt faction into other criminal activities, such as arms trafficking and especially burglary. By the early 1990s, Joey Bags's drug operations had expanded greatly. He had started selling cocaine out of Little Rascals, Tie Breakers, and Frank and Rosa's lounges and was also the financier of a large marijuana operation that imported weed from Aurora, Illinois. The marijuana was delivered by the carload from his connects in Aurora and sold out of an apartment on School Street.

Unlike Lucky, Joey had real concern for his underlings, especially those who got locked up. He made sure everyone who was incarcerated got a monthly payout of $200 and four magazines of choice. Joey Bags's sources of income and his crew continued to grow throughout the midnineties. By the fall of 1995 he attempted to add loan sharking and bookmaking to his repertoire, but Sal said, "That did not pan out too well for him." After suffering several weeks of losses and large payouts, and with the thought of having to chase people down for his money, he decided to stick with what he knew best. He involved himself with cartage theft: targeting trucks that were delivering or receiving shipments from electronics supplies stores. His crew included Dominic, a well-respected criminal who had just been released from prison.

Sal didn't want to talk much about Dominic or Sammy—I think it was because they were Italian—and he held back information about them. From what I could gather Dominic was born in Italy into a working-class family who immigrated to Chicago when he was an infant. As a teen, Dominic joined the C-Note$ following in his brothers' footsteps on Ohio Street and started out doing thefts. His family had moved to Elmwood Park, and he began to pull small burglary jobs that turned into a full-time job by the time he reached eighteen. He later started a small C-Note$ chapter in that suburb.

Dominic began various criminal ventures while working as a house painter. Sal explained that Big Wally's creative use of his day job of truck driving for the city had modeled the craft of using legitimate work—such as Dominic's painting or Lucky's plumbing—as a way to case homes and businesses and set them up for Outfit burglary crews. This pattern sharply contrasts with that of the black and Latino gang members I've previously studied. For them, regular work was not an option, and their entrance into gang life was a more or less an understandable consequence of dire living conditions. While for black gangsters, gang life was a choice, it was more of a desperate gamble in the face of a bleak future.

For C-Note$, on the other hand, a regular job was easy to get but secondary and functional to their criminal careers. With eventual admission into the Outfit in mind, Dominic worked his way up the criminal ladder through running his own very profitable burglary crew. Following a botched burglary he was arrested, and each member of his crew was charged with burglary, conspiracy to commit burglary, attempted grand larceny, and possession of burglary tools. They were found guilty and sentenced to serve time in prison. Less than a year after his release, Dominic found himself back behind the wall, this time for armed violence and distribution of narcotics. While he was locked up this time, he shared a cell with Francisco "Pimp Daddy" Garcia, the brother of the then street boss of the Maniac Latin Disciples, Rick Dog. Eventually, Dominic would serve as the C-Note$ institutional liaison to La Tabla, SGD's ruling body.

Sammy was the son of Italian parents who settled in the Jefferson Park neighborhood in the midseventies. He was close friends with Mo Mo, and for a while was partners with Mo Mo's mentor, Mickey the Pancake. Sammy was relentless in his efforts to gain control of various business ventures in the Jefferson Park area on Chicago's Northwest Side. Sammy's family was prosperous as well as Outfit-connected. Still, he had a violent youth. In the 1980s, Sammy was arrested and charged with multiple incidents of assault, battery, possession of narcotics, disorderly conduct, and by 1987 attempted murder. Although Sammy's record showed many assaults as a youth, he had served only one prison term, an eleven-month stint for aggravated battery. Sammy's reputation was so fearsome that in more than one case he would get blamed for the beatings of rivals that he didn't even do.

At only five foot seven with a medium build, Sammy was an old-school gangster who held onto the tradition of honor and respect for the family hierarchy. He was instrumental in carrying forward the wars with rivals of the past decade and had survived several attempts on his life. He had been shot, stabbed, and beaten on various occasions, but survived them all. He got along well with Mo Mo, since he also had modern ideas about where he wanted the gang to go. He began to reorganize Jefferson Park criminal activities to maximize profit. He masterminded schemes of cartage theft, boosting, bootlegging cigarettes, and narcotic sales.

Sammy was considered by Sal to be a "class act" who maintained close relationships with many of the organization's elite as well as the lower rank and file. Sal laughed that the young gang members liked serving under him because he would shower them with lush parties catering to all imaginable vices. These were the "side benefits" of gang life.

Sammy and Dominic were close to both Joey Bags and Mo Mo. When Lucky got locked up, they supported moves to strengthen and unify the C-Note$. The Jefferson Park and Ohio and Leavitt chapters were both C-Note$ turf, but Jefferson Park leaders kept their distance from their brothers in the Patch because of their disdain for Lucky's methods. They simply didn't want to be too close to him, and later events proved them more right than they imagined. Once Lucky went to jail on charges of conspiracy to murder, the two Hispanics started to talk between themselves. They agreed that the C-Note$ needed to turn Folks not only for protection of their members "in the joint" but also for the sake of maximizing profits. The two branches unified under joint leadership. For the first time, the C-Note$ were led by two non-Italians.

Sal saw unity as a sound practical matter as well as the precondition to bigger things with SGD. The Jefferson Park faction supplied the C-Note$ in West Town with weapons and narcotics, and sometimes the Ohio and Leavitt faction was expected to do the same thing. But more often than not they provided each other with stash houses where members could disappear while police searched for them in their own neighborhood. If one of the C-Note$ was wanted for any criminal act in the West Town area, Jefferson Park would make sure he had a good hideout in their turf or in one of the surrounding suburbs. The guest, Sal said, would be treated like a god and provided with any vice they wanted during their stay. This was the Outfit way.

MO MO'S LIFE STORY

Mo Mo was brought up in a conventional, two-parent Hispanic family who moved to Chicago when he was very young. As a Hispanic living in an Italian neighborhood, he worked hard to fit in. Sal said he was quite an athlete as a kid, and everyone in the neighborhood loved his parents.

His proud mother and father expected him to succeed in business, and he did, but not the kind of business they had hoped. There was nothing about Mo Mo, as far as I could see, that fit the broken-family, troubled-kid model of who becomes a gang member. Sal said that Mo Mo felt being part of the neighborhood was a "cradle-to-grave" kind of thing. He internalized a code of loyalty that exceeded those of many of the guys who had an Outfit pedigree.

English wasn't his first language, and at first he struggled at school, but he became a very good student and went on to take college courses. In his teenage years he drifted away from school and was attracted to the Young Notes, the C-Note$ junior group. In order to become a Midget C-Note you had to shoot a rival member. Everyone had to do that, and Mo Mo was no exception. This kind of initiation is common with gangs, but Sal said Outfit guys used it to determine who had both guts and potential.

In the 1970s, the C-Note$ were a large organization of more than a hundred members in their Ohio and Leavitt mother branch. They were age-divided like other gangs, with Midget and Pee Wee sections, a ladder everyone had to climb before they could become full members. The decision by C-Note$ leadership in the eighties to stay independent, however, led to increased gang violence and dwindling membership. Mo Mo would became the key player by the midnineties in the C-Note$ resurgence in part due to his advocacy of affiliation with Latin Folks.

Mo Mo had a tough time learning his place in the ethnic hierarchy. Sal told me of one time Mo Mo was at an Outfit guy's kids' house and the guy's sister "comes on" to Mo Mo, prancing in front of him in a negligee. "There are some things you don't do. Italians and Hispanics don't mix like that. Nuncio came in and knocked Mo Mo across the room. It was both that the rules said don't mix it up with another member's sisters, but we didn't really want to mix that way with Hispanics. Keeping them separate ain't wrong." It wasn't until he was older that Mo Mo realized he had to be Italian to be a made guy. From his early years, he told some amused associates, he wanted to be "bigger than Al Capone." He would overcome his Hispanic heritage by adopting the demeanor and speech patterns of Italian mobsters. This made him Sal's ideal candidate to liaison with SGD and the Latin Folks.

Mo Mo learned the dope game from Mickey the Pancake, a C-Note$ soldier who Sal disdainfully complained had a "flamboyant" style.

What Mickey didn't spend at the bar he would spend it on the bitches. He was being taken like a fool by these neighborhood coke whores, and he knew it, yet every week you could see him in the hood with a different one on each arm. Next thing you know he was buying a different car every other month. An Oldsmobile here, a Cadillac there—he was getting out of control. He was burning through money like water at all the hottest nightclubs, spending $1,000 to $2,000 a night. One would have thought that making that kind of scratch and knowing that all good things come to an end that he would have saved some money for a rainy day.

Mickey could get away with lots of stuff because he was connected. Aside from Mickey's father being an associate of the Grand Avenue Crew, his brother was a Cook County sheriff who worked at the jail at 26th and California. He once got time for drugs and ended up in a downstate prison cell with Sammy. He did his time and came back to do it all again. Mickey is one more example of guys who "coulda shoulda" made it, but were seduced by women, drugs, alcohol, or power. For every guy who made it, there were at least a dozen Mickeys. Mo Mo learned both positive and negative lessons from him.

As a teen Mo Mo thrived in the highs of gangbanging and also began to learn how to run a variety of criminal enterprises. One thing I realized talking to Sal is how much of a role chance plays in someone's life. While Mo Mo was known to have been grabbed by cops many times as a kid and involved in much C-Note$' violence and criminality, he never did serious time behind bars. He largely escaped paying consequences for his criminal life. Mo Mo was clearly one of the most intelligent of the C-Note$, and his IQ was fertile ground for Sal once they met. But Mo Mo's life would have likely taken a markedly different turn if he had been shot or spent time in prison like the other C-Note$ leaders.

Mo Mo started out as a Young Note, and when he was growing up it was all about colors. Gang sweaters were the thing back then, Sal said. A Young Note started out with sweaters with one stripe, then two as a Midget, and with three stripes you were a Pee Wee. That was as high as you could get before graduation. Getting your street diploma meant you entered a kind of criminal "draft," like the pros' draft of college football players. Pee Wee graduates got drafted by one of the crews.

Mo Mo as a kid always hung out with older guys, and his home became a gathering place for the mainly Italian C-Note$. He came to the attention of made guys early in life as their sons hung out with him, watching TV and rooting for the Cubs and other Chicago sports teams. What this did was put Mo Mo on a fast track into the C-Note$. He had a temper and streak of violence, but always was a thinker. Joey Bags picked him in that year's C-Note$ draft. Sal remembers Joey's standard advice to Mo Mo and his young charges that "anyone can be a thug, but it takes a real man to be a gangster." This was the credo of C-Note$ members who aspired to go up the ladder into Outfit ranks as made men or associates.

Mo Mo became part of the enforcer team that went after rival gang members and kept C-Note$ in line. As a teenage soldier, Mo Mo was brought in repeatedly for questioning on aggravated battery charges and was arrested several times, but the charges never stuck. In 1989 after having been involved in some retaliation shootings and with mounting police pressure, Mo Mo left the neighborhood and joined the armed services. Later he would tell Sal that Desert Storm wasn't nearly as violent as his life in Chicago. He was right at home with a gun, and he told Sal the war in Iraq was more "predictable" than Chicago gang wars.

Mo Mo led a wild life of trips to Vegas, blowing lots of money, and partying. But from his early twenties he also had a relatively stable relationship with Mercedes, a fun-seeking younger girl who knew from the start that she wanted them to get married. Mo Mo thus had a traditional relationship that Sal approved of, while he looked askance at Joey's philandering. Mercedes was constantly pushing Mo Mo to get away from gangbanging, which pressured him to slide more comfortably into a lower-key Outfit orbit. Competing pressures to settle down and go for riches and power haunted Mo Mo throughout his life. Mo Mo's more stable personal life is among the factors that convinced Sal that he was their man.

Mo Mo came back to the neighborhood at about the same time that the C-Note$ were considering the implications of SGD. But politics wasn't the first thing on Mo Mo's mind. He quickly hooked up with Joey Bags, and when Lucky went to prison, they began to make money together. The two of them sold TVs, given to them by a member of the Grand Avenue Crew, to employees and patrons of a local bar. In this scheme, he got Sal's attention for the first time. Joey told Sal that once two detectives had suddenly showed up and ask for their cut. To avoid having them confiscate the load, Mo Mo helped them load two TVs into the unmarked squad car. Sal said Mo Mo showed some street smarts, realizing that giving them a bite was the easy way out. Joey Bags gave him a substantial reward for keeping his silence and for not turning over the entire load to the authorities. Sal approved.

Mickey the Pancake's business partner, Sammy, was in jail at the time, so Mo Mo moved in to take his place. By the early nineties Mickey had developed a major source of supply from the Maniac Latin Disciples of Kedzie and Barry, and he was now dumping huge amounts of cocaine all over the Northwest Side to not only the C-Note$ but to members of the Gaylords, Royals, RS Heads, and other trusted independent drug dealers.

Mo Mo made quite a few deliveries, mostly to independent drug dealers. He would store the product at several of his most trusted members' houses. He used to hide the goods in garages, attics, and in storage spaces under stairwells, generally a few ounces at a time. The operation was being run by Mickey, and Mo Mo made sure that his own personal involvement would be hard to pin down by law enforcement. Mo Mo always kept a layer of intermediaries between him and deliveries and especially the collection of money. From the start, Mo Mo was calculating and cautious, while partying hard as one of the boys.

When Mo Mo made deliveries they were always to individuals whom he or his close friends knew. He never made transactions with strangers. Everyone he dealt with he had known for years, some of them since childhood. Knowing the people he was dealing with cut his chances of getting caught. Sal said in another context, "There was always a chance that someone you've known forever may go bad, but the likelihood with us was slim to none. Dealing with someone that you knew since childhood was always best because knowing the whole family would deter individuals from becoming potential informants. There was family honor involved and no one wanted their family to be labeled as a family of rats."

C-NOTE$, THE OUTFIT, AND TURNING FOLKS

The C-Note$ in the early 1990s were facing a dilemma. On the gang side, their successful businesses bought them temporary friends, but the rivalries between gangs kept their life unstable. The Note$ had business dealings with gangs of all sorts, but they were not in control of their fate. In Mo Mo's terms, warfare wasn't "predictable" as it was in the military. As Folks rivalries heated up, they were approached by representatives of the new families, Almighty, Insane, and Maniac, to link up with them. The maneuvering for advantage on the SGD board had begun.

For the C-Note$, turning People was out. They had hard feelings toward the Gaylords, their former UFO buddies, for "selling out." They were also in the process of destroying the LK chapter at "Heaven and Hell," and Sal had never gotten over his disgust for the Kings after their being sponsored by Chuckie English. Lucky had tried to make a deal with the Harrison Gents before he went to prison, and the C-Note$ thought they had made the right choice of joining the Almighty Family. On the other hand, they had had problems in the past with some Folks gangs, including the Cobras and Vikings, and had to push back an attempt by the Insane Deuces to grab some territory.

As soon as Lucky was in jail, the Gents tried to take over C-Note$ territory in the Ohio and Leavitt home turf. They moved in and claimed a couple of corners in the drug trade. Joey Bags would have none of that, and his response was typically violent and effective. The Gents withdrew. But they also stalled on their sponsorship of the C-Note$ into SGD. As time went on, Sal kept after Joey to figure out what was going wrong.

For many C-Note$, like the five core leaders, gangbanging was getting old. They knew they could make bundles of money as Outfit associates, and Lucky, Joey Bags, and Mo Mo had already been tagged by Sal to work a crew. Everyone realized that on the West Side nothing major went down without the Outfit getting their cut. Sal said, "To pull off major scores, open up a spot, or run any type of gambling operation, whether it was a card or dice game in the hood, you needed to be plugged in." In those days there was no way that you could do an illicit job without the Outfit finding out about it, so if you were wise you had to give them their share or suffer the consequences. There was a limit to how far the C-Note$ could take their operation on their own, even if they had wanted to.

Unlike black or Latino gang members, most of the older C-Note$ were now doing middle-class work for the city as tradesmen and laborers. Nearly everyone had a union job. As they grew older, the more criminally minded were now associated with one of two crews: Grand Ave or Elmwood Park. Elmwood Park was an extension of Grand Ave, having been made up of many neighborhood guys who had moved to the area in the late seventies or early eighties. Once a guy was known as an associate of a certain crew, word would be passed around to other members and associates letting them know of their affiliation. Sal said:

> Being a high-ranking member of the C-Note$ and affiliated with a crew was a two-way street. On one hand you had the right to basically call shots as you saw fit. On the other hand you were expected to obey all the orders we handed down with no questions asked. Here is how it worked.
>
> Once we summoned Joey Bags to the Aberdeen Club. A union carpenter had an outstanding debt that was long overdue to one of our guys who had currently been sentenced to do a twelve-year bid. The carpenter felt that he didn't have to pay since the guy would not be around for a while. Well he certainly thought wrong. We sent the C-Note$ out to collect the debt, and if the subject refused they were to give this guy a beat down that he would never forget.
>
> They put out the word on the streets they were looking for this clown. They searched high and low for this guy, and he is nowhere to be found. This idiot then goes to his girlfriend and gets her to pay off in full, and begged us to call off the Gorillas. He apologized for any inconvenience that he might have caused. I felt bad for the C-Note$ who coulda got in a good beating on that degenerate. That's how we gauged whether our minor leaguers were ready to move on up.

Mo Mo was obviously open to recruitment to the Outfit while he took over leadership of the Jefferson Park faction. He stepped up after Lucky's disastrous leadership style had left chaos within the ranks. With Lucky gone, Mo Mo brought order to the Jefferson Park crew and expanded C-Note$ rackets. What was also on his mind was to maneuver the C-Note$ into the Latin Folks fold. It was during this time that Joey Bags introduced Mo Mo to Sal.

I spent some time with Mo Mo back in those days, though it took a while before we talked about him representing us to SGD. I was worried about Joey and we needed a Spic to deal properly with the Spanish. I explained to Mo Mo how to carry himself. I said, look at the Old Man [Joey the Clown Lombardo] who was worth easily over $25 million. He could live anywhere he wanted to—Lake Forest, Glencoe, Winnetka, or Wilmette—with no problems. Yet he lived in a modest three-bedroom house since the early 1950s and drove a simple car. I explained to him how there was no need to dress flashy. I said the Old Man didn't have anybody to impress and was married with children. He went to work every day and could show everything he had could be covered by his income. The last thing you want to get pinched for is tax evasion like Capone.

Sal's advice to Mo Mo reads like a manual for the successful gangster. While much of this wisdom was also current within Latino and black gangs, the difference was that the Outfit represented a successful model and could offer a well-paying job and "professional" advancement to its recruits. The Outfit had lasted at that point for more than seventy-five years. In my terms they had *institutionalized* and were a living example of how gangs could do business over a long period of time. They had the experience necessary to give guidance to the young C-Note$.

I told him that there is enough money to go around and if everyone gets their cut you will not have any problems. If this is the life you want to choose, I told him, then make sure that you jump in both feet first, and be a hustler. You only get what you put into it. I recommended that he find himself a nice racket and invest his money wisely. I told him most guys start their criminal careers in their late teens or early twenties. If you get a good run of let's say ten to twenty years, you could be retired by forty living off of your earnings. Now if you happened to get pinched, hopefully you invested your money wisely and stashed some for a rainy day.

No one wants to go to the joint, but it's a risk of the trade. If you play your cards right, you will have more money than you'll know what to do with. Your kids and their kids will be set for life. If you do go to the joint, don't complain about it. Make sure that when you get out you grab yourself by the balls and get back to business. Whatever you do, don't be one of these guys that ends up doing life on the installment plan. There is nothing worse than hearing a whiner on how they are flat busted and how no one wants to give them a leg up. Don't depend on nobody. That way you won't owe anybody. You follow these words of wisdom and believe me it will all be worth your while. Be the best you can be.

With Lucky, Dominic, Sammy, Mickey, and Fiend all behind bars, the C-Note$ had to make their move. The Gents were stalling, so Joey's drug connection, the Insane Dragons, officially sponsored the C-Note$ into membership of SGD and brought them into the Insane Family. The Cobras also saw the invitation as a good thing, winning the C-Note$' loyalty away from the Harrison Gents, who belonged to the rival Almighty Family. But just as that phase of the C-Note$ history was getting woven, it almost came unraveled. The Aftermath bar incident was disastrous for the C-Note$, but also marked the beginning of the ascendance of Mo Mo to leadership.

THE AFTERMATH AND ITS AFTERMATH

Parties are a stable function of gangs and the Insane Family—popularly called the "I-Team"—was no exception. One party became infamous in C-Note$ lore, held at the Aftermath, at 835 West Evergreen near the old Cabrini-Green housing project and sponsored by the Insane Dragons. The C-Note$ had just joined the Insane Family, and their application to SGD was being sponsored by the Dragons. The Aftermath fundraiser followed a "holiday party" sponsored by the Insane Deuces. The grand prize at the raffle for that party was an AK-47.

Those I interviewed remembered the holiday party of December 8, 1995, as happening on a "dark and stormy night" with nearly a thousand

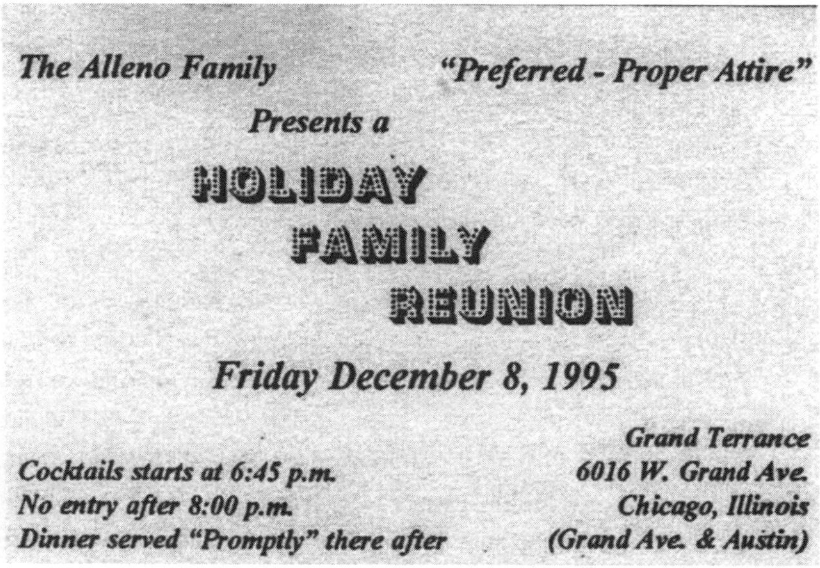

The Alleno Family   *"Preferred - Proper Attire"*

Presents a

HOLIDAY
FAMILY
REUNION

Friday December 8, 1995

Cocktails starts at 6:45 p.m.   *Grand Terrance*
No entry after 8:00 p.m.   *6016 W. Grand Ave.*
Dinner served "Promptly" there after   *Chicago, Illinois*
                                          (Grand Ave. & Austin)

FIG. 5.3. Ticket to Insane Deuces holiday "family" reunion

tickets sold. Soldiers of all the gangs were ordered to sell or buy a roll of tickets at twenty dollars a pop. The parties became popular way for Insane gangs to raise money. The holiday party at the Grand Terrace took place just after the C-Note$ joined the Insane Family. Mo Mo and Joey Bags, as the two Puerto Rican leaders of the C-Note$, represented their gang and without saying it out loud, the Outfit. The C-Note$ had thrown in their lot with the Insane Family and were eager to show their stuff, in other words to prove themselves worthy in a mainly Latino organization. For Sal, this was the move he wanted, and it opened the door for the C-Note$ to influence the direction of SGD.

After the successful Deuces party of December 8, all the Insane Family gangs were eagerly selling twenty-dollar tickets for the January Aftermath affair. Rival MLD soldiers had violated SGD rules and testified against Dragon members, and that added incentive for Insane members to buy tickets to this party, which would raise money for the Dragons' defense. All the C-Note$ showed up, including Dominic, who had just been released from prison. In the days before the party, Dominic had been acting up, trying to make up for lost time. He had been promoted to a section leader of Elmwood Park. Sal said he was on a rampage and he wasn't happy about it.

At the Aftermath party almost everything that could go wrong did. I interviewed several people who were there that night. Dominic had gotten rip-roaring drunk, and since many of the younger C-Note$ didn't know him, he felt he needed to prove himself with violence. At one point, standing outside the Aftermath, he confronted and humiliated a young member, "Lil Pit-Bull," asking, "What the fuck have you done for the nation lately?" and punched the unsuspecting Young Note in the face. A few minutes later, just as Lil Pit-Bull tried to stand up to an intoxicated Dominic, the police suddenly showed up in large numbers to raid the party. Joey, Mo Mo, and Dominic all ducked out and escaped arrest, but seventy-two people, including many underage juveniles, along with a few I-Team leaders, were arrested. A January 24, 1996, *Chicago Tribune* article about the incident Sal gave me reported:

> The man who allegedly rented the bar for the party, Abel De Jesus, 34, of 2646 W. Augusta Blvd., was charged with 70 counts of contributing to the delinquency of a minor as was the manager of the bar, Greg Rau, 32, of 2533 W. Chicago Ave., police said. Rau and another tavern employee, Alex Karfis, 33, of 3841 W. Touhy Ave., Lincolnwood, were also charged with failure to have a dancing and music license.

Joey Bags was angry with Dominic for causing a scene at an I-Team sponsored function, but Dominic was completely indifferent. He callously told Joey that the I-Team could "go fuck themselves." Joining the I-Team was still too new, and not everyone was fully on board with the decision. Sal said that after the incident, Joey Bags complained that this family stuff wasn't all that it was cracked up to be. He said he could control his own members, but this mixing it up with other gangs made things too difficult. Joey Bags was feeling the pressure and showing signs of retreat from C-Note$ leadership.

Sal wasn't pleased with Joey's response or the substantial fines the I-Team levied on the C-Note$. The C-Note$ had to pay for the guns that were confiscated and cover bail and legal expenses. This didn't get them off on the right foot in the Insane Family, and before long the violence would step up and draw everyone in over their heads. The events of that night led in the next few months to Joey Bags stepping back from C-Note$ leadership and Mo Mo being put forth as their representative to the Insane Family.

Being in a family was supposed to be the best way to protect the C-Note$ from violence as well as expand their vice markets. It linked them organizationally to SGD, which, in Sal's eyes, had the potential to evolve into a Latino-dominated organized citywide crime commission. But the unintended consequence of the founding of the families would instead be more violence that in turn would bring more police attention. This would make all the gangs' vice operations much more difficult and lead to catastrophe. The next chapter documents the origins of the families within SGD and the beginnings of their deadly rivalries.

6 Family Feuds

Document 6.1. Preamble to the SGD Constitution

Preamble

We, personnel of the union, are grateful to all of our brothers for their participation in our struggle across the years, and for the brothers who have given their loyalty to our Union's life. Through the decades we have enjoyed providing Security, Safety, and Domestic Tranquility among the lives of our people.

We personnel of the Union, must ordain and abide by the concept of our Constitution, In that we may . . .

1. Eliminate poverty and inequality among our personnel
2. Provide a structure of potential development for the individuals of our Union;
3. Maintain a liberty for our Children and a more gratifying style of Social Living.

We bless all of our folks along with their families and we will constantly try to obtain a future for the descendants of our union.

The noble sentiments expressed in the preamble to the SGD Constitution (document 6.1) were intended to create a new, broader, even progressive identity for the gangs signing on to the SGD concept. The out-of-control violence of the seventies and eighties set the stage for Latino gangs building a social institution that would bring peace while transcending, but not replacing, the neighborhood-based identities of Latin Folks gangs. One essential criterion for this goal would be broader and more effective leadership beyond the interests of individual gangs. We'll see that this quality of statesmanship and the weakness of what Paul DiMaggio calls "institutional work" was missing in the actual practice of SGD.[1]

The biggest threat to the success of building a new institution, Selznick gravely stresses, is "organizational rivalry." Rather than a common identity and strong overall leadership, factional identities and deadly rivalries would predominate and drag SGD to ruin. The most important aspect of Latin Folks gangs during this time was not their local roots or day-to-day activities. What drove Latin Folks gangs' activities in the early 1990s were their attempts to secure allies in organized power plays to control SGD. It was power, not neighborhood, that mainly shaped gang identity. This chapter tells the origins of Latin Folks' deadly family rivalries.

The C-Note$ were leery of joining either the People or Folks coalition largely because the Latino gangs seemed to be constantly at war, and bloodshed too often got in the way of making money. However, as we saw in the last chapter, incarceration of many of their leaders and the threat of war on all fronts convinced the C-Note$ to petition for membership in SGD.

The reasons for forming SGD were to control the violence, to lessen the impact of the incarceration of gang leaders, and to organize crime. It had less to do with contemporary economic, political, or demographic events. In Humboldt Park at the time, the Puerto Rican community was organizing to resist the encroachment of white yuppies who found the area conveniently located and housing inexpensive. Gentrification and displacement have been persistent themes for Chicago Puerto Ricans, and the Young Lords gang in the 1960s had transformed into a revolutionary organization in part through organizing against gentrification while working with other community organizations.

The early 1990s saw the struggle over the gentrification of Humboldt Park intensify when community activists defiantly erected Paseo Boricua— massive steel flags of Puerto Rico—which proudly marked Humboldt Park as a *Puerto Rican* community. A fierce battle against gentrification took place in that decade, led effectively by a core of community leaders that included alderman Billy Ocasio. The gangs meanwhile, were preoccupied with war among themselves.[2]

The principal dynamics pushing gang development in the 1990s were organizational rivalry within SGD, persisting violence against the Latin Kings, and efforts to evade and corrupt law enforcement. The Latin Folks

were intent on infiltrating the city political machine, but did not go beyond rhetoric in advancing a broader progressive or nationalist agenda.
This stands in stark contrast to the New York City Latin Kings, who
during the same period, with much fanfare, transformed for a time into
an independent progressive community organization.[3]

The main leaders of SGD were all incarcerated and the split between
the prison and the streets became increasingly significant. Since SGD was
seen by gang members as a legitimate authority to mediate and settle disputes, the major Latin Folks gangs sought allies to secure a majority on
the SGD board to get favorable rulings on territory and business conflicts.
The combination of tensions on the streets, a desire to control the decisions
of La Tabla, and lack of decisive leadership resulted in the formation of
families, or factions, within SGD. These factions would prove to be the
cracks that eventually shattered the entire edifice of SGD and with it Latin
Folks' hopes and dreams.

THE SIMON CITY ROYALS AND THE FORMATION OF THE ALMIGHTY FAMILY

The Simon City Royals (SCR) Social Athletic Club historically was one of
the largest and most powerful white greaser street gangs in Chicago. They
were formed by the merger of several small neighborhood gangs in the
late 1960s and were fierce rivals of the Gaylords and Latin Kings, among
others. The main rivals of the SCR were gangs that would become People
like the Puerto Rican Stones or Insane Unknowns.

The Royals' gang slogan, "Cross is Boss," referred to their symbol of a
cross with three slashes above it and could be found as graffiti on countless
buildings and walls across Chicagoland. Like other Chicago gangs, the SCR
were always about more than neighborhood, and they eventually claimed
over fifty sections within the city limits as well as spreading to suburban
Niles, Des Plaines, Franklin Park, and Skokie. In the 1970s they had more
members than any other gang in Chicago, white, black, or Hispanic.

The SCR violently resisted Latino encroachment of their traditional
area around Simons Park, a small green space near the much larger Humboldt Park. From time to time they united with white enemies like the

Gaylords and with their future allies, the Insane Popes, for a racist fight against what would be an irresistible ethnic succession of their neighborhoods. The Royals moved their main operations northward in retreat from what they saw as a Puerto Rican invasion. But they also were among the first white gangs to integrate their ranks with Hispanic members.

The Royals were engaged in warfare on all sides. The Latin Kings, Insane Deuces, and other nearby Latino gangs represented constant threats to their territory, but were met at every corner by violence. Their rivalry with other white greaser gangs, like the Gaylords, resembled in some ways traditional neighborhood ethnic rivalries, except the fighting spread over multiple neighborhoods and "fair fights" were replaced by drive-by shootings. In the 1970s, the Gaylords killed Larry "Larkin" Morris, the leader of the Insane Popes, which led to the building of an alliance with Simon City Royals called the Royal Nation, which became for the next decade the Royal Popes' Nation. Chicago neighborhood gangs have always been looking for allies and alliances.

The SCR earned the reputation as killers and in 1976 lured Capone, the leader of the Insane Unknowns, a Latin King ally, into a supposed peace conference and assassinated him. This led to a fierce war with the Unknowns and the loss of an SCR branch. But more importantly, it intensified wars against what would become People-affiliated gangs. Eventually the Unknowns were all but eradicated throughout Chicago.[4]

In their first decades, the Royals' main money-making activities, like the C-Note$, were burglary and the sale of narcotics. Sal told me their MO was to drive around an area in stolen vehicles around 6 a.m. and watch people leave for work. They waited for a few hours, rang the doorbell, and if no one answered, found a way into the house and ransacked it. They controlled drug sales on their corners throughout the North Side and, like most other gangs, saw many of their members get "high on their own supply." A new minimum sentence of four years for burglary and arrests on drug-sale charges of key leaders, like Frank "Fats" Fender and William "Shadow" Fender, devastated the on-the-street leadership of the Royals. It also created problems for their white members in the mostly black Illinois prisons, and this pushed the Royals to find new allies.

At the same time, a Black Gangster Disciple, Michael "Motto" Motten, moved into one of the Royals' neighborhoods. Despite the fact that he was black, his gang connections made him welcome. The Royals had a desperate need for friends in the prison system, and a working alliance with Larry Hoover's now united Black Gangster Disciples was common sense. In 1978, when Hoover proclaimed the Folks Alliance, the Simon City Royals would be a charter member. While there are unsubstantiated claims of a gun deal buying Folks membership for the Royals, at the time protection of the SCR leadership, now almost entirely incarcerated, was clearly necessary at all costs.[5]

Their Folks Alliance protected SCR members within the prison system, but the Royals' violence and criminal activities had taken its toll on the streets. A weakened SCR was vulnerable to threats from other gangs eager to encroach on their territory. By the mideighties, the SCR were battling on all fronts, and a bitter war against the Insane Deuces intensified when the Deuces turned People—in part to counter the Royals' alliance with Folks gangs. However, the Latin Disciples and Spanish Cobras would also encroach on Royal turf, foreshadowing the internecine wars to come.

The pressure on the Royals from all sides and the incarceration of their main leadership caused their street leader, John "Dollar Bill" Yonkers, to negotiate and sell to the Spanish Cobras traditional Royal turf at Kosciuszko Park. This bought the Royals temporary peace, but when the main Royals leaders, including the Fender brothers, started returning from the penitentiaries, they were outraged by Yonkers' deal. SCR leaders at the time, Agim Hotza, Frank "Fats" Fender, and William "Shadow" Fender filed a grievance with the SGD board against the Spanish Cobras, Maniac Latin Disciples, and Orchestra Albany. Yonkers simply had no authority to sell off SCR territory, the SCR leaders claimed. Their grievance became one of the first major tests of SGD's new La Tabla.

The SGD board was decisive in this instance, and the consequences of their action may have been a factor in their habitually indecisive actions from then on. The seventeen members of La Tabla at the time were nearly all Latino and ruled unanimously against the mainly white Royals. Their decision was not accepted by the Royals, and the SGD board was unable to enforce their edict. Violence between Cobras and Royals over Koz Park then broke out unabated. The war cost dozens of lives over the next several years.

I mentioned in the last chapter one of the major incidents of the war, the killing of Cobra member Jacobo Lozada by Simon City Royal soldier "Sammy" Sotirios Georgakapoulos, Lil Suzie Shelton's boyfriend. After the Royals rejected the SGD board decision as unfair, the Cobras were on the offensive and seized Jensen Park, another North Side area controlled by the Royals. According to court documents, seventeen Cobra soldiers, including the Lozada brothers, had occupied the park expecting trouble. At approximately 10:45 p.m. on July 1, 1994, a dark blue, four-door Oldsmobile automobile, occupied by Royals, slowly drove by, shouted out "Royals Love" and "Cobra Killers," and gunned down one of the lookouts, Jacobo Lozada.[6]

The Royals were outraged that Cobra members testified at the trial, in violation of SGD rules. They immediately took this violation to the SGD board and, in what would become characteristic inaction, La Tabla did nothing. Surely board resentment over the Royals ignoring their ruling over Koz Park was a factor, but the Spanish Cobras constitution explicitly forbade testifying in court, consistent with provisions in the SGD constitution.

The Cobras at the time were one of the two most powerful members of the board, and ruling against them was inconceivable. The board was sensitive to power, but the price of inaction was the further alienation of the Royals and impetus for them to set up the Almighty Family as a protective alliance within SGD. La Tabla failed, in sociologist Philip Selznick's words, "to bind parochial group egotism to larger loyalties and aspirations."[7]

The Cobras had flexed their muscles after both of these SGD decisions and along with their allies were in an expansion mode and not in any mood to conciliate. The Royals asked the two gangs with constant problems with the Cobras, the Latin Eagles and the Imperial Gangsters, to join with them. The last to join the Almighty alliance were the Harrison Gents. All of the Almighty Family members had territory that bordered each other, so there were further sensible reasons for forming a defensive alliance. The gangs in the new alliance all added "Almighty" to their formal names, a practice all the families would follow.

Document 6.2. From the Laws of SGD

LEYES

24. The Ex Board will maintain total jurisdiction over a personnel of this Union when he is in violation of the following acts:

    A) When an individual is positively known to be an informant;

    B) When an individual is positively known to be a homosexual;

    C) When an individual commits an assault upon another personnel of this Union;

    D) When a personnel of the Union is positively known to have lived or been there, under protective means;

    E) When a personnel of this Union abandons or is positively known to have abandoned another personnel of this Union in a situation where potential bodily harm was inflicted to a personnel of this Union.

Note: See appendix 9 for the entire list of SGD laws, or "leyes."

The Almighty Family proved very troubling for SGD and reinforced a family feud politics within it. The entire SGD union was threatened in 1993 when Stanley "Savage" Slaven, the leader of the Almighty Harrison Gents, signed as a confidential informant for the Organized Crime Division of the Chicago Police Department. He gave up information on rival gangs, particularly Insane Dragon Curtis "Curt" Coker and the Dragon's leader at the time, Abel "Green Eyes" De Jesus, who was introduced in the last chapter as the sponsor of the Aftermath party. A copy of Slaven's cooperating-individual request, reproduced below (fig. 6.1), was circulated at an Insane Family meeting.

More threatening, Slaven wore a wire at SGD meetings and led Chicago police to a street meeting of SGD representatives. As police zeroed in, the gang representatives had to run for their lives, reminiscent of fleeing mafia leaders in the infamous Apalachin, New York, police raid in 1957. Unlike that raid, where the FBI became aware for the first time of the existence of a nationwide mafia commission, the Chicago police and FBI failed to understand the significance of the Chicago SGD meeting they had disrupted.[8]

The SGD board ordered the expulsion of Slaven, and the Gents com-

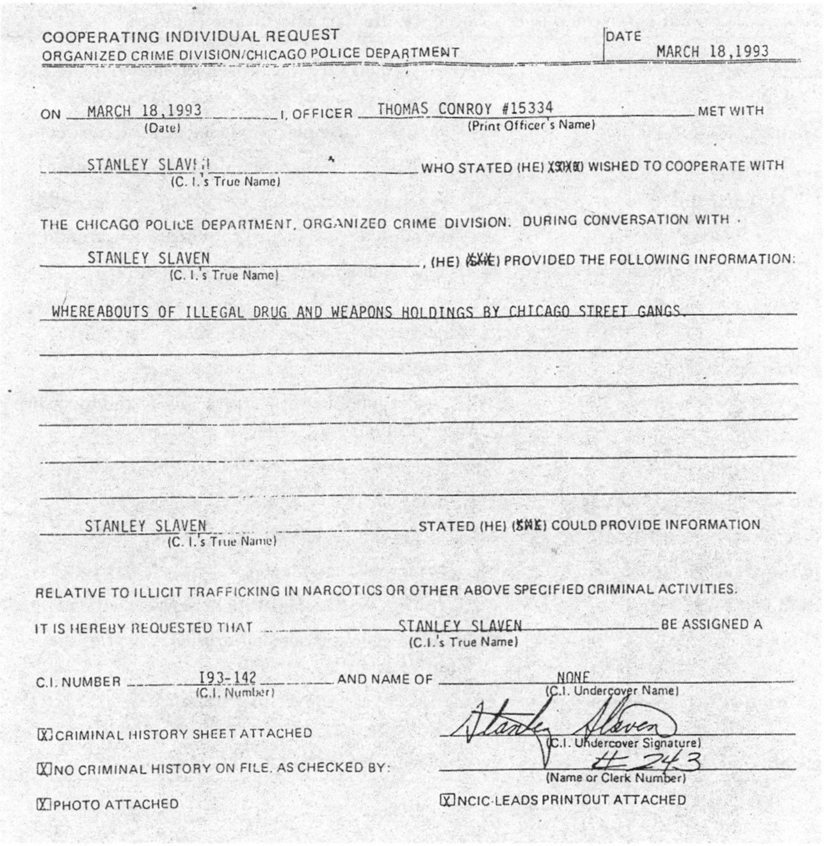

COOPERATING INDIVIDUAL REQUEST
ORGANIZED CRIME DIVISION/CHICAGO POLICE DEPARTMENT

DATE
MARCH 18,1993

ON __MARCH 18,1993__ I, OFFICER __THOMAS CONROY #15334__ MET WITH
(Date)   (Print Officer's Name)

__STANLEY SLAVEN__ WHO STATED (HE) (SHE) WISHED TO COOPERATE WITH
(C. I.'s True Name)

THE CHICAGO POLICE DEPARTMENT, ORGANIZED CRIME DIVISION. DURING CONVERSATION WITH ·

__STANLEY SLAVEN__ , (HE) (SHE) PROVIDED THE FOLLOWING INFORMATION:
(C. I.'s True Name)

WHEREABOUTS OF ILLEGAL DRUG AND WEAPONS HOLDINGS BY CHICAGO STREET GANGS.

__STANLEY SLAVEN__ STATED (HE) (SHE) COULD PROVIDE INFORMATION
(C. I.'s True Name)

RELATIVE TO ILLICIT TRAFFICKING IN NARCOTICS OR OTHER ABOVE SPECIFIED CRIMINAL ACTIVITIES.

IT IS HEREBY REQUESTED THAT __STANLEY SLAVEN__ BE ASSIGNED A
(C.I.'s True Name)

C.I. NUMBER __I93-142__ AND NAME OF __NONE__
(C.I. Number)   (C.I. Undercover Name)

[X] CRIMINAL HISTORY SHEET ATTACHED

[X] NO CRIMINAL HISTORY ON FILE. AS CHECKED BY:

[X] PHOTO ATTACHED

(C.I. Undercover Signature)
#243
(Name or Clerk Number)

[X] NCIC-LEADS PRINTOUT ATTACHED

FIG. 6.1. Signed CI agreement of Stanley Slaven with Organized Crime Division of the CPD

plied, but only after many years of resisting La Tabla's stricture. The SGD board was proving itself incapable of maintaining gang discipline in part because of the power of the newly formed families. The Gents eventually were expelled from SGD after the documents displayed in this book were presented to La Tabla.

THE MANIACS' POWER TRIP

Since the 1960s the Maniac Latin Disciples have been the second-largest Latino street gang on the North Side after the Latin Kings. Violence between these two gangs got its start with the Kings' killing of the MLDs'

Table 6.1. Dramatis personae in the Almighty, Maniac, and Insane Families

Frank "Fats" Fender and William "Shadow" Fender	Brothers; Simon City Royals leaders; filed grievance with SGD on sale of Kosciuszko Park to Cobras
Michael "Motto" Motten	Black Gangster Disciple, persuaded SCRs to turn Folks
Larry Hoover	Gangster Disciple leader; founder of Folks coalition
John "Dollar Bill" Yonkers	SCR leader; "sold" Kosciuszko Park to Cobras
Stanley "Savage" Slaven	Harrison Gent leader turned confidential informant
Albert "Hitler" Hernandez	MLD leader murdered by Latin Kings in 1970
Jacqueline Montañez	MLD female leader; murdered two Latin Kings in 1992; subject of an international clemency campaign
Prince Fernie Zayas	Leader of MLDs, mainly from Stateville
Hugo "Juice" Herrera	MLD leader; member of Herrera Family and the "Durango Connection" to Mexican cartels
Billy Ocasio	Powerful Humboldt Park politician with ties to MLDs
Enrique "Rick Dog" Garcia	Fernie Zayas's successor as MLD leader
Jose "Freckles" Cedeno	MLD street chief; indicted in 1980 sweep
Johnny "Loco" Almodovar	MLD leader who engineered Valentine's Day hits
Bum Brothers	MLD leaders, opponents of Rick Dog
"Juan"	Cobra Governor convicted of murder in war of the families
Anibal "Tuffy C" Santiago	Leader of Cobras; moved to prison in New Jersey to break his operational control of the streets
Blade	Insane Deuce leader and first chair of the I-Team

first leader, "Hitler" Hernandez, in 1970. Unrelenting violence with the Kings pushed the MLDs into the Folks Alliance, since the Latin Kings were also the largest Latino gang in Illinois prisons.

Even as tensions with other Folks gangs were growing, the violence against the Kings kept taking lives. For example in 1992, fifteen-year-old Jacqueline Montañez, along with Marilyn Mulero, twenty-two, and Madeline Mendoza, sixteen, shot and killed Latin Kings Jimmy Cruz and Hector Reyes, both twenty-one. Montañez had just been appointed by Prince Fernie Zayas as the leader of the Lady D's. She sought revenge after the Kings had shot and killed Ismael Torres, or "Mudo," a twenty-one-year-old MLD hanger-on.

The case highlights the factors that push poor and troubled Latinos and African Americans into gangs. It also demonstrates the cynical uses of youthful gang members by older gang leadership that marked the 1990s wars. Montañez at age thirteen had run away from her Latin King step-father, who had been raping and abusing her from the time she was an eight-year-old child. Understandably, when she finally escaped, she joined the rival gang to his, the MLDs. Her hatred of Kings and her stepfather was stoked by her new gang. She told me tearfully in Dwight Correctional Institution that when she pulled the trigger "it was her stepfather" she wanted to kill, not Reyes or Cruz.

Montañez's passionate personality, intelligence, and flair had brought her to the attention of MLD leaders. Soon after joining the Ds she was summoned to Stateville, where Prince Fernie stressed the importance of "family" to her. The MLDs, in truth, had become the family for a young girl who knew only pain from her own. The shooting of Mudo gave her the opportunity to show her bravado and proved her leadership as the newly crowned as leader of the Lady Ds. In fact her new family actually treated her as badly, if not worse, than her old one. Left without financial or emotional support by the MLDs, as a juvenile she was sentenced to life without chance of parole for her role in the killings. A worldwide clemency drive and possible resentencing will not bring back three dead young men or the fact that Montañez has already spent more of her life in prison than in the community.[9]

The killings of rivals, whether of Kings or other Folks, was conducted by young people who either carried out explicit orders, or like Montañez, implicitly understood retaliation as their duty. We will see how the ethic of violence, which had been embedded in Folks gangs in a blood feud with the Kings, transferred itself in the 1990s to internecine hatred toward rival families. SGD's self-image of Folks as a union of gangs peacefully settling their disputes never overcame what might be called rote scripts of violence.[10] Those who paid the ultimate price for the wars of the 1990s were more often than not young people like Jacqueline Montañez, who, while far from being innocents, were simultaneously offenders and victims.

The MLDs had grown for more reasons than an easy and copious use of violence. Key to the growth of the Ds was their member Hugo "Juice" Herrera, a drug dealer with family ties to the Mexican Durango drug cartel.[11] The MLDs distributed cocaine throughout the Chicago area, including a major stopover point in Aurora. Gangs who bought drugs wholesale from them paid a hefty street tax of thousands of dollars per month, and the MLDs grew rich and popular among youth. The MLDs also had ties to politicians, like alderman Billy Ocasio, who had grown up around them and worked closely with machine power broker Richard Mell. Some of the MLD leadership consciously wanted to follow the "Chicago way" of corruption and saw SGD as a promising way out of unending violence. We'll follow that shady story in the next chapter.

But federal law enforcement was taking aim at the Herrera Family and their connections to the MLDs. In July 1980, forty-six Latin Disciples were arrested in what at that point was the largest federal drug bust in Chicago history. The MLDs were running a $20,000-a-day drug business on the corner of Rockwell and Potomac, among other Humboldt Park spots. Among those arrested were Jose "Freckles" Cedeno, then the MLD street chief.

Their self-image as the real leader of SGD caused the MLDs to be almost universally despised among other Folks gangs. Hostilities toward other gangs prompted the MLDs to loosely organize their dependent gangs into a Maniac Family. We've already seen how MLD hectoring of the Latin Lovers drove that gang into the arms of the Insane Cobras for self-protection. For the MLDs even shooting another Folks gang member apparently was seen as within their rights. With Prince Fernie calling the shots from Stateville, Enrique "Rick Dog" Garcia assumed street leadership and appointed Johnny "Loco" Almodovar as his underboss, or don. It was Almodovar who engineered the Valentine's Day *Godfather*-style hits of Cobras reported in the preface that marked the actual launch of the war of the families.

The money and power of MLD drug businesses also led to internal disagreements. For Hugo "Juice" Herrera and one of his partners, "Evil Eddie," both from the Kedzie and Barry section of the MLDs, keeping the money coming in was the main thing. The formation of SGD meant the MLDs could use their power as cartel-linked suppliers to buy votes and get what they wanted from La Tabla. The war with the Cobras, which was originally started by Rick Dog, became more trouble than it was worth. As the violence appeared to have no end in sight, Rick Dog met with Cobra leaders and told them he wanted to quash the war. Supported by Hugo and

Evil Eddie, Rick Dog saw that violence was becoming bad for business. But he did not have unanimous support even within his own gang. Another faction, who coalesced around the "Bum Brothers," were not able to see past their thirst for revenge on the Cobras.

Within SGD, Prince Fernie took the side of Rick Dog, and wanted negotiations to end the war. It was at this time, one Folks leader told me, that the Bum Brothers began supplying Prince Fernie with large amounts of drugs to "keep him high" and "push him out of the picture." The Shakespearean theme of this book, between vengeful emotion and instrumental rationality, would catastrophically play out between MLD factions, eventually dropping the final curtain on SGD.

THE MANIAC FAMILY THROUGH INSANE EYES

The formation of the Insane Family was the result of what was seen as the arrogant power of the MLDs and their allies. How the MLDs were viewed can be understood through an interview I had with Juan, a former Cobra governor, or neighborhood section leader.

I had met Juan, a short Puerto Rican man in his late thirties, right after he got out of prison from a murder conviction he received from ordering a hit on an MLD during the war of the families. When we first met he was suspicious and said very little, but I kept in touch through a common friend. For some reason he mellowed over time and we agreed to talk about how the hostility between the Cobras and the Disciples developed.[12]

I drove to his North Side home, and after I parked my car one of his kids, a colorfully dressed preteen, yelled out to me, "Hey, Professor—he's back here!" I went to the garage and he quickly sent his son away. When we were alone he told me he was nervous about talking "nation business." "When I was a kid," Juan mumbled, "I was told that I could never even mention Tuffy's name." He is understandably emotional in discussing the origins of the hatred between Cobras and Disciples and their families. That rivalry, after all, cost him more than ten years in prison as well as the lives of many friends as well as enemies.

Soon after the formation of SGD, Juan said, "there was this wall" where the MLDs had drawn a hooded figure with a pitchfork, one of their main symbols. But now they had written over it the words "Real Folks." "Who do they think they are?" he said, raising a voice filled with indignation, even now, more than twenty years later. The Folks Alliance had promised a "New Concept" for all Folks, but apparently some gangs were thought to be more "Folks" than others.

Before 1987, he told me, Latin Folks were "one big happy family," or more accurately, he added, "more like one big Latino Family." In fact Cobras and Disciples had even shared some corners, splitting drug profits. "Relations between us were OK," Juan said, his face betraying mixed emotions. Memories seemed to be parading through his head, and those images were not mainly pleasant. During that time, he said, if there were disputes, they were taken to leadership in prison—Tuffy for the Cobras and Fernie for the Disciples. For example, Juan said, "the MLDs controlled Kedvale to Pulaski, Cobras Kedvale to Cicero. If there were encroachments, SGD leaders would simply say "Go look at the map," meaning the gang boundary lines that SGD had ordered surveyed and formalized. Things were settled peacefully and by law. The rulings of La Tabla, he said, were not contested.

While there had always been tensions, the Folks Alliance seemed to have meant a welcome peace and a way to settle tensions without violence. Juan then went on to explain that soon after the founding of SGD, at a party on Addison and Rockwell in the heart of MLD turf, an Imperial Gangster (IG), Goofy, was killed by the MLDs. The Cobras at the time had been buddies with the IGs, and in the spontaneous retaliation that followed, Cobras were shot at by Latin Disciples.

Rather than the dispute being settled by negotiation through La Tabla, Juan said there continued to be incidents over "women and greed—and I mean capital letters G.R.E.E.D." To Juan what was going on was that "the MLDs were getting too big for their britches." After the formation of SGD, he explained "the MLDs were much bigger and threw their weight around in juntas"—semiofficial meetings between gangs on the streets and at formal SGD meetings in Stateville.

Rather than SGD being a neutral forum of equals, the MLDs were emboldened by their power in numbers and drug connections. In disputes they coerced Cobra leadership to do their bidding, in Juan's words causing Cobra leaders to "appease" the stronger MLDs. Inside the jail and prison,

Juan said, "Cobra leadership often threw their own soldiers to the wolves," giving them violations after demands by MLD leaders. Sometimes, he went on indignantly, "the Ds would even violate Cobras if they did something that upset Disciple leaders."

"I'll give you an example," he said. "A MLD soldier wandered onto Cobra turf and was shot at. That happens. A carload of MLDs then invaded our turf to retaliate. The Cobras in that section called soldiers from another section to 'aid and assist,' which is one of our laws." At first the SGD concept seemed to work. "Higher authorities met and a group of MLDs later came by and played basketball with us. I thought the White House [SGD meetings in Stateville prison] had settled things. After the basketball game was over, they asked this guy who had been involved in the shooting his name and when he said it they grabbed him. They held his shooting hand down and one guy pulled out a short sledgehammer and smashed his hand."

The MLDs had violated a Cobra on orders from their own leadership. This appeared to be in violation of the SGD constitution, which said of violations: "For the personnel's concern, and for the firmness in discipline of the S.G.D.'s, we shall punish our own, unless otherwise instructed by the S.G.D. ranks." For Juan and many Cobra soldiers, MLD actions were in violation of the SGD concept. But what had actually happened was that the Disciples, secure in their dominance of SGD, decided on their own to violate a Cobra. They were acting in an imperial manner as if they were undisputed leaders of the union and could do whatever they wanted.

In our interview, Juan seemed to be almost reliving the incident and said it "infuriated Cobra rank and file. Our troops were getting fed up with this appeasing of the MLDs." This is not why SGD had been set up, he told me. Juan explained that incidents like this were why the Cobras felt they had to form the I-Team within SGD to combat the dominance and arrogance of the Maniacs.

"TRIPLE 8S" AND THE FORMATION OF THE INSANE FAMILY

The Insane Family was certainly the most organized of the three family factions within SGD. Since Sal learned of Insane Family meetings through

Joey Bags and later Mo Mo, we can follow the tragedy of SGD through the eyes of the Insane Family. We also have a comprehensive, and less biased, view of the Insane Family from Blade, the Insane Deuce who was part of the family from the start and one of its first leaders.

I asked Blade to describe explicitly how the Insane Family started and why.

> The concept of the Insane Family ... wasn't really about anything except keep the peace. That's what the Latinos wanted: to keep peace. A big war between the Spanish Cobras and the Disciples and it kept on going back and forth, back and forth. A couple of Cobras came to me and said, "We gotta make a concept" and I'm like, like "What?" "We need to make something to make it peaceful. But in case of war we have togetherness. Like NATO." You know you're pretty much following the guidelines of the big countries. I said "Like NATO?" They said, like, "Pretty much." So I say "OK, I have no problem with that, let see what you come up with." Bradley and Indigo from the Spanish Cobras. They were the originators.

For Blade, the establishment of the Insane Family tilted to the informal side, an arrangement of convenience. He insisted that the actual name of the Insane Family was "Triple 8s." He explained.

> We used to call it the I-Team, but back then it was pagers (used to call meetings). Lot of people didn't have cell phones. So we had to come up with a certain code that everyone would know. Let's try triple zeros, no. So we come up with triple 8s. We went all the way from 1, 2, 3. So no one had 8s. So we called the meetings the Triple 8s. So the only ones that would know about it would be ... you get triple 8s on your beeper, you know you had to pull over and make a phone call. Emergency call. That's basically what it was. . . .
>
> But everyone called us the Insane Family. If you would say "Triple 8" to someone who didn't know, they wouldn't know what the heck you're saying. That was our code. [If] we had people that came they didn't know what Triple 8 was, it was just a pager number.

But Blade understates the seriousness others imputed to the Insane Family. The conflict on the streets with the MLDs was not a small matter, and the Cobras were clearly preparing to make their own move on the leadership of SGD. Since by themselves they lacked the numbers and drug connections of the MLDs, the Cobras began to solicit gangs that had similar grievances with the Maniacs to join into a formal alliance: Blade's NATO analogy is pretty good. While NATO was formally a defensive alliance, it was not seen that way by the Soviet Union, who felt threatened and responded in kind. The Cobras, who were in one kind of war or another against both the MLDs and the Simon City Royals, built a formal alliance, with its own rules.[13]

For the Cobras, the Insane Family was a central link in their strategy to unseat the MLDs from power in SGD. The Insane Family's main task became the settling of disputes between their members, a task displaced from SGD. But the Cobras were also planning to challenge the power of the Maniacs, the underlying reason for creating the I-Team. The Cobra's formalization of a faction or family, in turn, sparked the consolidation of the Maniac and Almighty Families. Rather than "peace," as Blade so fervently desired, blood was shed on a regular basis and all was eventually lost. These dynamics of power were the prime motivation of Latin Folks gangs, although these processes were almost completely unknown to police, academics, and other outsiders. Without understanding the three families' will to power, much of gang behavior on the streets, especially violence, is simply incomprehensible.

Before I go on to describe the war of the families and the final demise of SGD, we need to look at why Folks gang members, and the C-Note$ in particular, believed that SGD as a Spanish mafia had a chance of success. The next two chapters look at corruption—the relationship of gangs to the political machine, as well as gang dealings with entrepreneurial cops. Corruption was the glue which bound the Outfit and Chicago's police and political machine together for decades, and Sal explains how that arrangement became the model for SGD.

part three

CORRUPTION

 **7** **Envelopes and Ethnic Politics**

JMH: Latinos are growing in numbers and they might even become the majority someday.

SAL: *Oh, absolutely, and the Irish and Italians have realized that. We figured out, hey, we gotta bring these guys in the fold, because they're growing, so we're utilizing them as a resource as well.*

The Latinos are making money, but not all of it is on the books. They're learning. They look and they say, "You know what, I'd rather have a piece of the pie than none of the pie." So they're starting to use the Italians and the Irish and their political connections. Say I'm a gang member and I go, "Look, I want to open up a club." You gotta go to the Irish and the Italians to get the permit [chuckles] to make sure you can get it done. The envelope has gotta be full.

OK. So they're learning that, because they're utilizing these clubs to conduct business. And in order to do so, you gotta take it past City Hall to get the permits to get this building, to get the permits to get this strip mall. I mean, they're learning—fast.

JMH: Yeah, it's not just one envelope, right?

SAL: *Right. There's a lot of envelopes being filled. They're learning, catching onto the game. And as they catch on, they're becoming the majority. And they're gonna start putting their own people in—and the Italians and the Irish will be gone. You know, it's just a matter of time. Now the whites are coming back in, but the younger generation, the yuppies, don't seem, in my eyes, to really want to be much involved in the politics.*

The envelope stuffed with cash has long been the quintessential symbol of Chicago politics, how the "Chicago way" really works. The Outfit was the Italian model of crime as an American way of life, and Sal was passing on the lesson that for today's Latino gangs to flourish lots of politicians and policemen would have to be on the take.

Francis Ianni, in a 1974 classic, *Black Mafia*, was one of the few researchers who looked seriously into the ethnic succession of crime, in his case in New York and New Jersey. Among his farsighted conclusions was the observation that cooperation between Italians and Hispanics far exceeded those between the mafia and black organized crime. In part, Ianni was skeptical that African Americans could overcome the racism that impeded even informal social relations with powerful white politicians and business leaders. He wrote: "It is difficult to imagine, however, that blacks will be able to insinuate themselves into the kinds of social relationships with white politicians that are the environment within which deals are made, bribes are offered and sought, and protection developed." Ianni, writing in the wake of the powerful 1960s social movements, saw black organized crime as a sort of social banditry, merging protest with illicit profiteering. I'll explore this theme more in the last chapter.[1]

Sal saw things like Ianni.

JMH: One of the things that interests me is that when I was talking to older Gangster Disciple leaders, they saw themselves as replacing the Outfit . . . they saw blacks taking over, that they would be the "new thing." But they weren't able to pull it off.

SAL: *They have no political background, no police background, nothing. They have nothing. I shouldn't say they have nothin'. They do have some politicians in their pocket. But I ask you, are those politicians powerful?*

JMH: Do you work with the black gangs?

SAL: *Well we're utilizing them as a resource as well. But the Hispanics, they're growing more, and that's the thing: the money, the drug route for all this money that's coming in is from them. And so it's better to align with them than blacks who gotta come get it. And after all, we're only gonna give 'em so much rope. You know, and you divide and you conquer . . .*

For Sal, organized crime provided rich lessons for Latino gangs.

SAL: *You know, if they had more brains they would utilize that money like the Kennedys did, you know, to establish themselves—to legitimize themselves as time progresses. Not a lot of people want their kids to do what they did or what they went through, you know? So you learn from these old timers like how Jackie Cerone [Outfit heavyweight for many years] didn't want his kid to be like him. His kid's a lawyer, you know—they put him through.*

So when you look at some of these old timers that did what they did, it was to provide for the family. And nobody wants their kids to do or go through what you went through. The struggles and the crime, I mean—all of the above. So, if these guys would wisen up or listen and start establishing themselves in the community and bring money back to the community, build the businesses, they'd be much, much better off.

But they're living for today, not for tomorrow, not for their kids, not for anybody else. So, and that's one of the big problems that they have. When you start looking at the big picture and looking at the future, and you're reinvesting that money into your community, it's gonna turn, you're gonna wash that money, that money's gonna come back to you, and then you don't have to do what you had to do ten years ago in order to survive.[2]

It would take an entire book, or maybe a bookshelf full of books, to put Chicago politics into perspective for the coming Latino era. But Sal's thoughts on ethnic succession need to be briefly contextualized before we describe Chicago's incipient Latino political machine and in the next chapter the Latin Folks' corrupt dealings with the Chicago Police Department.

FREDERIC THRASHER AND AL CAPONE

Everyone who has ever studied gangs has been influenced by Frederic Thrasher's *The Gang*, written in the 1920s about 1,313 neighborhood peer groups. But the power of Thrasher's study of kids on playgrounds had the effect of obscuring two words never mentioned in his classic text: "Al Capone." The Capone mob was wiping out Irish gangs like the O'Banions at the very same time that Thrasher riveted our attention on play groups and boy gangs. The beer wars brought levels of violence to Chicago not exceeded until the 1970s. Capone's use of extreme violence would consolidate Italian gangs across Chicago and wrest for his mob a monopoly on Prohibition-era beer sales. Capone's close relationship with mayor William Hale "Big Bill" Thompson and the Republican Party in both Chicago and suburbs like Cicero, Chicago Heights, and Joliet kept Capone protected even during the violent beer wars. The superprofits gained in Prohibition helped the Outfit fill the envelopes for politicians and helped it survive for almost a hundred years and running. The Outfit still is far and away the most important gang in Chicago history.[3]

Traditional gang researchers study the "group process" of wild neighborhood peer groups but have neglected the process of institutionalization of the Outfit; how after its victory in the beer wars it drastically *reduced* violence; how it dominated nearly every Chicago racket; and how it spread its influence to Las Vegas, Hollywood, and beyond. These processes were all models for SGD on how to grow and develop. More importantly, gang researchers have habitually neglected to investigate whether the systematic corruption of politicians and police that allowed the Outfit to thrive for so long is now being put into practice by current gangs.

Sal made sure his experience of how corruption worked would be lavished on his C-Note$. Under his guidance the C-Note$ paid off politicians and made special efforts to infiltrate the Chicago Police Department, all tried-and-true Outfit tactics. Along with other Latin Folks gangs, the C-Note$ cultivated corrupt relationships with dirty cops, like Joseph Miedzianowski, the SOS unit, and others. While popular lore has it that cops come cheap, scores of Chicago police officers saw the gangs as easy money and cashed in lavishly. We'll look at the different types of police corruption in the next chapter and how it paid off handsomely for both police and gangs. In Chicago it was Hispanic, not African American gangs, that made the most of their corrupt opportunities.

THE HISPANIC DEMOCRATIC ORGANIZATION AND THE MACHINE

The 1990s in Chicago was the decade that SGD rose and fell. Not coincidentally this decade saw the rise and fall of the Hispanic Democratic Organization (HDO), a political action committee founded in the wake of mayor Richard M. Daley's first successful mayoral bid. Both SGD and HDO represented rising Latino political power and corrupt influences in the machine.

Richard M. Daley, the old mayor's son, had defeated the city's African American interim mayor, Eugene Sawyer, in the 1989 primary and trounced the newly formed Harold Washington Party candidate Tim Evans in the general election. Racial politics is at the heart of how Chicago works, and during his six years in office black mayor Harold Washington had been fought tooth and nail by an assortment of white ethnic pols. These enemies included the Irish Richard M. Daley and City Council Finance Committee chairman Ed Burke, as well as the Croatian chairman of the Cook County Democratic Party, Ed Vrdolyak. Chicago has always been racially divided, and Washington had managed to win the 1983 general election by winning a majority of the Latino vote. Daley was a shrewd politician and realized he needed to prevent a future black/Hispanic coalition.[4]

Daley built on his already strong base with Latinos. In the 1983 three-way primary between him, Harold Washington, and incumbent mayor Jane Byrne, Daley got about a third of the Latino vote, Byrne got half, and Washington only 12.7 percent. Washington's Latino support was largely from community activists outside the machine structure. In the general election, however, Washington took almost three-quarters of the Latino vote against Republican Bernard Epton, who, fatally, ignored Latinos. Sal told me that Epton's single-minded racist campaign distributed stickers with one of one of the white community's popular slogans: "'Epton, Epton he's our man, we don't want no Afri-can.' In my neighborhood they were posted on stop signs and mailboxes, among other places." Washington's campaign paid close attention to Latinos, but racism plagued the Mexican as well as the white community. One of Washington's strongest Mexican supporters was Rudy Lozano, who in his race for alderman fell seventeen votes short of forcing a runoff with machine incumbent Frank Stemberk. It has been suggested Lozano made a mistake in tying his campaign so closely to Washington's, and Mexican racism may have cost him a chance at victory.

Daley used a high-tech campaign to regain full power of the city's machine in 1989, and he immediately began to cultivate the growing Latino population. Latinos in 1980 were 14 percent of the city's population, but by 1990 had risen to nearly 20 percent. Daley had won the allegiance of aldermen Juan Soliz and Luis Gutiérrez, who had both previously been Washington supporters. Guitérrez embraced the machine and in 1992 won Daley's backing in his successful congressional election. Daley was carefully building a Latino base, and the centerpiece of his strategy was the founding of the Hispanic Democratic Organization. HDO was an old-fashioned get-out-the-vote apparatus that used city jobs as incentives to win elections, just as in the old days. Hundreds of Latino city employees worked as "assistant registrars" for HDO, and they mobilized armies of workers to defeat Latino politicians who had worked within the Harold Washington coalition.[5]

The first victim of HDO was progressive state senator Jesus "Chuy" Garcia, an ally of the Harold Washington–inspired progressive coalition of blacks, Hispanics, and liberal whites. In 1998, the nascent Hispanic Democratic Organization backed political unknown and Chicago police officer Tony Muñoz against Garcia. Their flooding of Garcia's senate district, which contained strongholds for both Latin Kings and 2-6ers, with election workers resulted in a stunning upset victory for Muñoz. It was a classic display of machine power, but it also put into stark relief the crucial significance of Latinos to Chicago politics.

One of the key operatives in HDO was Al Sanchez, a former precinct captain for Ed Vrdolyak, the most outspoken opponent of Harold Washington. Sanchez was later sentenced to two and a half years in prison for his role in rigging the city's hiring system. The "Hired Truck" scandal of steering city contracts to powerfully connected firms and employing gang members took down another HDO official, Angelo Torres. HDO finally dissolved due to the scandals and was replaced by the regular machine democratic organization. HDO's job of integrating Latinos into the machine must have been reported to Mayor Daley as "Mission Accomplished." The black threat was decisively countered by Daley's apt maneuvers in winning the city's Latino population through HDO, the latest iteration of old-fashioned machine politics.

A political giant in the gang/machine nexus was powerhouse alderman

Richard Mell, who also is the father-in-law of infamous former governor Rod Blagojevich. Sal says this about the former governor.

You know Rod Blagojevich used to hang out with the Gaylords? Yeah, St. Gen's Boys. One of his guys, Squirrel—Dan Stefanski—he's got GL tattooed on his knuckles. Once a nice city employee. [Laughs.]

You know the St. Gen's Boys' favorite saying was "Black may have soul, but white has control." Back in the day Harold Washington might have been in office, but in reality almighty whitey was pulling the strings.

THE MACHINE AND LATINO GANGS

Blagojevich eventually fell out with Mell, and the machine then greased his slide into prison. Mell had built firm connections to Latin Folks gangs through one of his aides, Raymond Rolon, a principle leader of the Maniac Latin Disciples.

Rolon, along with Johnny "Loco" Almodovar, were named as key figures in the *Godfather*-style shootings of Spanish Cobras you read about in the preface. According to one newspaper account, "Over the past decade, Rolon has allegedly marshaled members of the Maniac Latin Disciples to work for candidates in Humboldt Park and Logan Square. Witnesses alleged that Rolon and gang members intimidated voters and pulled down opponents' campaign signs." This is indistinguishable from how Irish gangs or "social athletic clubs" had bullied their way into political power. Rolon died of natural causes on September 13, 2009, and Mell resigned in 2013 to be replaced as alderman by his daughter.[6]

Sal sees this all from the point of view of both the Outfit and Latin Folks. He sets me straight that business as usual *means* politics:

JMH: So both with the Gangster Disciple's Growth and Development, and Spanish Growth and Development, when they say "We're transforming"—they mean business, right?

SAL: *No, it's both business and politics, because with politics comes power. So you utilize this money to put businesses together, to get into your community, to put people in power—your power grows. There's a lot of money that gets funneled to* these politicians, to these services, to these schools, to the fire department—to charities. There are people that are involved—there's charities out there getting money from individuals that are involved in this game, and they say, "Why don't you make it legal?" There's too much money to be lost there.

JMH: Tearing down the housing projects [in the 1990s Chicago began to demolish its 99 percent African American housing projects] and dispersing the black population means that African Americans aren't as powerful any more, right?

SAL: Ha, OK—you split 'em up all over, their power is gone. The Hispanic neighborhoods, you're gonna have a tougher time because they don't live in projects; they live in single family homes and apartment buildings. That means you gotta work the old-fashioned way. Now, you got people like Raymond Rolon from the Maniac Latin Disciples, Humboldt Park area, city worker at one time [laughs] campaigning for his people in the Humboldt Park community. As far as HDO, they were in there. So, when you look at Ocasio, you look at Gutiérrez, and you look at Solis [Key Latino politicians]—guess who's behind them?

Election politics are standard fare for Latino gangs today, just as they have always been for their white ethnic predecessors. The Spanish Cobras, for example, were heavily involved campaigning for alderman Ray Suarez of the 31st Ward and made that point to fellow gangs at I-Team meetings. The Cobras were not as open as the MLDs in their ties to politicians and, as with all their dealings, they played the election game closer to the vest, but they played it constantly and well.

Sal pointed out, however, that the MLDs' Raymond Rolon was *not* a good example of how the gangs were learning to send respectable-looking members into the political system. College-educated gang members, not street hoodlums, were needed to get involved and use gang-derived campaign contributions to "get a seat at the table" of the Democratic machine. He says with a wry smile: "And, you know, they're not gonna put the black sheep in the front lines." What Sal means is that politics requires a different style for serious gangsters, a change from street smarts to being able to work the crowd of politicians, real estate executives, and the middle class. Sal speaks from his experience of more than thirty years in politics as well as organized crime.

Is the machine like it used to be? There's not too many savvy people like in the old days. The politicians are there, the police are there, the lawyers are there, the lobbyists are there, gang members are there. One of the things that I told Joey Bags and Mo Mo was this: "You wanna be a punk gang member or do you wanna be a gangster?" There's a difference. This guy here—the gangster—can go into different venues than the gang member. This guy there has his pants hanging off his ass—the gang member—standing on the street corner. This guy here is going to all the fine restaurants and nightclubs and going to political fundraisers, getting things done. This guy there has not . . . he's got tunnel vision, only sees this far. He don't see the big picture. We had lots of older guys trying to teach some of these young kids.

People as well as Folks were engaged with machine politics. Here is a Latin King leader complaining about the fickleness of Puerto Rican politicians. "But when they need to get elected who do they come to? They come to the Latin Kings because they need this little area to vote from. We help 'em out in exchange for jobs. And those are the backstreet politics that are played in this city. Everywhere. Right now I can guarantee—I could almost put my life on it—that there's some politician or commissioner somewhere making a deal that if everybody found out about it, it'd be over. It'd be the end of their career."

While Sal dislikes the Latin Kings, he agrees that the Kings have considerable political influence.

Yeah, you know the Latin Kings got their own people too, because they got territory. Whoever's gonna run in their territory has to have their backing in order to get into office just like the individuals you just mentioned. . . . They have to have their backing in order to get into office or you're not going to get into office. Believe me, because they're very influential—I mean they got parents, their uncles, their cousins, their friends—and that's how you get people into the office. When you have districts that only have X amount—a thousand people come out to vote [laughing]—you know you can win.

The Kings had been kept at arms' length by the machine, due to what Daley saw as Latin King ties to Rudy Lozano and his progressive, "black and brown united" politics. The 1983 assassination of Lozano, a prominent labor and antimachine activist, was tied to gang rivalries, particularly between the Latin Folks 2-6 gang and Lozano supporters in the Latin Kings. Latin Folks gangs from the start aligned themselves with the Daley machine and the Latin Kings with the insurgents. Despite family ties to Latin Kings, Lozano's house was squarely within 2-6 territory, which produced constant tension. Lozano's union activism, I was told by several street-savvy contacts, may have also upset cartel investments in local businesses Lozano was trying to unionize.[7]

Do not be mistaken: the Latin Kings in Chicago are not progressives; they are dozens of affiliated local gangs all trying to get protected and penetrate the system, but they are doing it less successfully than the Latin Folks. The Latin King leader I interviewed in 2003 went on to discuss their ties to now jailed former governor Rod Blagojevich. The Kings would later make a substantial contribution to Blagojevich through Alderman Mell and place some of their friends in his administration. "We have somebody that's running for governor for this state on the Democratic setting. He so happens to be the son-in-law of an alderman on the northwest side of Chicago [Mell]. Well, that alderman is very deeply involved with the Latin Disciples. That's the only reason this governor, Democratic nominee for governor, has made it to where he's landed. Because he's had unlimited funds by the street and drug dealers supplying that money, OK?"

Machine politics has always meant gangs. Latino gangs are merely the latest manifestation of that old ethnic tradition. I saw the gang/political nexus firsthand in 2009. I had taken part in a Pilsen neighborhood meeting after a spate of gang shootings between La Raza and the Party People, warring Latin Folks gangs. I was driven back to Union Station for my train home by a key aide to Danny Solis, the local Mexican alderman who was president pro tempore of the city council and Daley's floor leader. Clearly trying to impress me, his aide stopped at corner after corner talking to groups of youth whom he identified to me as different gangs. "Election time—we need them," he told me. "They get out the vote."

This was how HDO had worked, adopting the old machine tactic of getting gang members to bring their voters to the polls, intimidate the opposition's voters and rip up their campaign signs, and do whatever is necessary to get victory. The gangs, the alderman's aide told me, came pretty cheap: their payoff was entry-level jobs, mainly from city contractors who were instructed whom they should hire.

For the Outfit, jobs at places like the mammoth McCormick Place were perks of gang life. Italian mobsters by the score either actually worked as riggers at more than twenty dollars an hour or were getting politicians to get them ghost jobs that paid them for not even showing up. Sal explained the reality of jobs, even to Outfit-connected guys.

> That's another thing, too: we were able to buy union cards. For $500 you could get a union card, whether it was carpenters, electricians, plumber—and get your people to work. I mean, one of the best places was McCormick Place. Do a search on how many felons they got in there! We got several of our people working there.
>
> Sometimes that's the only work you're gonna get. That's a big problem that they have here—these individuals get caught with narcotics and stuff like that, they're not able to get legitimate work. So that's one of the things I try to influence. If you're not gonna go to school, learn a trade, because they can't take that away from you and you'll always have a job. Look at what they're doing, and it's not pretty out there, especially with the economy.

CHANGING OF THE GUARD

The Chicago way has always been about patronage, which has moved from direct city jobs to contracting with firms, like the trucking companies who were the locus of the HDO Hired Truck scandal. The gangs have made some headway in grabbing contracts themselves, but they still lack the Outfit's expertise. Sal explains that we are witnessing, in one way, the ethnic succession of patronage.

> Our day is receding ... because the old guard is on its way out and the new guard's coming in, so they're putting in their own people because they're finally realizing you don't have to pass out that many envelopes [chuckle] if your own people are in the loop ... you know, so the tide is changing. You look at the old guard and you look at the new guard, and that is what is transpiring. They're

saying, "You know what? Why am I giving Johnny Boy and Joey each an enve-
lope [chuckle] when I can give Jose one envelope?"

Dick Simpson of UIC's political science department has been track-
ing patronage over the years. Patronage jobs to African Americans stayed
steady for decades at about 12 percent even through the Harold Washington
years. Daley, Burke, and Vrdolyak kept control of the machine even when
Washington ostensibly ruled. Sal called Washington "a puppet," since he
didn't interrupt the flow of patronage controlled by the Outfit's friends.
In the last decade, Latinos have jumped past African Americans and now
command nearly a third of all patronage jobs.

Latino population today has almost reached parity with whites and
blacks. In 2010, Latinos made up 29 percent of Chicago residents, while
whites and African Americans each had 32 percent. Poverty is worse for
blacks than Latinos in Chicago, with almost a third of all African Americans living in poverty compared to less than a quarter of Latinos. Still the
drug game is a readily available and badly needed job for hundreds and
even thousands of desperate Mexicans, Puerto Ricans, and other Latinos.
And the gang is always hiring.[8]

Blade, the Insane Family leader, sees the increasing political sophistica-
tion of Puerto Rican gang leaders.

> I go to these politician parties. I got this Puerto Rican guy, one of the leaders,
> he won't talk; he's very deep into the politics. Every time he calls, he tells me
> there is this big fundraiser, this and that, and I say oh fuck it and he's shaking
> hands and I'm meeting Ray Suarez, I'm meeting this guy and that guy. It went all
> the way so I met Obama's secondhand man when he was running for president.
> He was some political advisor and he was hanging out right there at Coco's in
> Humboldt Park! And my guy was introducing me and do you know who this guy
> is? This is how it goes.

I could write an entire book on gangs and politics today, but I'm not
sure that book would contain much that is new. "Most Chicago pols have
a price," V. I. Warshawski said in one of Sara Paretsky's detective novels,
"and it usually isn't very high."[9] Latino gangs, and SGD, represented the

"changing of the guard" as a new set of gangs were looking to use some of their excess drug money for campaign contributions. Covert support from politicians is absolutely necessary for a gang to survive, and the parallel stories of SGD and HDO represent the recognition of lessons derived from an older white ethnic immigrant story. While African Americans may have thought they could ride their control of illegal markets in their own neighborhoods to political power, they were just plain wrong, as Ianni had speculated decades before.

Sal says gangs are about power, and power means money. In Chicago the key to making money is politics. Sal is a cold realist, and he recognizes that the Latino gang experience is part of the ethnic succession of Latinos into the system.

> We can influence individuals to vote. People been doing it for years, the Democratic machine. We can influence who's gonna vote—but if you're not able to vote . . . that's a problem. That's one of the things that the SGD—Spanish Growth and Development—was trying to establish. If we can keep ourselves out of the joint [chuckle], we can vote.
>
> You gain power by putting your people into office—when you look at Solis, when you look at Ocasio, when you look at Gutiérrez—they can offer jobs to the community. . . . When they talk to these gang kids they say, "Look—if I can get into office, this is what I have to offer you. You can give jobs to some individuals, I can't give you all jobs—there are not enough jobs to go around—but I can put some of you in there." And if we continue, we can put a little more in there, put a little more—that's how the Irish did it [laughs]; that's how we [Italians] did it.

In Chicago the coming Latino dominance of politics is a function of a growing Hispanic population becoming wealthier, the uses of superprofits from the cartel-controlled drug game, and eager and skillful participation in machine politics. The new Daley/Emanuel machine differs in some respects from the old, relying much more on big money from real estate and financial interests.[10] Consequently, the machine on the ground has somewhat atrophied. But getting out the vote is still crucial in aldermanic elections, and control of ward organizations can mean the difference between victory and defeat. Today, aldermanic elections cost considerably more money, and pols need to have rich friends in real estate and finance and of course stay on good terms with well-heeled machine bosses. Disguised drug money doesn't hurt either, and gang members who aren't "black sheep" find a warm welcome.

Aldermen influence contracts—the main way patronage is delivered in Chicago today—as opposed to simply dishing out jobs in the kind of patronage that has been severely curtailed by court decisions. This end of patronage may have been what Harold Washington meant at his 1983 inauguration when he proclaimed, "The machine as we know it is dead, dead, dead."[11] Sal, observing what has happened since the great mayor died, disagrees: "So, you know, the machine ain't dead. The machine is just rolling right along, just different names, different players."

V. I. Warshawski's conclusion about buying pols on the cheap still rings true. But Latin Folks gangs also learned from the Outfit the importance of police corruption to protect their businesses. And cops didn't come as cheap as politicians.

8 Police Corruption: From the Suites to the Streets

What the Don told me in chapter 3 nails it: "Without the cops, none of this stuff could happen." This chapter explains the centrality of police corruption to the persistence of Chicago's gangs.

Traditional gang research, much of it dependent on law enforcement funding, has almost nothing to say about police corruption. The assumptions of nearly all gang studies from Thrasher on imply that police corruption is irrelevant or at best incidental to the persistence of gangs. Police are typically conceptualized as key components of social order, their strategies of suppression of gangs being either more or less important than jobs or outreach work, depending on the politics and inclination of the researcher.

Police are almost universally defined by criminologists as being on the side of social control, working with the "community" against "disorganized" and violent criminal gangs. Corrupt or brutal cops, if they are mentioned at all, are "bad apples" in an apparently otherwise healthy forest of law enforcement. In Chicago, despite a storied history of police corruption—one CPD history has the inspired title "To Serve and Collect"—corruption is notably absent in contemporary research studies as a variable explaining today's gangs.[1]

When the Chicago Crime Commission released its latest Gang Book in 2012, highlighting Chicago's gang problem, I was invited as a speaker and criticized the report for having no mention at all of corruption or brutality. My comments were greeted with stunned silence by the mainly Chicago Police Department audience, who openly wondered what police misconduct had to do with gangs. This chapter may give them a more detailed answer. Still, I'm unlikely to be speaking any time soon to that august body.[2]

Studies today often conceptualize police corruption as the result of weak or failed states. Eastern Europe, for example, with the fall of socialism, had breakdowns in controls, and organized crime and corruption flourished. States are conceptualized as falling on a continuum from nations with only "cup of coffee" corruption to states completely taken over by corrupt actors.[3] American cities as well might be classified on some sort of urban corruption scale, with Chicago and New Orleans on one end, and perhaps Seattle on the other.

Wait! The late Bill Chambliss's highly touted studies of corruption were done in *Seattle*, and far from finding this social ill negligible in the "Emerald City," he concludes: "At the very least, I was convinced from my Seattle research that a symbiotic relationship between politics, law enforcement, legitimate business, and organized crime was absolutely necessary for organized crime to survive and flourish as it does in America."[4] Chambliss found organized crime to be an "integral part of the governmental and economic structures of our society." This is the polar opposite of the bad apples theory, and Chambliss's ethnographic work has the added benefit of insisting not only on concrete investigation into corrupt cops and politicians, but also on understanding their historical relationship to organized crime. In this chapter I extend Chambliss's method to explain new forms of police corruption by street gangs.

As far as police corruption is concerned, the bad apples theory has been found to be a bad apple indeed. The Knapp Commission, formed as a result of Frank Serpico's famous exposé of New York City police, explicitly rejected that theory in their 1972 report. The reform NYPD commissioner, Patrick V. Murphy, amplified: "The 'rotten apple' theory won't work any longer. Corrupt police officers are not natural-born criminals, nor morally wicked men, constitutionally different from their honest colleagues. The task of corruption control is to examine the barrel, not just the apples—the organization, not just the individuals in it—because corrupt police are made, not born."[5]

Other noted theorists of corruption, like Susan Rose-Ackerman, argue that scholars need to focus not just on bribery of patrolmen or low-level bureaucrats, but more importantly on what she calls "grand corruption."

She argues, Chambliss-like, that "of particular import is corruption at the top of the state hierarchy."

Contrary to Samuel Huntington and studies from Transparency International that find corruption is the product of weak states lacking strong bureaucratic controls, the persistence of corruption in machine-controlled Chicago supports Chambliss's view that corruption can be functional for the workings of cities. And while Rose-Ackerman is skeptical of an "ethnographic" approach to corruption, what Chambliss's work shows is that corruption is an institution that has a history, and it can be studied. In Chicago that history shows that police corruption has always been strongly related to organized crime, and with the rise of street gangs in the 1960s, it continued, adapted, and expanded.[6]

THE OUTFIT'S STRATEGY: CORRUPT
THE POLICE FROM THE TOP DOWN

The close ties of gamblers, bootleggers, red-light house madams, and other vice lords to Chicago politicians and police is legendary. Richard Lindberg's fine history of police corruption ends with the 1960 Summerdale scandal, and he concludes on an optimistic note that "there would be no more scandals of this magnitude." On the contrary, the worst was yet to come.[7]

The Outfit had flourished with covert and at times open support of the city machine and police. The Chicago Crime Commission's 1971 study found that organized crime "persists and prospers because it is not unacceptable to the power structures" in Chicago communities. Art Bilek, storied Chicago crime fighter and vice president of the Chicago Crime Commission, said that as late as the end of the 1960s, every police commander in Chicago got their monthly envelope to distribute to the troops. Sal laughed: "Like I say, you've got police captains that have retired millionaires." Literally. For example, Lindberg reports on Tommy Harrison, whom he calls one of Chicago's "millionaire cops," who apparently supplemented his $5,200-a-year pay in the post-Depression era with enough graft to afford a "deluxe country style house in Sauganash" (a posh suburb) and other amenities. And the tradition is not only past history. Recently the head of the CPD sergeant's union was sentenced to twelve years in prison for stealing over $1 million in union funds.[8]

The Outfit relied for protection on regular cash-filled envelopes to influential pols and high-ranking cops. This modus operandi was handed down from its origins with Irish Mike McDonald and Big Jim Colosimo, the first Italian crime boss. Then, from Johnny Torrio to Al Capone to Frank Nitti to Tony Accardo, the Outfit made sure they always had lots of stuffed envelopes for police commanders and local politicians, as any reader of Lindberg's book can attest.[9]

Even after the 1960s, the Outfit maintained their strategy of penetrating the highest levels of the Chicago police. For example, William Hanhardt, CPD's chief of detectives and deputy superintendent in the 1980s, was convicted in 2001 of running a jewel ring for the Outfit that stole more than $5 million in diamonds and other gems. Hanhardt used CPD computers to get information on jewel traders to set up his burglary operations, protected and run by police.[10]

Hanhardt's sponsor for promotion to chief of detectives was none other than alderman Fred Roti, son of the Outfit's Chinatown crew chief Bruno Roti. Brother Fred was named by the attorney general as a made man in the mafia even while he served for twenty-three years as alderman of Chicago's notorious First Ward. This ward contains the downtown Loop, but has been dominated by organized crime since the nineteenth century and included such aldermen as the infamous "Bathhouse" John Coughlin and his grafting mate, "Hinky Dink" Kenna.[11]

The Outfit web of influence goes even higher than chief of detectives. Robert Cooley is especially qualified to appear in this chapter, having made a journey from dirty cop to even dirtier judge-bribing lawyer to a snitch testifying against Outfit heavyweights. Cooley reported on the "bad apples" he knew in the CPD, but by the early 1980s, he said, "the bad apples were in position of command."[12] One "bad apple in chief" was Chicago's police commissioner Matt Rodriguez, who was forced to resign in 1997 for his ties to Outfit figure Frank Milito. This mob-tied businessman was a good friend of the police superintendent, but also owned a string of local gas stations, was—incredibly—a gun-toting deputy sheriff, and was a popular restaurant operator to boot. Superintendent Rodriguez, who worked his way to the top from being the son of a Mexican American precinct captain in the Daley machine, vacationed with Milito in Italy, Israel, California, Arizona, New York, Colorado, and the Bahamas.[13]

It was apparently on a New York City trip to see Broadway shows that Milito encouraged Rodriguez to protect Pierre Zonis, a Chicago police officer who was being investigated as an Outfit hit man in multiple murders.[14] These hits included the killing of oil company executive Charles Merriam, whose uncle and grandfather were both famous antimachine reformers. Merriam had taken away Milito's gas station franchise after he was convicted of tax fraud, and Milito was suspected of paying Officer Zonis to do the hit.[15]

The CPD Internal Affairs (IAD) officials who initiated the investigation into Rodriguez's mob ties were thwarted by the superintendent in getting Zonis fired from the CPD. Raymond Risley, the head of IAD and his chief lieutenant, Eugene Karczewski, were removed from their positions by Rodriguez, who instructed IAD investigators to focus on corruption by beat cops, not higher-ups. Rodriguez's edict fit nicely with the Outfit strategy of working from the top down and deflecting attention from the Outfit to street gangs.

The Outfit bribery machine also made sure Chicago's Cook County sheriff would be on the payroll. In February 1990, Outfit boss Ernest Rocco Infelice told a bookmaker who was secretly wearing a wire, "Between you and I the Sheriff [James O'Grady] gets ten [thousand dollars]. Five goes to another guy [Deputy James Dvorak]. Sheriff never bothers us. Then we got a guy in the state's attorney's office. We got another guy downtown."[16]

The point is that the Outfit has historically bought police protection from the top down. To reinforce this point, let's give the last word to Renato DiSilvestro, a former Chicago cop who was suspected as working as an Outfit hit man. This mob-tied Chicago police officer came under investigation in the 1986 gangland slaying of Giuseppe Cocozzo, quickly retired, and skipped town, moving to Las Vegas. He told *Tribune* reporter David Jackson with a chuckle, "I'm not gonna spell out nothing, but everybody knows how it works. You know that everybody is on the take. Everybody who's been in Chicago for years knows how Chicago operates. It's always been like that and it ain't gonna change." DiSilvestro goes on to insist that the Outfit had a special focus on the city's police commanders. "They'll never stop. You understand that, don't you? It will never stop. What draws them together? The green stuff."[17] Enough said.

CHANGES IN THE STRUCTURE OF POLICE CORRUPTION

The 1960s gang takeover of retail drug sales described in chapter 3 by the Don represented a fundamental change of pace in Chicago police corruption. While the Outfit handed over its street-level drug businesses to the gangs, it kept its police and political protection for itself. In other words, the street gangs would be selling drugs retail, but the envelopes that protected Italian networks didn't extend to protect the hundreds of new black and Latino gang drug sellers. As Sal said matter of factly when I asked him if my analysis of the changes from the Outfit to the street gangs made sense: "It makes some sense for the simple reason—look at the color of the gangs."

These new conditions meant that since police officers weren't being paid off by their commanders to protect black and Latino gangs' drug businesses, the gangs had to strike deals with individual officers and units. For example, in the 1970s, the Marquette Ten were officers who made their own deals with the Vice Lords and West Side gangs to pay them protection for drug operations. One drug seller at the time described to me officers going house to house—drug houses, he means—demanding that the gang drug dealers pay protection.

The Marquette Ten were examples in many ways of the ambiguity of law enforcement at the onset of the war on drugs. James Tuohy and Rob Warden, in their brilliant exposé *Greylord*, were convinced that the Marquette Ten were framed by an out-of-control federal prosecutor, Dan Webb, going after police officers in his attempt to nail judges for corruption. Nine sitting judges and a host of court personnel were felled in the 1980s by Operation Greylord, but the Marquette Ten case was confined to examples of low-level street corruption. Higher-up CPD officials escaped indictment, and Webb could not nail down a connection between cops and judges. Among those higher-ups were future CPD superintendent

Phil Cline, whose search warrants were rejected by the US attorney as bogus. But Webb may not have understood that a new day of police corruption was dawning, one where the action remained mainly at street level. "In the twilight world of drugs," Tuohy and Warden write, "police and dealers live in a murky symbiosis, feeding on one another." It is this "twilight world" that the Latin Folks gangs exploited to protect their illegal businesses.[18]

CATEGORIES OF THE NEW CORRUPTION

While Latin Folks drug operations were far-flung, gang leaders saw it as essential to have gang- and tactical-squad cops on the take for manipulation and protection. This is not to deny that street-level corruption needs covert support from CPD higher-ups and other supervisory officials. For example, one CPD officer I interviewed who served time for robbing drug houses told me he became the focus of investigation once his arrests of gang drug dealers included guys who were paying off higher-ups. Self-serving stories like these must be listened to cautiously, although Ianni notes that such bribery of higher-up police officials was a mainstay in New York.[19]

While supervisors and command personnel may be regularly turning a blind eye to drug corruption, this is a different modus operandi from the old-style "pay the commanders and pass down the envelopes" corruption. The war on drugs and the gang control of retail sales have made the streets, not the command posts, the center of the action. Thousands of drug transactions take place on a regular basis in neighborhoods, and it would be unworkable to protect all drug sellers from determined, honest police. At the heart of policing, especially in the drug war, is the contradiction between enforcing the law and what Peter Manning calls the "impossible mandate" of actually accomplishing this goal.[20]

From the gangs' point of view, since police have extensive networks of snitches, the only way for drug enterprises to be sure to flourish is to establish working relationships with street cops and give them information on their rivals in order for their own businesses to survive. Additionally, as Sal said, there are few high-level black or Latino police officers. Most minority cops who have relationships with gang members are street-level officers. This bottom-up corruption is essentially different from the traditional Outfit way of buying protection from the top down. While it is widely estimated only 5 percent of all police officers are corrupt, in Chicago that 5 percent are enthusiastically targeted by street gangs.

From the police officers' point of view, it is impossible to do their jobs without making deals with one enemy in order to get another. There are so many drug transactions going on that arresting everyone is impossible. Good police work in the war on drugs means discretion, and discretion means police officers are always making decisions on who to arrest, who to make a deal with, and who to leave alone for a time. This means difficult decisions for honest officers and golden opportunities for corrupt ones.[21]

Police corruption by gangs in the money-mad war-on-drugs era can be fit into six categories:

1. Warden and Tuohy's morally ambiguous "twilight" world of protecting one dealer to get another, where police officers justify, to themselves, their buddies, and bosses, corrupt or questionable methods in order to get the "really" bad guys;
2. *guisos*, or robberies of drug dealers, by crooked cops;
3. direct payments to cops, either as protection or as what are called "bones" which are paid to police as a percentage of the profits from a drug bust or robbery;
4. police working as major drug suppliers or "kingpins" selling drugs to gangs;
5. infiltration of the police force by gang members working with or protecting their own street gang; and
6. the "blue code of silence" of officers declining to report corruption of fellow officers.

I'll illustrate all of these methods, beginning with Sal's inside information on the Latin Folks ties to one of Chicago's most infamous cases of police corruption.

Table 8.1. Dramatis personae in police corruption

William Hanhardt	CPD chief of detectives and deputy superintendent; ran jewel burglary ring for the Outfit
Matt Rodriguez	CPD superintendent forced to step down after protecting CPD officer and Outfit hit man Pierre Zonis
Marquette Ten	Police officers convicted of extorting drug businesses; the beginning of bottom-up corruption
"Baby Face" Nelson Padilla	Latin Lover and business associate of CPD gang squad officer Joseph Miedzianowski
Joseph Miedzianowski	Highly decorated and corrupt CPD gang squad officer; later convicted as a drug kingpin
Juan "Casper" Martir	Imperial Gangster leader; later major drug distributor from Miami for Miedzianowski
Alina "Ala" Lis	Drug dealer, lover to Miedzianowski and Joey Bags
John Galligan	Miedzianowski's corrupt CPD gang squad partner
Keith Hernandez and Jerome Finnegan	Special Operations Squad (SOS) officers indicted for conspiracy to murder fellow officers; worked with C-Note$ and Latin Folks gangs in drug conspiracy
Saul Rodriguez and Gary Lewellen	La Raza drug dealer and CPD officer running a Latin Folks drug operation

GANG SPECIALIST JOSEPH MIEDZIANOWSKI

I asked Sal about Joseph Miedzianowski early on in our interviews.

JMH: Tell me about Miedzianowski.

SAL: *The way the Note$ got involved with him was through Ala, Alina Lis. She got hooked up with Joey Bags when her boyfriend was locked up. At the same time she was having a relationship with Miedzianowski, she was also banging Brian from the Imperial Gangsters. Now, her girlfriend Yolanda was going out with Gallo from the Kings. So here is a cop putting everything aside that he has supposedly believed in for twenty, thirty years—to make money with all these people.*

Miedzianowski got his start in corruption, as I showed earlier, through his relationship with Baby Face Nelson Padilla and the Latin Lovers. Nelson was given a break by Miedzianowski in 1980 and in exchange became a snitch and helped the gang-squad cop to run up impressive arrest totals. Miedzianowski swore at his trial that he had "never betrayed his oath" and that his seeming friendship with gang members was solely for the purpose of getting information. He claimed that his actions, however questionable, were motivated by a desire to get the bad guys. He once said: "We need some bad cops to keep the public in line. I'm not talking bad as in thieves. You need a couple guys that can do the job right. I do what I have to do to get the job done. I always have done it. My bosses know how I work."[22]

In the twilight world of the war on drugs, the pursuit of glory and results compels gang and drug officers to make deals with unsavory characters in order to get even more unsavory guys. I'm convinced most police officers on drug details are honest, but the pressures are intense, and right and wrong are not always clear-cut. The reader needs to put him or herself in the difficult position of an honest cop on the street trying to enforce drug laws that are being violated by thousands of people daily with drug dealers seemingly on every block.

For example, I interviewed one police officer who was convicted in another scandal at the time Miedzianowski was on the streets. Like Miedzianowski, this officer insisted he was always trying to do the right thing and got caught up with taking money from one dealer and trying to bust another. "When did you realize you crossed the line?" I asked him. "What line?" he calmly replied, staring directly into my eyes. "Everyone was doing it," he insisted, meaning his fellow officers played one gang drug dealer off against another. The line between honest and criminal may not always be as clear as it seems from the outside.

Joe Miedzianowski, like other gang-squad officers, may have worried about crossing a line early in his career as well. But before long the concept of any "line" lost all meaning. By 1987, Miedzianowski realized that ripping off drug dealers was a no-lose proposition. Who would drug dealers complain to? Who would try to kill a cop? Miedzianowski, called "Papa" by his gang buddies, kept piling up the official commendations (fifty-nine of them in all) for his busts of rival drug dealers and turning in some (but not always all) of the drugs he confiscated. He enlisted the Latin Lovers' Baby Face, along with Imperial Gangster Juan "Casper' Martir to begin what on the street are called *guisos*, robberies of drug dealers. These robberies gave them product to sell back on the street, and Latin Folks gangs were quick to take advantage. Sal describes how it worked:

SAL: *So the guys were telling Miedzianowski where the dope was, and they were raiding the houses and taking the product.*

JMH: Miedzianowski was raiding ... ?

SAL: *Yes. His squad was ripping off the drug houses. Then if there were twenty bricks, only ten were put into evidence.... So that's what he was doing. Not only that, but our guys were also giving tips to their people [telling him] "these houses got dope" so they can rob 'em. So, they were robbing drug dealers, and then they weren't charging our guys full price. To get rid of the stuff they were charging discount prices and the C-Note$ were buying product at discount prices.*

JMH: He had dealings with the Kings too, right?

SAL: *I don't know the extent of what he was doing with the Kings, but what he was doing with the Imperial Gangsters here and the Latin Lovers, they would tell him where dope was and he would go do the raids and grab that dope. And what they [Imperial Gangsters] would do is sell it back to us at a discounted rate. So if a brick was going for $18 thousand, they were selling it for $15 thousand, so who wouldn't buy it if you're in the game? Joey Bags was buyin' 'em left and right. They were robbing other drug dealers and selling it to other people.*

Sal's comments were backed up by testimony at Miedzianowski's trial. The success of the Latin Lovers in making money through Baby Face's entrepreneurship prompted attention from other Latin Folks gangs. Fredrick Rock, or "Sweet Pea," was an MLD drug dealer who was indicted along with Miedzianowski. Rock testified that the gang-squad cop approached him to do a *guiso*, telling him not to worry because "you have the best insurance policy in the world," meaning Miedzianowski himself. Rock testified to buying more than ten pounds of cocaine from Miedzianowski and how Joe and his team, including his partner John Galligan, stole from rival drug dealers. Miedzianowski was also reported as selling drugs in a church parking lot and, incredibly, making a crack sale directly behind the West Side police station where he worked.

In the early 1990s Miedzianowski, on loan to the Bureau of Alcohol, Tobacco and Firearms, was angrily confronted by ATF supervising agent Diane Klipfel. She claimed he stole thousands of dollars in a drug raid, charges that CPD's Internal Affairs later could not confirm. According to the *Chicago Tribune*, in February 1992, Miedzianowski told Klipfel, whose husband also worked for ATF: "Your husband and you both work in the city. Remember that. Always remember that. And you better watch your darling kids. Your house could get lit up."[23]

Joe had a business to protect, and his techniques became commonplace for corrupt cops. Later I'll show how extensive this kind of corruption is and how it continues today. What was most significant about Miedzianowski's thefts of drugs and money was that in order to make the big time he had built an alliance with the Imperial Gangsters and then other Latin Folks gangs. The trigger, so to speak, of his success turned out to be the hit of Robert Detres by Joe's favorite snitch, Baby Face Nelson Padilla.

MIAMI VICE

Once Miedzianowski's main man, Baby Face, was being sought for Detres' murder, Joe had a decision to make. He and his partner John Galligan hid Nelson out in Juan "Casper" Martir's apartment. Martir had become an informant and business partner for Miedzianowski in the early 1990s when Joe arranged for him to have sex with his girlfriend while he was locked up. As police looked for Baby Face Nelson, the man he called his "mentor," Joe Miedzianowski, made preparations to get him out of town. He sent him to Miami, where he was later joined by Casper Martir, at the time a high-ranking Imperial Gangster. Their displacement to Florida would prove to be a golden opportunity for Joe, though like many such stories, the high price of his womanizing lifestyle would eventually bring him down.

It was at this point that Joe's career as a drug kingpin intersected with a woman with both high spirits and high aspirations: Alina Lis. Sal explains Joey Bags's dealings with Ala and how her charms and Joe's greed clicked to the financial benefit of everyone. Ala was well known on the West Side prior to her meeting Miedzianowski in a North Side bar in 1996. Sal typically sees Ala's "affairs" as mainly about business. "She was a party girl and got involved with Joey Bags. So they were messing around for a minute. This girl, she was smart and a hustler. Her boyfriend was Brian, an Imperial Gangster. Juan Martir—Casper from the Imperial Gangsters—

she grew up with him and Frankie and all them. She was doing my guy, she was doin' Joseph, she was doin' several others, but it was all business."

Ala had childhood connections with Latin Folks gangs, and her girl-friend, Yolanda Navarro, was dating Gallo, a Latin King leader. While Sal was not aware of Miedzianowski's dealings with the Latin Kings, the Kings had found ways to work with Papa. One Latin King leader told me their dealings with Miedzianowski were much less extensive than his re-lationship with Latin Folks gangs, but were based on an incident of quid pro quo.

> As for that cop [Miedzianowski], he did a lot for the Nation mostly because one of his girlfriends was "sister-in-law" to the Inca of Spaulding at the time [a top gang leader at the Kings mother chapter at Beach and Spaulding in Hum-boldt Park]. The cop was riding around with the feds one day [while Joe was on loan to ATF as a "gang expert"] and they grabbed the Inca. The Inca had a written list of who owed what in dues. The feds had an onboard copier in the car and made a copy. When the feds got out the car the cop took the copy and destroyed it. They let the Inca go and drove off. They got a few blocks away and they started to look for the copy and when they didn't find it they looked at the cop and accused him of destroying it. So they sped back to where they had dropped off the Inca, but by then he had already tossed the paper in the sewer. They had lost evidence and started getting into an argument with the cop. We believe that was the start of the feds looking more seriously into who the cop knew and what he was doing for them.

But it was Alina Lis's ties to the Imperial Gangsters and numerous boy-friends that opened up major opportunities for both Miedzianowski and the Latin Folks gangs. Sal comments on how Ala flaunted her status after she hooked up with Miedzianowski: "Ala was driving around the neigh-borhood in a white Mercedes. Guys asked: 'Who's Mercedes is this?' It was her old man's, which happened to be Joseph Miedzianowski."

Joe was expanding his drug operations when he met Ala. According to the federal indictment, by 1995 he was demanding $10,000 per month in protection payments from an assortment of Latin Folks gangs. For Mied-zianowski, $10,000 per month was actually small potatoes compared to what came next. With Casper making a connection with major drug importers in Miami and his direct ties with Latin Folks families, Joe saw the potential for a major expansion of his business, moving from reliance on *guisos* to becoming what prosecutors called a drug kingpin.

SAL: *Nelson Padilla was with Miedzianowski, and when he got the hell out of Dodge he went to Florida and he got hooked up again with Juan Martir. Nelson Padilla was a Lover, Latin Lover. So you had these two individuals and what they were doing was they had a police officer down in Florida. So the police officer would put the girls [drug couriers, including Alina Lis] on the plane and they would get picked up by another police officer at O'Hare. They just walked off the plane. That's how they used to do it.*

JMH: They had police protection in both Chicago and Miami?

SAL: *Right. A police officer in both places. Put on there and picked up here by a police officer.*

Miedzianowski's case deserves a book, and I wish my attempts to interview him and Alina Lis had been successful. But by 1997 as the drug pipeline went into high gear with Ala as one of the main couriers, Joe found that all the money he stole was barely enough to keep Ala in her luxury cars, trips to Vegas, clothes, and high lifestyle. Miedzianowski was married with kids, but Ala thought that he would leave his wife and marry her. Sal was impressed that while Cobras, Lovers, Maniacs, and Imperial Gangsters all testified at Miedzianowski' trial to get a break off their sentences, Ala alone refused to snitch.

I mean she was going all over the fucking place—on vacation, in Florida, and all over and Vegas. So he couldn't keep up, and she thought that he was going to leave his wife. He was living over on Cumberland—by Cumberland and Lawrence was where his house was—and I remember when they came and raided him.

But out of all those people, the word was that for every person that Martir—Casper—turned in, they would cut off five years off his sentence. That was the deal and he told on a lot of people—I mean that sentence took out a whole bunch—Ala ended up getting thirty years. She never informed on anybody and neither did Miedzianowski—he got life. But everybody else—Padilla ratted, Yolanda ratted . . .

According to both Sal and testimony in court, Joe had upped the price for protection to $22,000 per month. He once reportedly spent $40,000 in one month on Ala, though such wild spending was denied by both Miedzianowski and Lis. But Joe's arrogance and demands were getting out of control, and at some point, Latin Folks gang members began to tip off law enforcement. While I've heard different stories on how it happened, it is clear that the Latin Folks did Miedzianowski in. Just go over the list of those who were indicted with him, all of whom, except for Ala, testified against him.

- Mohammed Omar, 29, Spanish Cobras
- Juan "Casper" Martir, Imperial Gangster
- Jesus "Flip" Cuevas, 29, Spanish Cobra section chief who dined with Miedzianowski on his yacht in Puerto Vallarta
- Joseph "Pote" Deleon, 32, Imperial Gangsters, Miedzianowski's major customer and main local business partner
- Francisco Figueroa, 28, Imperial Gangsters
- Alina Lis, 34, grew up with Imperial Gangsters
- Yolanda "Jolly" Navarro, 26, roommate of Ala and girlfriend to Gallo of the Latin Kings
- Rolando "Biggie" Otero, 30, Maniac Latin Disciples
- Nelson "Baby Face" Padilla, 34, Latin Lover
- Marvel L. "Rico" Passley, 29, Imperial Gangsters
- Fredrick G. "Sweet Pea" Rock, 30, listed as an Imperial Gangster, but actually MLD
- David "Viejo" Ruiz, 28, Imperial Gangsters
- Lissette Rivera, Imperial Gangsters
- John Galligan, Miedzianowski's CPD partner[24]

The CPD Internal Affairs investigators told me they had no information that Miedzianowski had been doing *guisos* or operating a drug business before 1997, although his cooperation with Latin Folks gangs dated back to the 1980s.[25] IAD cleared him of Klipfel's ATF charges. In court, however,

Baby Face testified that he and Miedzianowski had committed at least 15 *guisos* over the years, totaling nearly eighty pounds of cocaine and more than $250,000 that was split between several different police officers.[26]

No one ever ratted on Miedzianowski until he got out of control in 1998. His demands to increase his protection payments to $22,000 per month prompted the Latin Folks gangs to turn on him, beginning with his main business partner, Juan Martir. What needs to be pointed out, though, is that corruption is not only committing criminal acts, but also keeping quiet about them. It was the blue code of silence that had protected Jon Burge, notorious Chicago police commander, when he physically tortured more than a hundred black gang members on the South Side. At that time no one came forth to report the torture—screams in police stations and all—from the 1970s through the 1980s. This blue code reappears in corruption cases like Miedzianowski's. It is simply implausible that a drug conspiracy of this extent would escape the notice of *every* Chicago police officer investigating so many Latin Folks gangs for more than a decade.[27]

IT GETS WORSE

The *Chicago Sun-Times* editorial after the Miedzianowski trial asked indignantly:

> Has the huge cache of money from the illegal drug trade created a culture of corruption among urban police officers? If so, what can the Chicago Police Department do to reverse this trend and restore the trust that has been undermined? An investigation by FBI officials focusing on individuals suspected of similar crimes may well uncover more corruption. But while such investigations snare criminals, they do not get to the root of the problem. Answers to the critical questions posed should be addressed by an independent task force with powers to review the process that allowed Miedzianowski to stay on the street. It is time to look beyond specific incidents and focus on the overall internal operations of the department's drug and gang units.[28]

Indeed. But ceremonial task forces and pious denunciations of "bad apples" would be shattered over the next years by scandal after scandal.

While I've shown how the Outfit worked from the top down, the street gangs, particularly Latin Folks, systematically reached out to individual cops and entire units to provide protection and buy drugs on the cheap.

Although individual corruption of rogue police officers—the 5 percent—continue to plague the CPD and police in every US city waging the war on drugs, what is most significant in this story are the organized efforts of gangs, particularly Latin Folks gangs, to build working relationships with police. One egregious example, the infamous SOS corruption scandal, had more to it than the public read in sensational media exposés.

MAKING THEIR BONES: SOS AND THE C-NOTE$

In 2006, the Cook County State's Attorney's Office indicted members of the CPD Special Operations Section (SOS) for aggravated kidnapping, theft, burglary, and other police misconduct, including, but not limited to, home invasion, armed violence, and false arrest. SOS had been on a reign of terror on the streets, and their actions caught the attention of the US attorney. Originally formed as a response to the 1990s spike in homicides, the citywide SOS unit's officers brutalized those they arrested, stole money and drugs, then made up false police reports and lied in court. They did whatever was necessary to get the bad guys off the street. "The bad guys didn't play by the rules," SOS leader Jerome Finnigan told *Playboy Magazine*; "why should we?"

Finnigan went on: "I was a good cop. I really was. I didn't intend to go bad. But once I started I couldn't stop." Both he and his partner Keith Herrera described how they crossed the line from taking a few hundred dollars in a drug raid to splitting more than $600,000 in drug money they appropriated for their own uses. SOS leaders were given awards and praise from superintendent Phil Cline in 2004, who then had to eat his words two years later when the indictments were announced. Herrera described to CBS media star Katie Couric how he and other younger officers learned corruption from Finnigan and more experienced cops in a real-life example of Patrick Murphy's line that corrupt cops are "made, not born."

SOS's cowboy behavior, including multiple *guisos* and flat-out thefts of money and drugs, caused US attorney Patrick Fitzgerald to persuade some SOS members to testify against others, a tactic typically used against gang members. Then the case took a bizarre turn. The two main targets of the federal investigation, veteran Jerome Finnigan and his young protégé Keith Herrera, discovered that their SOS brothers in crime were saving their own skins by testifying against them.

Depending on whose story you believe—Finnigan's to *Playboy* or Herrera's on *60 Minutes*—one or both of them concocted a scheme to hire a hit man to kill John Burzinski, one of the wilder and more violent members of the SOS crew, when they suspected he was wearing a wire. When Finnigan reported he could get a "paint job"—a term for a hit Finnigan got from a book on the supposed mafia killing of Jimmy Hoffa—Herrera said he could hire 2-6 Latin Folks gang members cheaper. In the course of their frenzied discussions, they added three more SOS police officers to a "kill list."

Both Finnigan and Herrera ended up arrested for their murder scheme and were convicted of reduced charges and sent to prison. Finnigan got thirteen years and Herrera, although he was by all accounts one of the most violent and reckless of the SOS crew, was given a mere two months. That unbelievably light sentence was justified, said assistant US attorney Brian Netols (who was also Joe Miedzianowski's prosecutor), since Herrera wore a wire and assisted in nailing Finnigan and eight others. Snitching apparently pays, and I'll give an example of how much in real dollars a bit later.[29]

As bizarre as this story is, Sal explains how SOS was also deeply entwined with Latin Folks drug businesses. SOS raided houses for the C-Note$ and regularly were paid "bones," or bribes. SOS also exemplifies how gang members eagerly have infiltrated the CPD, particularly the city-wide units. Sal ripped to shreds the public sob stories of Herrera and Finnigan that they were simply good cops who were mainly out to get the bad guys. Like Miedzianowski, some SOS officers may have started out with good intentions, but Herrera and Finnigan ended up running a criminal conspiracy on the streets with Latin Folks gangs.

The C-Note$ had direct dealings with Keith Herrera, who was in his midtwenties when he first joined SOS.

The one that approached us was Keith Herrera, because he's closer to the Note$ age group. And he was a club hopper. He used to go to the clubs downtown. The

Note$ controlled the ecstasy scene in those nightclubs downtown. And those cops have eyes. They're told, these are who the players are, and he thought because he was a police officer that he could try to muscle in.

He was Finnigan's little errand boy, so he wasn't gonna do shit himself, he was gonna go back to Finnigan and try to get them to try and squeeze us. But you know what? Police officer or no police officer, they would have had one comin'. When Herrera approached some of our memberships in some of the clubs downtown he gave one of the Note$ his card, telling him if you ever need anything, there it is. They were actually trying to muscle in, trying to get a piece of the pie. We were on to them. We had friends too.

By this point, SOS was not just going after the bad guys; they were in the business themselves. Like other corrupt police they demanded payment for the drug rip-offs that are called "bones" on the street. Sal explained to me patiently that bones are a cost of business in the gang world, and are the "new normal" in bottom-up police corruption. He explained how the C-Note$ would get tipped off by SOS on the location of a rival's drug house and the 10 percent bone the Note$ gave SOS:

SAL: *You know you gotta throw them a bone every once in a while, that's how it works.*

JMH: What do you mean by that? And give an example. We gotta be big on examples here rather than just general statements here, right?

SAL: *Throw a bone. They get their cut depending on the job. Normally it was 10 percent. Whatever you'd do, we get the product—if we got the house, two hundred pounds of marijuana, we hit that house [rob the drug house]. We're selling—for pounds of marijuana at the time was fifteen hundred dollars, and they get 10 percent of that total for telling us.*

JMH: So who did you pay? How did this happen?

SAL: *We paid them directly*

JMH: So you just meet 'em somewhere and give them the—

SAL: *Absolutely. The cops hang out at the same places as our young guys. They go to the same gym, they go to the ball games together. You just slip them the envelope.*

I asked him to give me another example of cooperation with SOS.

SAL: *OK. SOS was looking at the Harrison Gents, and they informed Joey Bags where the house was at.*

JMH: Who was it in SOS?

SAL: *I don't want to say, but he grew up with the guys. He was our people.*

JMH: OK.

SAL: *You know, if you spread the wealth, they're going to tell you what you want. So they tell ya, we're investigating this person, this is where the person lives, this is what we believe is in the house. The Note$ send our people and surveillance the place ourselves and they hit the house. In this case they got two hundred pounds of marijuana. It happened so many times. Then they get paid their bone. Ten percent. Do the math.*

In fact, SOS and other citywide units were prime targets for infiltration by C–Note$ and other gangs, particularly the Latin Folks.

SAL: *The C-Note$ had three of our people in SOS at the time.*

JMH: Tell me about that. How did you get three of your people in there? What does that mean?

SAL: *Well we first got 'em into the police department. Once they're in the police department then you start talking to people who are already in the units. And we get them to select our people for their units. Influence. You get 'em in and from there it takes off. And what we utilized those people was for info. Intelligence. They go out there, they're on the streets—they're legit, they can go out citywide and pressure other organizations and get information that would assist us conducting our business.*

According to several angry, honest police officers I talked with, SOS really stands for "Sons of Supervisors" and they were well connected within the CPD. I asked Sal for more examples of collaboration with SOS. He doesn't have any trouble.

Well, when the C-Note$ were at war with one of their rivals, we had individuals who were 13th District [police district in the area] and as well as in the SOS unit. So when they were fighting them, the Note$ would get girls to infiltrate the opposition and would find out where their stash houses were. Then we'd have our *guys in SOS to go hit those houses and they'd take their guns, take that dope. That would leave the rival gang with no guns, so they can't defend themselves. So that took place. We helped the Note$ with some of our people in the 13th to assist some of our young guys who had gotten arrested with product and they would step in on their behalf to try to get them off.*

I never could get clear, and I think Sal didn't want me to know, whether the "we" in some of his examples of police corruption was the Outfit or the C-Note$. But Sal has a sober view of how corruption works, and a balanced perspective on police. Gang infiltration of police is both conscious and also a function of the career paths of young men—and women—in the Patch and other gang neighborhoods.

SAL: *It always helps to have your own people in there. You gotta remember not all of the cops are dirty. One of the things that we did do was get individuals that we grew up with to take the law enforcement test—get into the police department—and once they're in our district, not only our district but the C-Note$ enemy's district as well, so now they're pressuring them. Whoever the Note$ were fighting, we put our people in that district and they're going to be hassling them [rival gangs].*

JMH: So did you really do that? Can you tell me—you can name names or not—did you really get people to join up and then use them?

SAL: *Absolutely. One of the best was the girls. This one kept calling to let us know that cops were gonna hit one of the Note$' houses. She worked the 911 line in our district . . .*

Sal explains clearly how gangs and cops are drawn from the same population, and corruption naturally follows:

Nothing's changed, but you gotta realize this, too. A lot of the people that I went to high school with and went to grammar school with—not only me but other guys in other neighborhoods—guess who's in law enforcement now? Johnny who was sitting next to me for fourteen years going to school. I know him, his mother, his kids—everybody. You think he's gonna jam me up? He's gonna call me and say, "Hey, you gotta lay low" or "Hey, get outta Dodge"—because you

have those relationships built in already—just like the old timers did. I mean
every generation—and it will continue.

There are many more examples of gang members who joined the CPD. One of the most notorious was Pac Man Jackson, a Vice Lord leader who worked the West Side Austin CPD district. He raided rival gangs and sold some of the drugs he confiscated to his own set. Tommy Marquez, who was caught up in another scandal at the Shakespeare CPD district, was a Latin Count and worked as a tactical officer. He took envelopes of cash from drug busts and admitted to taking more than $25,000 from drug raids over two years. Then there was Sonia Irwin, who was a CPD officer convicted in 1996 for aiding and abetting her boyfriend, a high-ranking Gangster Disciple, Gregory "Shorty G" Shell.

The Latin Kings do not take a back seat to anyone in getting their members into the CPD. A recent indictment charged that between 1996 and 2006 two Chicago police officers, Alex Guerrero and Antonio Martinez, confiscated drugs for the Latin Kings in what appeared to be drug busts. Eight specific incidents or "overt acts" were cited of the two King members/police officers seizing money and drugs, all of which was turned over to Latin King leaders. The list could go on.[30]

To end this litany of corruption, let's return to a final story of cops as drug kingpins. When Joseph Miedzianowski was first tried, US assistant attorney Scott Lassar said, "This is something we haven't seen before." He called Miedzianowski "the most corrupt police officer ever prosecuted in this district." He'd get a chance to reconsider a few years later, and perhaps the Saul Rodriguez case would give the US attorney's office the opportunity to ponder their own culpability.

In 1996, as SGD struggled to survive and the war of the families was waged on the North Side, Saul Rodriguez, a South Side La Raza (Latin Folks) member established a drug conspiracy with Chicago police officer Glenn Lewellen. Saul Rodriguez had been arrested for drug dealing by Lewellen on February 8, 1996, and was told he could escape being charged if he cooperated with the CPD. Rodriguez, Lewellen said, could be paid $1,000 per kilogram of drugs the CPD confiscated based on his snitching. Yes, $1,000 per kilo in the feds' money. That's almost as good as selling it, and safer!

However, Lewellen got some bigger and more lucrative ideas and told Rodriguez to keep on with his operation and he would be protected. The next sentence needs to be quoted from court documents verbatim so the reader will not question my veracity.

Glenn Lewellen delivered payment to Saul Rodriguez in cash. Saul Rodriguez' CPD CS file reflects that between 1996 and 2001, he was paid approximately $807,859 [my italics]. Glenn Lewellen told Saul Rodriguez that the IRS was unlikely to audit him or other CPD informants. Saul Rodriguez did not declare the money the CPD paid him on his tax returns, and therefore did not pay taxes on that money.[31]

More than four-fifths of a million dollars for information, all while running a major drug operation, robbing and turning in your competitors, and even committing murder for hire. Paying for information is how federal agencies get convictions, and I think the amount of money paid to snitches should call the entire drug war into question. Lewellen at one point found out the Drug Enforcement Agency had discovered that Rodriguez was continuing to deal drugs despite his confidential informant agreement. Lewellen intervened, telling the DEA Rodriguez was acting as a CI for the CPD, and the DEA dropped their investigation. Lewellen even stole cocaine recovered by other CPD officers and brought it to Rodriguez to resell. What did Lewellen get? He took a portion of the money from his and Rodriguez's robberies of other dealers and on one occasion even cheated Rodriguez out of his share.

Enough! We are approaching saturation, having covered all of the categories of police corruption, even though I have many more cases I could cite. However, I'll leave the rest of the material on my hard drive and let's summarize what we've learned.

CONCLUSION

Years ago, I told a friend of mine who had been an official in the Drug Enforcement Administration that my gang research was leading me to investigate police corruption in Chicago. He had decades of experience with the CPD, and he said with a wry, knowing, smile: "Be careful. In-vestigating police corruption in Chicago is like having sex with a porcu-pine." Ouch. It is not only the gangs who have much to hide. Now let's be fair. Not all cities have police departments like Chicago's. But if we are to understand gangs, police and official corruption can no longer be off limits to gang research, no matter how difficult research on the topic proves to be.

The main point is that you cannot understand gangs without under-standing how they find ways to work with police. Because of the ubiq-uity of drug dealing in many neighborhoods, and the heavy presence of law enforcement, gangs must make accommodations with some street-level police officers. The cops in turn, make their own accommodations with gangs, and some corruption is inevitable. It is shocking that police corruption is nearly unmentioned in traditional gang research and that drug war police tactics are, when mentioned at all, depicted as unprob-lematic. One goal of this book is to challenge researchers to show some independence from law enforcement and include police corruption in their studies.

To summarize, from the gangs' perspective, and surely for the Latin Folks, police corruption is a standard tactic, one of many skills neces-sary for successfully operating a drug business. In Chicago, following Bill Chambliss, I've explained how corruption has its own unique history from a top-down Outfit strategy to the bottom-up Latin Folks strategy. In the 1970s the black and Latino street gangs' takeover of retail drug sales, along with the massive law enforcement resources thrown into the war on drugs, created the perfect conditions for corruption to flower on the streets. It still does.

From the perspective of police officers, the war on drugs has created thousands of criminals selling illegal substances in an immense market. This gives police unprecedented discretion over whom they arrest, ignore, or make deals with. This situation is fraught with moral danger and in-escapable temptation. I've argued that Joseph Miedzianowski, SOS, and Glenn Lewellen are not just specific cases but also ideal types who diffused learning to other officers of how to use their badges for private gain. This cancer is not a minor aspect of what we call the "gang problem." Latin

Folks gangs and their commission, SGD, were among the most aggressive gangs in suborning police and using them to guarantee their profits.

These two chapters on corruption bring us to the final section of this book, the violent resolution of the tragedy of SGD. But before I lead you through how the war of the families undermined the legitimacy of Latin Folks gang leadership to its members and fractured its organizations, I need to conclude my story-within-a-story on the C-Note$.

This "junior mafia" rode high in the 1990s, monopolizing Chicago's ecstasy market, practicing deception, and expanding their businesses. They were the link between the Outfit and Latin Folks gangs, and within the Insane Family they argued the gangs should put business before revenge. Their cleverness and ties to the Outfit allowed them to flourish and escape the worst of the consequences of the Latin Folks civil war. Still, *catastrophe* is an apt term for what happened to most of their leadership.

part four

CATASTROP

Ecstasy and Agony

The C-Note$ of the 1990s were not what the public would consider a typical street gang. Most of their members grew up in white working-class communities and were not desperately poor. Over the years, an increasing number of Hispanics joined the C-Note$ as their West Side neighborhood changed. Many adult C-Note$ held full-time jobs, particularly with the City of Chicago. Some were Outfit associates, and a handful of the Italians grew up to become made mafia members. While the C-Note$ acted out violently like other youth gangs in the 1990s, they also developed a diverse set of creative and very profitable criminal activities.

The C-Note$ were not major players in the prison-dominated Latino leadership of SGD, but they are important to this story because they were the conscious link of the Outfit to Latin Folks' gangs. While street gangs and organized crime have long been considered by scholars as separate topics, the history of the C-Note$ demonstrates that this approach is too narrow.

There is both an organizational and cultural influence of organized crime on gangs, whether from the Mexican drug cartels, the mafia, or other professional criminal organizations. In my view, this has generally produced two extreme institutional responses: while law enforcement tends to see organized crime on every corner, most academic gang researchers pretend it doesn't exist at all. This book should add some balance to the discussion.

Groups like the C-Note$ bring the rationality of organized crime into the world of gangs. Their stance within SGD for the regulation of violence in some ways echoes that of Donald Black, who argued that violence was essentially a form of social control. For example, gangs need to make sure their customers pay and rivals don't take over their markets. Since the rule of law is weak in ghetto areas—the courts or police surely would not help a drug dealer collect what he is owed—gangs and criminals must enforce their own laws through the threat or use of violence. Thus for Black, a utilitarian or "self-help" morality arises in low-income areas where the state is relatively absent.[1]

I question this aspect of Black's argument. The source of this "self-help" outlook in Chicago did not mainly come from "stateless" ghettoes, but historically derived from social institutions like the Outfit. While groups like the mafia, for example, may have originated as poor "social bandits" in rural Sicily, today organized crime is not a mechanical product of poverty. Once constructed as an institution, organized crime becomes a conscious social actor with its own instrumental, adaptive culture. Sal and the C-Note$' main goal was to embed within the I-Team and SGD an instrumental culture of organized crime that justified violence to make money and cunningly understood corruption as their ticket into conventional society.

I'll grapple with what all this means for the future of gangs a bit later. This chapter describes the 1990s C-Note$ as a criminally creative and violent street gang. But I'll also show how C-Note$ leaders pressed the I-Team to put business first and slow down the killings. We'll see how catastrophe lurked around the corner as the C-Note$ tried mightily but unsuccessfully to embed this instrumental culture of organized crime into the Insane Family and SGD.

JOEY BAGS AND THE I-TEAM

The arrests that ended the Insane Family's Aftermath party, as you read in chapter 7, rippled through the C-Note$ leadership and led Sal to make a decision. He met with Joey Bags, who said he'd had enough: "He told me Mo Mo can take over, that he couldn't handle it anymore." Sal, like any good corporate executive, at first took Joey's resignation under advisement. This was what he had wanted for quite some time, but he thought the transition to Mo Mo should happen naturally rather than through his intervention. With an out-of-control, alcoholic Joey Bags, Sal would not be able to effectively argue to the I-Team the importance of putting business first.

A week after the Aftermath party, Joey Bags showed his frayed nerves at a C-Note$ party. Alina Lis (Ala) was there with Joey, but walked out on him. Joey was hung up on her, but Ala at this time was more preoccupied with her own business dealings than with settling down with a man. Her obsession with Joe Miedzianowski a few years later was what brought her relationship with Joey to an abrupt end. At the party, Mo Mo criticized Joey for jeopardizing business by his treatment of Ala and Joey blew up. As the party ended, there was a drive-by shooting against the C-Note$ and Joey stressed out even more. Mo Mo reported what was going on to Sal, who told me he had been watching Joey's demise "in slow motion."

The very next month the Maniac Family attacked the Insane Family in the *Godfather* movie-style hits described in the preface. Sal says,

> Joey Bags sorta went nuts. I couldn't talk sense into the man. He wanted to go out himself and hit the Disciples, like some kinda Braveheart. That's not how its done, I told him. I even met with him and Mo Mo. My other guy, Dominic, had just been locked up shortly after that bust at the Aftermath. Sammy was behind the walls too. Lucky was there, but I never cared for him and didn't really trust his judgment anyway. It turned out I was right about that prick.

Sal goes on:

> Joey was gonna screw everything up. I know Ala did her best to talk him into chilling out. But Joey wouldn't even listen to her. I told Joey doing it back to them, simultaneous, like in the Godfather, was the best way to go. These things take time and planning. What was important was business, and if you do a hit right, business gets better. If you don't do it right, you lose both money and your life. Sometimes you gotta use your head more than what your gut tells you.
>
> But Joey said to me again, "Let Mo Mo represent us to the Insane Family. I'm out." I have to admit I was pleased.

Dominic had been caught up in the moment during the Aftermath raid, and indeed he was mainly responsible for the disturbance that brought the police. It wasn't long after that fiasco that he was arrested for narcotics trafficking. Once in custody, he was paid a visit by the FBI and was told that he could beat the rap if he cooperated in the prosecution of an Outfit burglary ring that included Joey Bags and Big Wally, a guy the feds wanted badly. He refused, living up to the "no-snitching" ethic with which he was raised. This got him respect from the C-Note$ and Outfit guys, but also got him five years in prison and immediate deportation to Italy once he was released.

Many of the C-Note$' key leaders were also facing jail terms, and there was a brewing crisis in leadership. Burglary was a big-time Outfit enterprise, and it had gotten Joey in trouble.

By 1994 over three-quarters of the Grand Avenue Crew members and associates had arrests for burglary or were suspects in major unsolved burglaries throughout the Midwest. In the West Town neighborhood bars like Knights Out, Easy Inn, and Jerry's, Joey Bags had met with his crews to hand out orders, many of them burglary and cartage theft schemes that either others couldn't do or weren't interested in doing. Joey was tied to a crew whose members were currently fighting a 1992 case where Chicago police recovered more than $2 million worth of stolen property and cash. All this added to Joey's stress level. By 1996 the kid was ready to break.

When Mo Mo attended the I-Team meeting after the Aftermath party, he was hammered by leaders of the other gangs, and the C-Note$ were forced to pay restitution to cover bail and reimburse for all confiscated weapons. I-Team leaders told me at first Mo Mo wasn't fully trusted since he was not from an original Latin Folks gang and the C-Note$ hadn't been formally voted into the SGD union yet. Their initial application was being held up by the Harrison Gents, and it would be up to Mo Mo to get this settled.

There followed a series of I-Team meetings that according to Sal, "laid out an agenda for the 1990s." The problem with this agenda, as we'll see in the next chapter, was that the Spanish Cobras, as leaders of the Insane Family, were more concerned with battling the Maniac Latin Disciples for control of the SGD board than making sensible business decisions.

The SGD union was proving incapable of solving problems between its members, particularly the growing number of falling bodies in a bloodier and bloodier war of the families. Sal said bluntly, "The Cobras had had enough and decided to force the hand of La Tabla by conjuring up a plan to take majority control of the board." The desire of the Cobras to eradicate the Maniacs from SGD was matched by the Maniac Family's desire to eliminate the Cobras and their entire family. To Sal and the C-Note$ leadership, this was crazy. What SGD needed was to concentrate on business. Sal urged the C-Note$ to show them how.

THE BUSINESS OF ECSTASY

For Sal, the war over who was going to control the cocaine distribution on the North Side of Chicago no longer made any sense. Too much blood had been shed, and there was no end in sight. The Outfit had been caught up in their own internal battles over the years, but had learned war was only necessary as a last resort. The C-Note$ membership had also dwindled, and Sal knew something more was needed for them to make an impact on the I-Team.

> In the 1970s I remember the Ohio Street faction had membership in the hundreds, and by the time the 1990s rolled around, their ranks were now comprised of no more than thirty members depending on who was coming or going. Although they had had their ups and downs in recent years, the neighborhood ties were still strong, and with the new upswing many relatives of old members were now claiming affiliation with the various crews. Gone were the days when guys got beaten up or killed over dumb shit. There was a new motive, and that motive was for everyone to get paid.

The snitching problem was pretty serious in the street gang world, and cocaine use, arrests, and violence created major problems.

> By the 1990s, law enforcement had developed a vast network of informants. The network was made up of individuals who at one point or another had been caught and charged with being involved in the sale, distribution, or possession

of narcotics. Rather than do their time, they chose to turn state's evidence. Rats were beginning to infiltrate many of the larger organizations, and with jail sentences becoming harsher every day, there was no shortage of individuals willing to become snitches. Because the penalty for dealing in hardcore drugs was far greater than dealing in recreational drugs, it became a no-brainer to stay away from dealing them.

It seemed like every other day you'd hear about a large shipment being seized or a person getting killed over what was presumed to be a drug-related incident. Organizations like the Latin Kings were becoming prime targets for federal and local law enforcement agencies. Their image was in the toilet as they were portrayed by law enforcement and the media to be creating a world of death and destruction with their high level of involvement in the drug trade. A ban was put into effect where the Note$ were not only not supposed to deal in crack or heroin but members were now not allowed to indulge in either one of them as well.

Sal thought he could show the Insane Family a better way to avoid the "bad rep" of dirty violence. He noted that the ecstasy market was almost completely open, very lucrative, still relatively violence-free, and thus not at the center of law enforcement's attention. He explained the situation to me so vividly that I'm going to reproduce his words verbatim:

While violence was erupting on almost every street corner of the Logan Square and Humboldt Park neighborhoods of Chicago, Jefferson Park functioned as a distribution point for more than 240 pounds of ecstasy per year—I estimate worth $16 million a year. Overseeing the distribution was a crew known as the X-Men. The C-Note$ had entered into an arrangement with associates of the Israeli mafia, and due to the amount of money that they were now generating for them, the Israeli mafia was willing to provide not only the product for distribution but also gunmen and muscle at a moment's notice.

The Note$ revolutionized their drug network by investing in the ecstasy drug industry, realizing that the product was easier to transport and store. At the time the penalty for dealing in ecstasy was very minimal compared to the penalties individuals faced who were dealing cocaine, heroin, and marijuana. Ecstasy pills arriving from their manufacturers' laboratories in Las Vegas were nearly impossible to detect. Shipments of cocaine and marijuana were easily detected by drug-sniffing dogs. Their mere bulk and odor made it difficult to transport from one end of the city to the other.

Part of their revolutionizing strategy was the guaranteeing of their product line. In the beginning when a customer was not happy with their product they simply took it back, repackaged the product, and sold it to one of their other customers. This was done by either of two methods: one was by crushing the pills and then putting the powder into capsules that once housed vitamins and supplements or by simply spraying the pills with food coloring to change the color of the pills giving the impression to customers that it was a totally different batch of goods. The Note$ would then market the product by giving them different names.

Realizing this practice was bad for business, they began to demand a better product from their manufacturers. A meeting took place over a weekend in Las Vegas where all expectations were ironed out. The quality of the product increased drastically and soon they were cornering the market. If a customer was not happy they would switch out their product, no questions asked. The Note$ were making quite an impact in a relatively short period of time. Ecstasy dealers from all over the city were seeking to purchase their products from them. What started out as two local dealers soon was employing hundreds of people, including dealers, mules, distributors, and muscle—thus the beginning of the X-Men crew. In the 1990s nobody moved more ecstasy pills into the Chicago area than the X-Men.

The Note$ opened up new drug markets in surrounding suburbs that stretched from Las Vegas to Illinois, and by year's end they had earned over $1 million. They began to monopolize the distribution and transportation of the product operation throughout the city. They soon had dealers in every community and from every walk of life, from heterosexual to homosexual and from every race, color, and creed. They now had several stash houses in the city were they could store and distribute their product without raising any eyebrows. With the high percentage of college students and nightclubs in the Chicago area, it was an ideal business to get into, and they jumped in with both feet. "X" was being sold at underground rave parties all over the city in mass consumption.

The Note$ started to capitalize on this venue and was soon hosting their own underground parties at various locations throughout the city. They were making money hand over fist. Not only were they profiting from the cover charge to enter the party, but they also had a multitude of party favors. You name it, they had it, from nitrous-oxide balloons to mushrooms. You had individuals who did nothing but roll at these events.

Day or night, you can always count on a party going on somewhere. To avoid law enforcement detection most parties were promoted via fliers with a contact number which would have an informational voice message for the individual calling. On the day of the event, the message would change to give the caller a new location. Upon showing up at the new location, individuals purchased their ticket to the party and were pointed in the right direction. Parties were commonly held at warehouses, empty storefronts, and multiple apartment buildings and on occasion rented halls.

By the late 1990s two associates of the C-Note$ had opened up teen clubs. One was actually named XTC in Chicago and the other one was called Industry in unincorporated Northlake. Things were going great—and then Mr. Daley went on a crusade and had the downtown Chicago location closed. Having the club named XTC was funny but didn't help the Note$' associates beat the closing.

The Industry in Northlake lasted two years before shutting its doors as well. The Industry owners decided to close the doors rather than paying the local Outfit guy more street tax. This individual—I don't wanna give you the name— was already getting paid $1,500 a month, and after seeing how much traffic was coming in and out he decided to up the ante and proposed a higher street tax. While the Note$' associates were thinking it over, the local Outfit member had some of his cohorts start towing vehicles out of the rented parking lot as though to send a message. This was despite the fact they were already paying to utilize the lots as additional parking! They decided rather than pay this greedy fuck another dime they would simply close shop.

They simply moved operations to other teen clubs in surrounding suburbs, Zero Gravity in Naperville, the Mission in Elgin, and Nitro in Stone Park. It was business as usual as they continued to push their product on all the patrons that visited these establishments on a weekly basis. Shorties were first sent out with twenty hits apiece to test the market, and within minutes of arriving at these establishments they were sold out. With this new intel they then were deployed with a hundred hits at a time at fifteen to twenty dollars at a pop.

The boys began to distribute the club drug to several different organizations and soon became the main supplier in the Chicago area.

Many gangs began to receive their X from the C-Note$, but none were bigger buyers than the Insane Deuces from their Villa Park section. The demand for the drug was so intense at the time that whatever the C-Note$ supplied, the Deuces had no problem dumping it to hundreds of customers. Their orders began at five hundred hits a week, which soon swelled to five thousand a week as they built themselves a very lucrative business in Aurora and eventually expanded their operation to another one of their satellite sections in Addison, Illinois.

The whole operation was based on muscle and loyalty; the Note$ used muscle to take control of the rackets and took care of those that provided loyal service throughout the years. Noting that the real power came from those that worked behind the scenes, they maintained a low profile and allowed other organizations to assert themselves in the public eye and media. Unlike some of their counterparts, they did not seek public acclaim for crimes committed. Following this ideology they were able to build an uncontested empire that would last for at least a decade.

This "ideology" was precisely what Sal wanted to get across to the I-Team. While "muscle," the threat of violence, is always a necessity, its actual use in the ecstasy game paled in comparison to the bloody wars then being fought over control of cocaine markets. The "low profile" route pushed by Outfit leaders like Tony Accardo and later Joey Lombardo was in contrast to the flashy "gangsta" mentality of many Latin Folks gang leaders and some of the youthful and more reckless C-Note$.

Sal saw the I-Team as a natural arena for the extension of C-Note and Outfit influence and their member gangs as new partners in crime and profit. But he knew he had to slow down the senseless Latin Folks wars, and the best way to do it, he thought, was for the C-Note$ to model an "ideology" of putting business first.

BETTER THAN SLICED BREAD

Sal tells, with some pride, of the creativeness of the C-Note$ in their money-making schemes. Expanding the number of businesses gave the

C-Note$ a growing reputation in the Patch, and their ranks swelled. Their added numbers and growth of their businesses, in turn, got them respect and influence within the I-Team.

Sal told me of the merchandising skills of the C-Note$ with laughter. One of our interviews took place driving through the Patch. Sal had rented a car with tinted windows so we couldn't be recognized, and he showed me the railroad yards nearby that were major hunting grounds for the enterprising C-Note$. The C-Note$ were among the best at changing with the times.

> In 1995 the best thing since sliced bread was invented: E-Bay! It marked a new era of moving stolen merchandise. In the beginning mostly collectibles were being moved through the system, and as the years passed the Note$ began to move anything ranging from power tools and motorcycle parts to ceramic figurines and designer clothing from Marc Jacobs. The majority of this swag was lifted from railway freight containers at various locations and yards. By 1999 the Note$ were moving hundreds of items a month through the online auction website. Appliances, computers, televisions—everything was being sold, and the best thing about it all was that you usually got more money than what you were asking for it, so it was a win-win situation.
>
> Eventually the boys would face a hiccup here and there due to new and improved technological tracking devices that were being utilized by shipping companies. In reality all those devices did was force them to become more innovative. They were constantly changing it up to stay one step ahead of the law. One week they would burglarize houses on the North Shore; the next week they would be jacking Union Pacific boxcar loads; and the following month they would be boosting from chain stores. The key to their success has always been their ability to diversify their operations and never putting all their eggs in one basket. Authorities estimate that approximately over $10 billion in merchandise is stolen from stores every year. Diversity at its finest: the boys certainly have gotten their share.

This "diverse" criminal orientation was in contrast to the narrow drug dealing activities of other Latin Folks gangs. Sal explained this as one the advantages of Outfit culture.

You have to remember that most of these guys were born and raised in the same "hood" that they operated in, so it was a close-knit family. They were accustomed of doing anything to make a fast buck, and even after landing some good paying jobs old habits were hard to break.

The majority of the guys were in their midtwenties to early thirties with only a handful of them being considered connected guys. These guys always had something brewing. They always had loot on them. They were constantly flipping goods. You needed a TV; done. You needed a leather jacket; no problem. You needed a five-gallon bucket of paint, they could get that too.

Whatever someone needed or asked for they would get it for you. These crews would hit job sites, stores, trucks, cribs—nothing was untouchable. One of the older guys had an antique car that he was restoring and was looking for a piece, so he came to the spot and offered one of the guys $100 to get him the piece. He even told the guys where one could be found by providing the address of a garage where the car was being stored. Within a week the brother had his piece.[2]

PROVOCATIONS AND VIOLENCE

While their business ventures were calculated to maximize profits and minimize violence, the C-Note$ were still a street gang with plenty of bravado and territorial enemies. Sal's efforts to get his minor league team to "put business first" didn't always meet with success. He tells me, with somewhat of a "boys will be boys" attitude, of how the C-Note$ creatively contributed to the violence, and the Internet again featured in their mayhem.

One of the C-Note$' old-school tactics had been to ride public transportation from one end of the city to the other and incite conflicts between their rivals. They crossed out graffiti, making it look as though it was crossed out not by them but by a different, rival gang, provoking disputes between them. Now with access to the Internet old grudges could be solved by using the same tactic but with the click of a mouse. Their objective was to help take out as many of their rivals as possible without suffering any casualties themselves in the process.

They realized that by participating in various Internet chat rooms they could instigate war between gangs they hated, a tactic that has become common today. Their main targets during this campaign were the Insane Satan Disciples, Latin Jivers, Maniac Latin Disciples, and the Latin Kings. The C-Note$ would go to local libraries and Internet cafes and eventually would use boosted laptops with wireless systems and get on unsecured lines so as to not have anyone track where the message was coming from. They would sit in locations where Wi-Fi was offered free and go to town "assaulting" anyone they encountered in the online chat rooms, pretending they were from a different gang.

As an example, I'll take an actual transcript of one C-Note "insult" chat which had been saved for posterity and provide simultaneous translation and interpretation.

> What's up Putos? I'm Cholo D from Ohio and Marshfield [Satan Disciples branch], Bow down to this Baby Devil, IGSDN till the End [give respect to the SD Nation]. HGK, IGK, LJK, LKK, SLK, VLK [All rival gangs with a K on the end, which disrespects them, e.g., Harrison Gents Killer]. Cum get you sum bitches" [Come to our turf and try your luck].

Responding to the chat, an actual Harrison Gents (HG) gang member disrespects the supposed SD member, who was actually a C-Note:

> IGSDK [Insane Gangster Satan Disciple Killer] All Day Fuck you Shitty Diapers [i.e., SD, an insult to Satan Disciples]. Hustlas and Gangstas World [**H**arrison **G**ents **W**orld], Gotti Rots [Gotti was a fallen SD soldier and to say he "rots" means disrespect]. Almighty Harrison Gents Ashland and Cortez 187 [AHG, first, eighth, and seventh letters of the alphabet as well as, weirdly, the California penal code for murder] your Soggy Donut ass [more childish SD insults].

The undercover C-Note pretending to be an SD then responded:

> Ohio and Marshfield run up and get gunned up [daring the Gent to come to SD turf]. Grapes [Disrespect to the Gents, whose colors are black and purple] ain't shit. S/D Crazy, never lazy ride down to Murderfield and test your luck niggas [more daring the Gents to come to SD turf for drama and violence].[3]

Soon, according to Sal, "They had half of their enemies going at each other's throats" as they sat back and watched all the chaos they had created. The Note$ found themselves inciting war between members of the Almighty Family and the Maniac Family as well as various members of the People Alliance. These teen antics were tolerated by Sal, and he said with a smirk while shaking his head:

> Folks were killing Folks and People were killing People and nobody had a clue that it was all the results of the click of a mouse. There is no doubt in my mind that hundreds of individuals were victims of drive-by shootings due to the onslaught of propaganda that was offered by the boys throughout the years.

Trading in arms was also one of the C-Note$ specialties, and while joining the I-Team was for Sal about business, the "judicious" use of violence could not be neglected. Sal explains:

> With money comes power and with power comes respect. In order to maintain this respect and power they had to be willing to protect it by all means necessary. We taught the C-Note$ they could do this by utilizing their resources. The boys had three pipelines for weapons available to them; one was from West Virginia, one from Texas, and the other from Wisconsin.
>
> Their guy in West Virginia used to come in once a month with duffle bags full of guns. He used to sell half for cash and trade the rest for dope. The way he would get the guns was by reading through the Trading Times and want ads.
>
> The Texas connect was a member from the Ohio Street faction that was on the lam for several crimes that he was being sought for back in Chicago. He found that all you needed to purchase a weapon in Texas at the time was a Texas driver's license. Before long he opened up his new line of money making, purchasing and selling guns illegally.
>
> Their guy from Wisconsin would come in with loads more frequently, since he was more centrally located. Each of these individuals would purchase the weapons from various sources then tack on twenty-five to two hundred dollars depending on the caliber and brand. In return the Note$ would do the same on their end by providing weapons to the I-Team and passing along the cost to

them. It became a very profitable business, and at the end of the day everyone involved was happy.

Members of the I-Team would put in orders and the Note$ would deliver the caliber that they were seeking. 9mms were the weapons of choice. Everyone wanted 9mms—there was such a high demand—and besides, this is the weapon that was the most profitable. Some of them, like the Vikings, only wanted small-caliber weapons, which were easier to hide. Others, like the Cobras and Deuces, wanted the cannons like the Mac-10s and Tec-9s. The Note$ kept the pipelines open as long as they could, for they knew that the weapons would be put to good use by the other families. One of the guys ended up getting busted for transporting weapons and drugs across state lines. He eventually beat the case on a technicality, and before long he was back in business.

The C-Note$ knew that the threat and occasional use of violence was always necessary for their kind of business. They also shrewdly used their arms dealing to get others to do the shooting and safeguard their own members, while watching their rivals get eliminated. By avoiding direct involvement with revenge killings and playing a more laid-back role, the C-Note$ managed to escape police attention during the war of the families. Sal told me with pride that "no police arrests of any C-Note$ members were ever made during this time in connection with any crime tied to this conflict."

In fact, one tactic the C-Note$ employed was to take advantage of the Chicago police mandate to "get guns off the street." When C-Note$ were caught in a drug bust, the Note$ offered firearms to the arresting officers if the charges would be dropped. In one case, the cost of dropping charges was a .22 rifle with a 30-shot banana clip and a 12-gauge shotgun. These guns were put in a box and placed in the alley behind Oakley Street. The cops were called as instructed, and then C-Note members sat back and watched as the officers came and picked them up. The charges were dropped.

This type of request became more frequent, and soon it was customary to ask to make a deal. Sal remembers one Young Note had to give up thirteen pistols just to get out of going to the joint for driving on a revoked license. Sal laughed and said it was "win-win." The Note$ didn't go to jail and the cops got brownie points for turning in guns. But most of Sal's attention was to more important matters.

FORMAL APPLICATION FOR SGD MEMBERSHIP

Even before the Aftermath party and the *Godfather*-movie attacks of the Maniacs on the Cobras, the C-Note$ had made the decision to become Folks and register with SGD. Their initial sponsors were the Harrison Gents, and the souring of relations with them prompted the C-Note$ to ask the Dragons to be their official "first cousin." The expectation that a decision would be quickly forthcoming was, in retrospect, foolish, as politics delayed C-Note$ registration for four more years. Soon after they applied for membership, the C-Note$ began attending I-Team meetings. Sal provided me with their application letter, which documents the formality of the registration process (see appendix 8).

At their first I-Team meeting, the Deuces objected to the C-Note$ presence: the two had a history of conflict, but the Note$' sponsors, the Dragons and the Cobras, assured the family that the C-Note$ would be team players. The Dragons, for their part, were intrigued by the potential of broadening out their business to burglaries, safecracking, arsons, and cartage thefts. They were in a war with the Latin Kings at the time, and as goodwill, the C-Note$ agreed to provide them weapons. The Note$ hated the Kings as well, and they privately reasoned that it was better for Dragons to be dying against the Kings than C-Note$ losing their own lives.

Sal told me more war stories from those times than I can include here. What Sal stressed to me, however, was that while the C-Note$ joined in the war of the families of the 1990s, he was working behind the scenes to channel their gangbanging behavior into more rational actions. Tit might have to lead to tat, but still there was business to do. For Sal, it all started with getting the C-Note$ registered as Latin Folks, to formally become members of SGD.

Joining the Insane Family was the first step, and a factional "family" structure, even more so than SGD, became the basic gang organization on Chicago's West Side. This would have some ominous implications, which we'll explore in the next chapter. According to Sal, the I-Team's "objective was to force communication in order to resolve some of the conflicts that were taking place. The I-Team organized several organizations across the city under one umbrella, each with duties and responsibilities as well as set borders across the board. Their main interest remained the sale and distribution of narcotics."

One result of the formation of the I-Team was to put the squeeze on some of the smaller organizations. For example, the Campbell Boys were grabbed by larger, adjacent groups and split into Maniac and Insane factions. Both factions of the Campbell Boys eventually dissolved as independent organizations. Their once lucrative drive-up drug sale business was now controlled by the MLDs and Cobras. The formation of the families was forcing consolidation, which worked for profit but also strengthened the families for war against one another.

The I-Team gave the C-Note$ a forum to address the gangs' common problems. One serious issue that organization was thought to be able to solve was rivals testifying in court after acts of violence. SGD laws, as well as the Outfit code, prohibited even testifying against enemies, following their own "golden rule" of "don't testify against them because they might testify against you."[4]

The C-Note$ tried to work within the structures of SGD, and especially the Insane Family, to settle grievances rationally, through juntas or organized sit-downs. Within the Folks Alliance, the C-Note$' worst enemy was the nearby Satan Disciples (SD). In 1996, just as the Note$ joined the I-Team, the SDs were in the midst of their own civil war, the periodic battles between old and new members that most street gangs experience. An attempted hit by one faction against the other on C-Note turf was stopped by C-Note$, but that infuriated the SDs. They returned and picked a fight, but Armando "Mando" Rodriguez, an SD solider, was shot and killed. The driver, Ruben "Professor" Martinez, and a passenger, Latin Jiver Juan Ocun, told police they were assaulted by C-Note$ and testified in court against a C-Note$ member.

Joey Bags and other C-Note$ leaders met with the SD leadership at Smith Field in the Patch, prior to the court date. Joey invoked SGD rules to argue that Martinez and Ocun should not testify, but they did anyway. The C-Note was sentenced to sixty years, angering the C-Note$ membership. This sparked what would turn into a fifteen-year war with the Satan Disciples, who had violated the basic principles of SGD that mandated no snitching.

There was little that Sal or any of the older guys could do to cool things down. C-Note$ used their Internet chat-room strategy to inflame tensions between the SDs and the neighboring Milwaukee Kings and Latin Kings, both rivals of the C-Note$. The Note$ used their connections with arms dealers to provide weaponry to the Ashland Vikings and Dragons, who as Insane Family members, faced the same tensions that their brothers the Note$ faced. Thus the enemy Satan Disciples were decimated at no cost to the C-Note$. In fact, in true capitalist fashion, the Note$ even made money on the war by selling guns. But this drama worried Sal, who was concerned that violence was taking too much of a toll on business.

As Mo Mo took over representing the C-Note$ (and Outfit) to the I-Team, his job was to influence the Insane Family to stay away from "counterproductive" acts and to concentrate on neighborhood rackets. At a 1997 junta in a seafood restaurant on Ashland Avenue, the main leaders of the I-Team gathered. The Cobras explained to the rest of the I-Team that they now had the votes to control the SGD board. The Maniacs' eradication of the Latin Lovers had pushed them into the Insane Family but not out of SGD. The dissolution of the Campbell Boys subtracted another vote.

At the junta many different points of view were expressed on how the Insane Family had arrived at a position of taking power. While some stressed the victories in battle, Sal knew that peace, not war, was the key to long-term success in SGD. For the C-Note$ to be a major player in SGD, they had to go "behind the walls" to get La Tabla to sign off on their registration. They also needed to take further steps to consolidate their own organization.

CONSOLIDATION AND FINAL REGISTRATION

Mo Mo's responsibility as the de facto leader of all C-Note$ branches meant that he had to first attend to organizational development. He began a recruitment campaign of "only relatives of existing members" in order to minimize snitching and build trust. Along with the profits from the booming ecstasy business these measures more than doubled their ranks. Given relative peace, Mo Mo proved adept at handling business on the street the old-fashioned way. Mo Mo grew to admire the political fixer and thus became a firm devotee of negotiating deals both internally and externally.[5]

Sal advised Mo Mo to seek out new markets where violence between gangs wouldn't break out. The ecstasy business was sensible, we've seen, because the C-Note$ had little or no competition. This contributed to their building up a broad and more affluent customer base in suburban and rural areas. The Note$ cultivated markets in Chicago's Northwest Side and in surrounding suburbs like Schaumburg, Crystal Lake, Elk Grove, Park Ridge, Bensenville, Norridge, and Elmwood Park as well as in other states, like Wisconsin, Texas, and West Virginia. There was more money in the suburbs than in the city—a "real gold mine"—and the Note$ went after it.

Sal simultaneously pushed Mo Mo to cement membership into the Latin Folks Alliance. Sal said Mo Mo knew that under the SGD concept, "no outside family could come into his territory without being invited by the host family, and he was not inviting." This move alone bought an uneasy peace to the C-Note$ throughout the 1990s, with the stubborn exception of the war with the Satan Disciples.

Sal told me the stalling of the SGD board on C-Note$ registration seemed mainly political, but it stood in the way of full C-Note$ legitimacy as Latin Folks. Within the I-Team, the C-Note$ had established themselves as major players with a consistent, rational message of putting profits before warfare. The next step was to take this message to the entire Union, La Tabla of Spanish Growth and Development.

La Tabla held its meetings behind the walls, and any serious decisions had to occur there. Dominic, who had been sent to prison after refusing to snitch shortly after the Aftermath incident, became the C-Note$ representative. At one point he shared a cell with "Pimp Daddy," Francisco Garcia, whose brother Rick Dog at the time was the MLD street leader. The negotiations concerning the C-Note$' registration application would take place in various Illinois correctional facilities.

By 1999, Mo Mo had become chair of the I-Team and moved to force a decision from SGD, now delayed for four years. At I-Team meetings, often at a bar on Fullerton Avenue where the girlfriend of one of the

I-Team leaders was the bartender, the I-Team met to discuss disputes among themselves, business ventures, and rising hostilities with the Maniacs. The Maniacs had ambushed Stoney, a Cobra leader, and there seemed to be no end to the hostilities in sight. In order to have the legitimacy to mediate peace, the C-Note$ moved decisively to formalize their SGD membership.

The decision was made to meet with La Tabla at the Galesburg correctional center, which at that time housed many of the main shot callers. An added problem to be solved were threats by the Simon City Royals to an incarcerated C-Note for problems that had taken place on the street. This violated SGD laws that said that what happens on the streets has to stay on the street. On March 11, 1999, I-Team members visited various SGD board members in Galesburg. One by one, the shot callers of Latin Folks gangs were called out to meet their visitors and took their places at long tables in the courtyard while the guards looked on unaware of the "criminal conspiracy" taking place right in front of their eyes. At this meeting, the Royals' problem was settled, and any final objections to C-Note$ SGD membership were answered. All that remained for C-Note$ registration was a formal vote, which in fact came in the next months.

Sal was pleased the C-Note$ were about to accomplish one of their main objectives. However, at the same time they were losing many of their key leaders.

AGONY

This story doesn't end well for all of the C-Note$ top dogs. I asked Sal early on whether it would be sensible to try to interview the 1990s C-Note$ leaders who were still alive. He told me to put feelers out, but he doubted anyone would talk. He was right, and I stopped my efforts to contact Mo Mo, Sammy, and Dominic, in part to safeguard Sal's confidentiality. From what I could gather, Sammy was released from prison and was working, older and wiser. Mo Mo left the city and the street life and returns occasionally to talk about old times. But for the other three of the "Two Dagos, Two Spics, and a Hillbilly" the end was nastier.

Joey Bags's decision to retreat from active leadership of the C-Note$

left him to concentrate on making money, and he became increasingly erratic. In 2003, he was "caught red-handed," according to a press report, as an operative in a major Outfit burglary ring, "one of the top crews in the Midwest." He was headed for prison, but he never got there.

He had married a Polish immigrant—Sal said it was a scam for her to pay Joey to marry her so she could become a citizen. In 2005, he was arrested by Cicero police for domestic battery. According to the police report, which I received by a Freedom of Information request, on February 18, 2005, police responded to a report of "a man beating a woman in a black car and the woman yelling for help." They found Joey Bags "jumping up and down on the hood of a black Mercedes, and kicking the front windshield." The police report then said Joey "fell and hit his face against the broken windshield while standing on top of the hood of the car." In the report, this strangely appears to have occurred *after* he was arrested. This may be the officers' way of explaining extensive and suspicious facial injuries to Joey, who had no love of the police.

Once back at the Cicero police station, Joey's injuries were determined to be worse than they had seemed. He was taken to Cook County Jail and then rushed to a nearby hospital, where he died. A lawsuit by his "widow" was quietly dropped.

For Lucky, the Hillbilly, the end was a bit less dramatic, but even more offbeat. He served time in prison, and while he was gone Joey Bags and then others had taken over the crews. Lucky had been so erratic when in charge that no one wanted him in any position of responsibility, and Sal and the Outfit didn't trust him either. He began robbing drug dealers and lived in fear of his life.

Sal also suspected that Lucky was making deals with the police, and that that was what kept him on the streets. He was allowed to "retire" from the C-Note$ and Sal said he "degenerated." As I was beginning to write this book, on April 27, 2012, Lucky went to the dentist to have four wisdom teeth extracted. He suffered an allergic reaction to the medication and ended up suffocating when his air passages were shut due to the swelling. Sal said, "The kid survives prison, multiple gunshot wounds, stabbings, and ball battings, and ends up getting taken out by a dentist."

Dominic is still alive today, happily married and living in Italy. Upon release from prison after his arrest for narcotics trafficking, immigration agents detained him. Apparently after his family emigrated from Italy Dominic had never followed through and applied for citizenship, and he was deported. Sal says he wants to come back, but there is little chance that can happen.

I began this chapter by saying that it was difficult to see the C-Note$ as a typical street gang. They were indeed a neighborhood gang, but also had organizational, local, and blood ties to the Outfit. The reader should also note that none of the "Two Dagos, Two Spics, and a Hillbilly" died as a result of gang warfare. The C-Note$ were adept at provoking violence, but also largely avoided becoming its victims.

These were surely sound survival skills. They were also learned Outfit traditions passed down from elders like Sal in the manner described by the classic criminologist Edwin Sutherland. While the C-Note$ engaged in youthful violence and provocative behavior, they also consciously represented Outfit interests to SGD. Those interests were fundamentally to bring an end to war in order to increase profits, consistent with the aims of some, but not all, of the leaders of the Latin Folks. In the end, however, the C-Note$' advocacy of the Outfit's instrumental culture proved ineffective. It never overcame the vicious cycle of factional revenge that ultimately shattered the SGD experiment. It is to that final story we now turn.

 **The War of the Families**

The People and Folks coalitions and later SGD were formed out of the need for the safety of gang leaders in prison, to slow down and regulate violence on the street, to build a shared identity, and to create a better business climate. As we examine the 1990s war of the families it is reasonable to first ask whether "violent street gangs" even have the capacity to come together and stop their own violence. Of course they do, and there is ample evidence outside Chicago to support this.

No one has more to gain from a halt to violence than gang members. The truces called by Mara Salvatrucha and 18th Street gang in El Salvador and Honduras and subsequent drops in violence in those countries are a recent example that gangs can indeed restrain violence, at least for a time. MS-13 and 18th Street gangs are multinational in scope, and have members with a strong gang identity. They have leaders who their members concede have legitimate authority to regulate violence. Thus a press conference in an El Salvador prison by gang leaders announced a ceasefire to the nation and to their own members. Gang truce meetings have been held in nearly every city in the US over the years and I suspect internationally as well. Such efforts have had a significant, if unmeasured, impact on gang violence.[1]

For another example, look at the twin cities of El Paso and Juarez, separated by only a bridge. While war between gangs or cartels rages in Juarez, El Paso has been consistently anointed as the "safest city in the United States." This clearly represents differences between Mexico and the US, but the cartels operate transnationally, and as the data show, have nearly complete control of *where* they kill.[2]

While in Mexico a war rages between cartels, on the US side of the border a different dynamic is at work. Latino prison gangs like La Eme,

Table 10.1. Homicide in two cities, 2010

City	Population	Number of Homicides	Homicide Rate (per 100,000)
El Paso	800,647	5	< 1
Juarez	1,300,000	3,075	229

the Mexikanemi, Nuestra Familia, and the Texas Syndicate have extended their influence from their jail cells to the barrios. They have developed strong, vested interests in peace on the streets, both for their members' safety and for their businesses. As with SGD in the 1990s, in Texas and California incarcerated gang leaders meet among themselves to discuss how to both stay safe and make money. Coincidentally we are witnessing record lows in homicide throughout south Texas and California. Consider San Antonio, where in 2010 there were only *five* drug-related homicides—a bad weekend in Chicago.[3]

Law enforcement always wants to take credit when homicides drop but blame the gangs when it goes up. However, the reasons the Mexican cartel war has not spilled over to the US side surely reflect more than policing and include the conscious, rational decisions of both cartel leaders and powerful US prison gangs.

To better understand this dynamic, we can turn to the 2011 United Nations *Global Study on Homicide*. It points out that levels of homicide in most times are related to lack of development and inequality. It is the most undeveloped areas, like sub-Saharan Africa, with high numbers of desperate young men, that have the highest rates of killing. The report adds that when homicide rates shoot up stratospherically it is typically because gangs go to war, as in Colombia between the Cali and Medellin cartels, the 1990s mafia wars in Italy, and more recently the Mexican Sinaloa vs. Zetas cartel wars. The report adds that violence often sharply declines when wars end.[4]

The standard notion by US criminologists that "neighborhood characteristics" of social disorganization predict homicide rates makes little sense at times of war when murders double or triple in a single year. Is it reasonable to believe measures of local "social disorganization"—unemployment or single-parent families—double or triple in a year, then correct just as fast as homicides fly up and then fall down? Of course not. Something else must be the cause of such sudden changes. The UN report implies that we need to look at gang warfare as the principal cause for the sharpest increases in violence, while more traditional criminological variables may apply at other times.[5]

HISTORY, INSTITUTIONS, AND IDENTITY IN CHICAGO

Following the UN study, to understand variations in gang violence, it is necessary to study the history of gangs and their wars, not just levels of poverty, inequality, and social disorganization. For example, homicides in Chicago hit record highs in the 1920s during the beer wars of Prohibition when the economy was booming. Capone's mob defeated his rival Irish and Italian gangs, and when Prohibition ended, Frank Nitti enforced a peace that sharply curtailed the killing. The homicide rate in Chicago stayed low from the Great Depression through the prosperous 1950s.

The Outfit victory in the beer wars also resulted in the consolidation of a unified single family controlling organized crime in Chicago. Made members and associates all had a shared identity and worked under the control of the legitimate authority of an Outfit boss of bosses, from Al Capone to the present day.

Similar processes were at work with contemporary street gangs, but with a different result. The 1970s jump in gang violence led to the 1978 founding of the People and Folks coalitions. People and Folks were new kinds of identities beyond the individual gangs that sought to realign friends and enemies and bring violence under control. This is similar to the master identity of belonging to "Our Thing," or Cosa Nostra, which transcends an Outfit soldier's local membership in the Grand Avenue or Chinatown Crew. Similarly, SGD's Latin Folks was intended to be a new, shared identity that would overcome past differences and rivalries. Recall the extreme reaction of the Spanish Cobras when the MLDs declared themselves True Folks, threatening that shared identity.

The data, however, show the manifest goal of SGD to bring violence under control was not accomplished. Homicide rates in Humboldt Park skyrocketed in 1989, the year of SGD's founding, reaching rates by the

1990s twice as high as their 1988 levels. These rates did not substantially drop until after SGD's demise in 2003 (see fig. 4.2). On average during each of those years nearly forty young people lost their lives in Humboldt Park alone. This book in a way represents my journey to understand why SGD could not stop the violence on the West Side and instead degenerated into family warfare.

I was puzzled for a long time as I asked various Latin Folks leaders to give me their opinions on why SGD, whose premise was the control of violence, couldn't do it? From reading their constitution you might assume SGD was a strong, rule-governed institution with clear-cut mechanisms for resolving conflicts. But if that is so, why did their member groups go to war against one another, and why were SGD leaders unable to stop them? Why couldn't they succeed like the Outfit or Latino prison gangs on the border? I'll share some of the gang leaders' opinions in the final chapter, but in short, they were as puzzled as I was.

Part of my problem was that I needed to think differently about institutions. In fact, SGD was far from stable. Theorists Christine Oliver and Lynne Zucker argue that institutions are characterized more by entropy than stability. This means institutions like SGD have a normal tendency to disintegrate that, if unchecked, will lead to their demise.[6]

Consistent with this perspective, individual gangs and their families were constant stresses within SGD, promoting their own interests and maneuvering for power, sometimes with violence. La Tabla leaders simply were not able to rise above factional rivalries and assert overall control over the families. Once the broader identity of Latin Folks was replaced in practice by factional "family" identities, SGD deteriorated into little more than a battleground for warring rivals. That battleground would also take its toll on the individual gangs, particularly the Maniac Latin Disciples, who imploded, in part, over how to manage family relations.

What occurred, borrowing from Oliver, was "the failure of organizations to accept what was once a shared understanding of legitimate organizational conduct." This means that the individual organizations or gangs at one point simply would no longer accept the rules governing peace and commerce between families. The Insane, Maniac, and Almighty Families abandoned the "rules of collective behaviour [i.e., SGD's laws] in favour of self-interested gain and individual protection." The result was catastrophe.[7]

I'll go more deeply into this issue in my conclusion, but this chapter illustrates the erosion of the more universal identity of Latin Folks by factional identities of rival families. Unlike gangs in Central America or South Texas, SGD's La Tabla of leaders possessed neither the will, the capability, nor the authority to stop the violence once the gangs on the streets saw their family and individual gang identities as more important than membership in SGD.

RETALIATION

The Insane Family had already called a meeting to plan their own attacks on the Maniac Family when the Maniacs struck on February 13, 1996, in the attacks you read about in the preface. The war was on, and the Insane Family had no intention of backing away. Coldly assessing the situation, the Insane Family met a few days later in a hotel room at the Days Inn on Mannheim Avenue near O'Hare airport. What did not happen was a formal grievance to SGD, the commission that was founded to settle disputes between gangs. Violence is a "raging fire," the philosopher of violence René Girard says, and while there are always ways to prevent it, nothing less than victory was on the minds of the Insane leaders. No punishments or sacrifices of individual members would appease the Cobras, as they were dead-set on punishing the Maniacs and seizing power for themselves on La Tabla.[8]

The leadership of all the individual I-Team gangs were present at the Mannheim Avenue meeting after the February 13 *Godfather*-style hits. As the delegates entered the meeting, a "bug wand" which had been stolen from the Chicago police was waved over each member to see if he was wearing a wire. The bug wand was passed between individual gangs, and for each meeting one gang was responsible for security as well as for providing a lavish layout of food and drink.

I-Team meetings began in ritual fashion. After a call to order, the largely Catholic Puerto Rican delegates were led in reciting the Lord's Prayer. Being religious was part of their culture, and few thought it contradictory to being a gangster getting ready for war. As the Lord's Prayer ended, the chair directly led the group into reciting the official prayer of the Insane Family:

> Again we gather in an unbreakable bond of unity, loyalty, honor and respect for one another. We are all recognized by our accomplishments. Because of that, we welcome with embracing hearts, yesterday's memories, today's achievements and tomorrow's dreams. Together, combined as one for all that's righteous, we are a growing body, we are the stepping stone of our future lives, we are the Insane Familia . . .

The I-Team, as one, then chanted: "Amor de Insane!" The rituals of the I-Teams strongly enforced family identity.

The meeting followed *Robert's Rules of Order*, with announcements, minutes of the last meeting, and treasurer's report followed by old business and new business. Typically, the main item on I-Team agendas was resolving turf or business disputes of family members. But this meeting quickly dispensed with everything else and zeroed in on what the I-Team would do in response to the Maniac attacks. The Spanish Cobra representative said matter-of-factly: "Those hits by the Maniacs mean we need to counterattack to show in force what we're all about!"

Please note that what the I-Team was all about was not mainly being Latin Folks, the broader identity they shared with the MLDs and all of SGD. The assembled gangsters mainly self-identified as the Insane Family, beleaguered and victimized by the Maniacs. With the two largest members of SGD, MLDs and Cobras, facing off, La Tabla was helpless to mediate. Recall that it had also been unable to mediate the dispute of the MLDs with the Latin Lovers reported on in chapter 1. The result of SGD's inability to enforce its rulings was the recruiting of the Lovers from the Maniac to the Insane Family as both Cobras and MLDs counted votes on La Tabla. The *Godfather* hits of the Maniacs led to the planned Insane retaliation that said, in effect, control of La Tabla will be settled by war.

And war it was. The Cobras said at the I-Team meeting that every individual gang would be given a task. The plan was for each Insane gang to hit the MLDs at a specific location. For example, one hit would take place in the "Twilight Zone," the MLD home branch at Rockwell and Potomac, and others took place in Logan Square, East Village, Hermosa Park, Albany Park, Ravenswood, Ukrainian Village, and Elgin. The Latin Lovers gunned down an MLD soldier, Jose "Fonzie" Soto, in Waukegan, and the Insane Deuces did a hit in their stronghold of Aurora.

Making sure each member actually carried out their mission was regulated ingeniously by the use of police radio scanners, with leaders of each gang glued to the scanner to follow actual police reports of shootings, which would serve as evidence that each I-Team member had done their job. Joey Bags brought a scanner to Sal and they listened, with satisfaction, to the first days of the carnage.

> Listening in on the scanner was so that we were sure everyone was doing what they were supposed to be doing. You're listening to the various sequences to make sure that you were within that district, that police district, that band. So, you know, the ball was in motion and everybody did what they were supposed to do. I think the Maniacs were surprised in this tit-for-tat. They didn't know that the I-Team was as strong as it was, as united as it was.

Sal had a certain, Outfit-engendered satisfaction with "hits well done," but went on to worry about the dysfunction of SGD at the time. He said that SGD "was not meeting how it was supposed to be meeting. It was basically the I-Team's meeting. The Almightys are meeting and the Maniacs are meeting and then they're sending their grievances or kites [secret letters to prisoners] to their own leadership. It was total chaos."

Sal seemed to take pride in the violence of the I-Team's retaliation, but he was also becoming increasingly aware that SGD might not survive. During Prohibition, Al Capone had waged war on the Gennas and O'Banions and consolidated his victory by force of arms. But once the Outfit was established, war between crews was prohibited and problems of greed, individualism, and factionalism were quickly settled by surgical violence from the top. By Frank Nitti's time, all the crews and individual soldiers recognized the legitimate authority of the leadership and identified as a member of a crew that was subservient to the Outfit. This was not the path of the member gangs of SGD.

The result of the Insane hits was to up the ante within the Latin Folks. The MLDs were not expecting to be hit from so many directions and by so many different gangs. In a surprising comment, one Insane gang leader told me bitterly as this was being written in 2013, "The Insane retaliation is still taking place to this day." Girard says, "When internal strife, previously sublimated by means of sacrificial practices, rises to the surface, it manifests itself in interfamily vendettas and blood feuds."[9] In other words, fraternal hatred, like that between Cain and Abel, and kinship-based rivalries like the Hatfields and McCoys, run deep and long. SGD, the legal authority who should have taken charge and squelched any war, was not up to carrying out its responsibilities.

RED TAPE AND INTERNAL TENSIONS

SGD's record of mediating between the larger gangs was not impressive. From what I could see, La Tabla's most decisive action, ruling against the Simon City Royals in their dispute over Kosciuszko Park with the Cobras and others, was simply ignored by the Royals, and a bloody war resulted. Smaller issues of jurisdiction and disagreements were settled by bringing the dispute to the "White House" in Stateville and other prisons where SGD leaders were incarcerated. But problems between the larger gangs were almost always tabled. The board felt it could not afford to offend its main constituencies, and thus it lost legitimacy to all.

One example I was told about from several sources was when a Cobra soldier, "Bean," was "infractioned" for shooting another Cobra in the early 1990s. He was being harbored by relatives who were MLDs. The Cobras drew up a grievance and presented a copy to every SGD gang leader, and La Tabla voted. In this case, the MLDs were ordered to break the shooter's arm for violating SGD rules. The MLDs decided to put the shooter's arm on a garbage can lid and smash it with a baseball bat to carry out the ruling. But when the MLD soldiers tried to hit the offender with the baseball bat, I was told, he "took off running." Amazingly, the MLDs didn't pursue him, and nothing more happened. Resentment simmered within the Cobras and Insane Family at the failure of the MLDs to mete out justice to one of their own.

Some of the problems with SGD were surprisingly caused by the bureaucracy of the process. SGD instituted a set of rules and regulations that required extensive paperwork and documentation of infractions. For example, if someone was discovered to be a snitch, it wasn't enough to just accuse him; the accuser had to have "paperwork" and present it to La Tabla. We saw earlier how Stanley Slaven, the Harrison Gent who wore a wire to an SGD meeting, was confirmed to be a snitch when SGD leaders were given his CPD confidential informant agreement (fig. 6.1), which was circulated as proof of Slaven's breaking SGD rules. Action came only after what Latin Folks leaders told me was "due process." Sal was irritated by the paperwork necessary for SGD to act.

> There was a lot of red tape. Before they could take action, unless they caught someone red-handed, they had to wait. There was a grievance process. They had to wait until that paperwork is brought up. They even had "lawyers" who would demand paperwork. Then there was the waiting for La Tabla to make a decision. What kind of stuff was happening in the meantime? Waiting for that red tape to clear, a lot of people were suffering. So I got fed up just listening about the bureaucracy. It ain't like that with us.

Sal looked at La Tabla as failing in its mission mainly because of the "corrupt" politics of SGD. Things were different in the Outfit, he assured me. He chided me when I pointed out the difficulties SGD must have had keeping everyone satisfied.

> Come on now. When you have individuals that say, ok, that board—the commission, La Tabla, whatever you wanna call it—had all these leaders from all these different Latin Folk gangs, OK. The process was corrupt, so they could never come to a consensus, because some of those families, the smaller families, were being bought by the bigger families for their vote. So, if my family [Sal means individual gangs] has a hundred infractions of the policy but I'm buying you, you're voting on my side. So discipline is never being taken on my people. So you're part of the problem, not part of the solution.... The main reason was because the money is in the millions and they were greedy.

A typical example of SGD inaction was a dispute between the MLDs and Insane Dragons over a corner drug-selling spot on California and Thomas. This had been Dragon turf for more than fifteen years and they had paperwork that documented their title to the land. Despite juntas and formal grievances, La Tabla hesitated to offend the MLDs. The Dragons told SGD leaders that unless they made a proper ruling, there would be violence, but still La Tabla stalled. The Dragons resisted MLD incursions and were angered by lack of support of their "just cause" from SGD.

SGD's inaction carried over to the families. Like the incident with Bean, who was never fully punished by the MLDs, an incident involving Curt of the Insane Dragons was related to me by several Insane leaders. It seemed that a "junkie Cobra" was ripping off car stereos, and Curt, a high-ranking Dragon, caught him and struggled with him over a gun. Blade, from the Deuces, who was the first chair of the I-Team, gave his take on what happened when Curt discovered the Cobra trying to rip the stereo out of his car:

> They start struggling. Curt has a gun, then "wham"—gun goes off. Now Curt's dead. He is a Dragon. He was just trying to defend his car and now the dude that did it was a Cobra. That is how it started, just stupid stuff. Next thing you know the Dragons have a chip on their shoulder. "Hey what the fuck," they say. "Give that guy up." The Cobras say, "We don't know nuttin'." They are hiding him back and forth. They say, "He's not a Cobra no more. Ta da da da da." But the dude *is* a Cobra. So that's how it started, stuff like that.

Cobras and Dragons were both "cousins," meaning members of the Insane Family, and this was an incident that should have been settled by the I-Team through normal channels. With SGD inertia as a model, the Cobras dragged their feet. When the Dragons found out where the shooter was staying, they went to the house and confronted Bradley, a Cobra leader who was there, demanding he turn the guy over. Bradley let the accused Cobra skip out the back door and the Dragons never were able to exact punishment for the death of one of their members.

The Dragons' demands for justice from the Insane Family in this case went on for years. Finally, one of the Dragon leaders came to an I-Team meeting and said: "You know, we've been going at it for three years. We honor the Insane board. We are no longer going to be a part of this organization. We honor it on the street and behind the wall, but we're not coming to any more meetings because we feel that we were grieved by your actions."

The Dragons walked out of the I-Team meeting and never returned. What was clear was that the inability of both SGD and the families to resolve internal problems led to increasing tensions between families and gangs, as well as within each family and gang. The constant pressures on the families to fracture were combatted in some cases by demanding stronger family loyalty, and in others, like the Dragons, stronger individual gang loyalty. But the Cobras and Insane Family's problems paled in significance compared to the civil war that ripped the MLDs apart.[10]

THE ASSASSINATION OF RICK DOG

The MLDs' main leader, Prince Fernie, was serving life in prison and would eventually be transferred to solitary confinement in the supermax Tamms prison, which has since been closed. While at Stateville, like other gang leaders at the time, he was in day-to-day communications with his street gang. He had a down-to-earth business mentality and personally directed "mules" to transport drugs for Hugo "Juice" Herrera's Durango Connection drug distribution network. He was a strong voice for settling disputes through the formal rules and decisions by his fellow leaders on La Tabla. According to people who knew him back then, he considered the MLDs as his family and saw himself as their father figure and decision maker. He must have surely approved of the *Godfather* hits in February 1996. News travels nearly instantaneously between the neighborhood and prison cells.

The leader on the streets of the MLDs was Enrique "Rick Dog" Garcia, a confidant of Prince Fernie who was a close business partner with Juice Herrera. It was Garcia who ordered the shooting of a Lover named Cook Dog which began the conflict with their then fraternal gang, the Maniac Latin Lovers. As a result, the Lovers dropped the moniker *Maniac* from

Table 10.2. Dramatis personae in the war of the families

Prince Fernie Zayas	Head of Maniac Family and MLD leader of SGD board in Stateville
Enrique "Rick Dog" Garcia	MLD street leader assassinated in power struggle
Francisco "Pimp Daddy" Garcia	Leader of Rick Dog's MLD faction; cellmate with Dominic of C-Note$
"Carlito"	Emissary of Pimp Daddy's faction; murdered at peace conference
Jamie "Tuffy Bum" Ruiz	Soldier in Bum Brothers faction; assassinated Rick Dog and was killed in retaliation
Juan "Bum" Hernandez	Leader of Bum Brothers faction until incarceration
David "Little Bum" Hernandez	Took over Bum Brothers faction after Juan was incarcerated
Thomas "Outlaw" Ross	MLD drug dealer and shooter of Carlito
Raymond Rolon	MLD leader; aide to alderman Richard Mell and supporter of Rick Dog
Johnny "Loco" Almodovar	MLD don and organizer of Godfather hits on Cobras; supporter of Rick Dog
Hugo "Juice" Herrera	MLD drug supplier from Herrera Family; supporter of Fernie and Rick Dog
"Hi Lo"	MLD leader shot by Cobras in 1996
David Ayala	Leader of 2-6ers; SGD leader in Stateville; neutral in war of families
Stanley "Savage" Slaven	Leader of Harrison Gents who wore a wire to an SGD meeting; caused Gents to be expelled from SGD
"Blade"	Leader of Insane Deuces and first chair of the I-Team
Anibal "Tuffy C" Santiago	Cobra leader and head of Insane Family
"Indigo"	Cobra founder of I-Team, mentored by Tuffy C
"Chiefy"	Cobra street leader at 1999 peace conference

their names, and Rick Dog was furious. He ordered the violation of "Bam Bam," a Latin Lover locked up in Cook County Jail. The Lovers formally complained that Rick Dog had violated due process by not even presenting Bam Bam with the charges against him before a violation "beat down." The Lovers eventually joined the Insane Family for protection as the war heated up.

Similar in some ways to the SGD coalition of Latin Folks gangs, the Maniac Latin Disciples were a network of neighborhood gangs that had tenuous and sometimes hostile relationships among themselves. Like all institutionalized Chicago gangs, they were beset by internal rivalries, contests for power, and personal greed. The vast amounts of money produced by the drug trade makes control within gangs sometimes a lethal issue, and snitching was a constant worry. As with SGD, the dominant tendency within the MLDs was not stability but *entropy,* or pressures toward deterioration unless checked by strong leadership.

With Fernie calling the shots from the White House and supporting Rick Dog with his profitable operations at Talman and Wabansia (called by MLDs the "Real Side"), other factions within the MLDs were envious and desired a bigger share of the profits. One set of gang leaders known as the Bum Brothers, whose stronghold was in the MLD motherland at Rockwell and Potomac, planned to depose Rick Dog, but Fernie was in their way. According to various Latin Folks leaders, the Bum Brothers began supplying Fernie with as much hard drugs as he could consume. Fernie, like most other major gang leaders, had no hope of parole, and he soon became lost in his own drugged-out world. As he lost touch more and more with reality, the Bum Brothers faction had him violated and he was forced to give up even the formal trappings of leadership. I was told he eventually renounced his MLD membership to get out of solitary confinement at Tamms prison.

This opened up a path to power within the MLDs and an opportunity to seize control over the prosperous Real Side chapter. Fernie's demise meant Rick Dog was next. The Bum Brothers skillfully maneuvered MLD/Cobra hostilities to their advantage. When Hi Lo, an MLD leader, was shot by Cobras in early February 1996, the die was cast. Rick Dog, being pressured by the Bum Brothers, ordered the *Godfather* hits on the Cobras you read about in the preface. Ever cautious, Rick Dog had his underboss, Johnny "Loco" Almodovar, and brother Pimp Daddy assume operational control of the hits. Immediately after what became nationally prominent shootings on February 13, Pimp Daddy and Loco were arrested as the Chicago police got MLD members—presumably Bum Brothers followers—to snitch to them about who did the shooting. One gang member even provided police with the ledger of the meeting Loco had called to plan the hits! The crackdown was intended by the CPD to defuse what clearly was a volatile situation. The Chicago police were unaware, however, of the full implications of what was transpiring and were being manipulated by the Bum Brothers faction.

Rick Dog knew at that point that he needed peace in order to control the violence—even if he had been one of its main instigators—but also to keep his own job as prince. He approached the Cobras through SGD leaders in prison and asked for a junta to settle past disputes and stop the killings. A wave of shootings continued in March, however, and confusion reigned within the MLDs. The Bum Brothers faction waited to make their play.

It came on April 3, 1996. While Rick Dog talked on his cell phone to his minister of information, Ray Rolon, Jamie "Tuffy Bum" Ruiz walked up and fired three shots to his head, killing him instantly. Panic gripped the Humboldt Park neighborhood where Cobras and Ds had their main chapters, and the Bum Brothers spread the word that the hit had been done by the Cobras and called for more war.[11]

Three days later, the reach and strength of the MLD nation would be clear. Chicago newspapers reported incredulously that more than a thousand mourners showed up at Rick Dog's funeral. There were blue and black flowers (MLD colors) arranged in the shape of pitchforks surrounding the casket. The Maniac prayer was recited graveside, and members threw guns into his grave as his casket was lowered to its final resting place. To longtime observers of Chicago's gangland, this brought back memories of the funerals during Al Capone's beer wars.[12]

This funeral was organized by Ray Rolon, who would later be an aide to alderman Richard Mell. At that time, Rolon worked as a twenty-five-dollar-an-hour employee of the City Water Department, a patronage job that required little real work. Rolon was everywhere at the funeral and coordinated the attendance of gang members from suburban areas. Soon after, police arrested "Tuffy Bum" Ruiz for the shooting, and it became apparent to MLD soldiers that a civil war would rage at the same time they were being hit by the Insanes. Their long-standing war against the Latin Kings hadn't gone away, either. David "Little Bum" Hernandez assumed leadership of the Bum Brothers faction in open rebellion against Pimp Daddy, Loco Almodovar, and Rolon.

Major law enforcement campaigns against MLD drug businesses continued, like Operation Devil's Head, which resulted in seventeen indictments of MLDs in 1999, including their main drug supplier, Thomas "Outlaw" Ross. Such investigations are an ongoing risk of the drug game.

They upset business when arrests occur, but with institutionalized gangs like the MLDs, they typically lead mainly to turnover in who is running things and to displacement, not elimination, of the drug sales. The thousand mourners at Rick Dog's funeral attest to the depth of gangs like the MLDs. What I have been trying to show in this book is that the demise of the MLDs, like that of SGD as a whole, was largely due to internal, not external, causes. I don't think there is firm evidence that law enforcement has ever completely destroyed *any* institutionalized gang in Chicago, whether the MLDs, the Gangster Disciples, or the Outfit.

CARLITO'S STORY

The Maniac Latin Disciples were feeling the heat from the Insanes and now were consumed by internal war. Rick Dog's assassination left his brother, Pimp Daddy, in control of the main factions of the organization, although he had been locked up for his part in the February 13 attacks. It was during this time that Pimp Daddy was the cellmate of the C-Note$' Dominic, and they were both the liaisons of their respective organizations to La Tabla. Attempts by SGD behind the walls to mediate the bloody dispute were unsuccessful. With the defection of the Lovers to the Insane Family, the dissolution of the Campbell Boys, and distancing by South Side Mexican gangs like La Raza and the Party People from the factional family structure, no clear majority existed on La Tabla. Both the Cobras and the MLDs were determined to control the board, and warfare was their main tactic. Sal said resignedly: "Everybody wants to be the top guy. That's why people brought their issues to the table, to try to resolve those issues before they escalated. Unfortunately, some of these individuals were not in the right state of mind, were influenced by others, and bad decisions were made. When it spills out to the streets, you see what happens."

What happened was hit after hit, a war of the families that left everyone constantly watching their backs. It was during this time that the C-Note$ tried to refocus the I-Team on making money and dove deeply into the ecstasy business. But the blood thirst was too great, and within the MLDs, the contest for power could not be settled. Rick Dog was dead and Fernie was out of the picture, violated for his drug use and no longer able to lend support to Pimp Daddy's loyalist faction of the MLDs. From the 1996 assassination of Rick Dog to spring 1999, the situation remained unpredictable and violent. It seemed to Sal that the logical answer was to have a junta and calm things down, make peace, get on with business, and remove the constant fear of being killed.

After many false starts, the various MLD factions agreed to a peace conference with the I-Team to be held at the YMCA at 1834 West Lawndale. For the YMCA and their hardworking outreach workers, the immediate reason for the meeting was to negotiate a ceasefire during the Puerto Rican Day Parade. Tensions between gangs had brought violence to the parade in the past, and on the surface bringing the rivals together and making an agreement to keep the peace during a festival celebrating Puerto Rican culture was surely sensible.

Behind the scenes, the Maniac and Insane families gathered their principal leaders to come together and try to bring an end to the war, making the peace conference a much more sweeping and significant event. I interviewed several of the participants in that meeting, and the anticipation at the time was palpable. A YMCA van traveled through the Cobra's sections, picking up various governors and major leaders. Other Insane Family leaders gathered as well, including representatives of the Ashland Vikings, Latin Lovers, and C-Note$, but they came warily, and on their own. They were suspicious of Maniac intentions in any meeting and came fully armed. "Chiefy," the Cobra street leader at the time, came into the meeting with bodyguards tightly walking on all four sides of him, forming a human shield. Cobra leaders never appeared in any public setting without tight security, and they saw this meeting as exceptionally dangerous. They were right.

For the MLDs, both factions had agreed to attend. Bull Dog, Ray Rolon, Pimp Daddy, and Carlito were the leaders of the loyalist faction, and they had been meeting with the Insane Family on and off. Carlito was a rough solider who seemed to always have a gun on him. Over the past year, though, he had been solicited by the YMCA to become active in their activities and had even gone to Stanford University on an educational trip with Ray Vazquez, the YMCA outreach program director. He was seen by YMCA officials as someone with promise, one of the many gang leaders who were maturing out of a life of violence. For every gang leader who continues on the road to organized crime, a dozen or more leave the life and settle down. Maybe half that number are killed or incarcerated for long prison terms.

Before the meeting even started, YMCA officials watched as cars filled with young men drove up and down the adjoining streets. Unknown to the YMCA outreach workers, in the cars were MLD leaders, including Thomas "Outlaw" Ross and others who had their own plans for the meeting. It was only afterward that the significance of these cars filled with Bum Brothers leaders and soldiers—who did not attend the junta—would be understood.

At the YMCA, Cobra leaders quickly agreed to a ceasefire at the Puerto Rican Day Parade. They asked YMCA officials if the alderman could get paint to pretty up some buildings and various other political favors. All this is possible, they were told, and things seemed to be going well. As the Insane leaders waited for the Cobras to return after their private meeting with YMCA officials, they began to get even more nervous. Carlito was there, and Jaws from the MLDs' Murdertown section. But instead of a host of governors and other leaders in their thirties or older, the MLDs present were mainly teenagers, terribly out of place at any high-level junta.

The YMCA officials, mindful of the dangers of being a formal part of negotiations that could be seen as a conspiracy, left the room, allowing the gangs to negotiate among themselves. There already was agreement with the Cobras about the Puerto Rican Day Parade, and Carlito was on board with that as well. Unaware of who was at the meeting representing the MLDs and who wasn't, the YMCA staff was shocked when they returned to the main room. The thirty or so MLD teenagers were in one corner, and when they were asked about peace at the Puerto Rican Day Parade, they yelled out, "Hell no!" There was pandemonium, and the I-Team leaders quickly and carefully withdrew as the MLD kids kept yelling gang slogans.

What was also unnoticed was that after their loud rejection of the peace proposal, the teenaged MLDs left suddenly as a group, leaving Carlito behind by himself. As he walked out of the YMCA alone the worst possible result shocked everyone. Two gunshots echoed through the ears of those still inside the hall. The cars that had been driving around before the meeting had returned, and Carlito had been shot dead on the steps of the YMCA. The shooter was "Outlaw" Ross, a major MLD leader, which indicated how important the Bum faction saw the hit. The Bums wanted no part of any peace deal with the Insane Family. With Carlito's dying breaths, they got their wish. And with Carlito's death, SGD died as well.

POSTSCRIPTS

What began as an experiment to replace the factional identities of individual gangs with a broader, more inclusive Latin Folks identity that could keep the violence under control in the end completely failed. The war of the families continued after Carlito's assassination, but exhausted itself as leaders of both families were killed or incarcerated. Rank-and-file members questioned the wisdom of leadership who could offer nothing to them but death or prison. Snitching was normalized, and even more than before, it became every man for himself. The largest Latin Folks gang, the Maniac Latin Disciples, fractured even more, each governor more concerned with his own corner than with the Nation. This is what Sal meant by his comment that "things had changed" and was an underlying reason for his interviews with me.

For Sal, Carlito's murder was the last straw. It had been increasingly difficult to sell SGD to Joey the Clown and other Outfit bosses. The Outfit were having their own problems, which surfaced at the 2005 Family Secrets trial where Joey and thirteen other mob leaders were convicted of murder and conspiracy. What the Outfit didn't need was entanglement with gangs who didn't understand the simple logic that business comes first. I asked Sal:

JMH: What was the Outfit's take on all this craziness going on? I mean, Carlito's murder and the whole war of the families?

SAL: *It brought too much attention. We have been successful because we've been under the radar for the last hundred years, OK? SGD, at the end, it wasn't worth it. And basically what the bosses said was that the good intentions are there because they see the possibilities of what can take place. But to continue on* *that route is to jeopardize other individuals. It's just not worth it. No money amount is worth messing up a process that has been successful for all these years.*

So the daring plan to create a Spanish mafia drained away with Carlito's lifeblood. SGD itself ceased to meet. For what point? No one was abiding by SGD rulings anymore, and the leaders of member gangs were not delivering benefits, only bloodshed. Their credibility was put in question by rank-and-file members of Latin Folks gangs. The Outfit model and the very purpose of SGD, a commission to rule over disputes, was no longer valid or functional.

In many ways, this oddly resembles the complaint caught on an FBI wiretap in New Jersey about the failings of the mafia's own regulatory commission, which had been the original model for SGD: "If these people don't enforce what's right and what's wrong" one mafia soldier complained to another, "then what's the use of having the Commission?"[13]

Indeed. The end of SGD provided difficult lessons to gang leaders on how hard it is to mediate disputes, stop the violence, and organize crime. Entropy is the norm, not stability, which means that adopting a shared identity requires ongoing "institutional work." The SGD leaders just weren't up to it. But SGD's demise provides us with both some new ways to understand gangs and hints about the future of gangs in Chicago, the topics of my last chapter.

 **The Future of Gangs in Chicago**

T he story of SGD is unique to Chicago, but I believe it contains lessons
for those who want to understand gangs in their own city. I am arguing that if we pay attention to history we are likely to question what we
think we know about gangs. This might lead us to some different conclusions about what *we think we should do* about gangs.

SGD was a product of the experience of Chicago Latino gangs in forming cross-neighborhood alliances in the 1970s to fight racist white gangs.
Neighborhood became less important than power as incarcerated Latin
Folks gang leaders met together to plan for their own security, decrease violence on the streets, and organize crime. To accomplish this, they actively
sought to corrupt police and politicians and saw the Outfit and the mafia
commission as an organizational model. They emphasized their Latino
identity and built a complex organization separate from more numerous
African American gangs. The Outfit tried to take advantage of this bur-
geoning Spanish mafia, and used their protégés, the C-Note$, to try to
influence events. Their attempts failed as Latin Folks factional violence
soared to unimaginable heights, bringing catastrophe to all.

To make sense of this history I had to go outside of conventional ap-
proaches of both law enforcement and criminology. I was guided by Salvatore Lupo's notion of *polygenesis*, his term for how he understood the Sicilian mafia. He said: "The history of the mafia cannot be reduced to a single
scheme, applicable to all situations and all periods." Like Lupo, I looked
inductively and historically at factors that don't fit well in standard analyses. For example, in Lupo's mafia history, corruption and violence by the
state are crucial variables, facts often left out in traditional gang research.[1]

This neglect can be readily seen in a recent Justice Department funded study that purports to tell "The History of Gangs in the United States." Unsurprisingly, this essay contains no mention of mass incarceration or police brutality, or any hint that official corruption might be important in understanding gangs. Writing history, Eric Hobsbawm says, means selecting some facts and ignoring others.[2] How could I tell the tale of SGD without an analysis of the impact of locking up gang members by the thousands, the importance of the Latino vote for Chicago's machine, and the police/ Latin Folks conspiracies of Joseph Miedzianowski and SOS? Polygenesis means we need to "bring the state back in" to the study of gangs—even if it offends those who pay for the research.[3]

Many of the finest case studies of gangs implicitly follow this model. Deborah Levenson's chilling history of Guatemala City gangs, *Adios Niño*, Joan Moore's *Going Down to the Barrio*, Carl Taylor's *Dangerous Society*, Diego Vigil's *Rainbow of Gangs*, and Susan Phillips's *Operation Fly Trap* are richly draped in history. They also are deeply critical of repressive state policies while being brutally honest in explaining the context of gang violence.[4] The majority of gang studies are still ahistorical, but writing a history of gangs means more than reciting a list of drive-by shootings or detailing neighborhood statistics on poverty.

This final chapter asks, "What is the legacy of Spanish Growth and Development?" A decade after SGD's demise, Latino gangs, as well as the Outfit, have summarized their experience and are planning for the future. While I think the current breakdown in gang leadership presents some important opportunities, my own summary revolves around an ominous conclusion: given the vast amount of money in the drug economy, I fear new forms of organized crime are inevitable.

This is not good news. However, Chicago's African American and Latino gangs as well as the Outfit are following different trajectories. An honest review of the patterns of gang history is the first step toward thinking creatively about what we should do today.

PEOPLE AND FOLKS, PUBLIC HOUSING, AND RICHARD SPECK

The demise of the People and Folks coalitions has fundamentally changed the nature of black gangs. Their current disarray, far from being a reason to encourage further repressive measures, is a red flag for activists that they must act now to intervene with youth on the streets.

From the 1970s on, leaders of black gangs believed that they would be able to use illegal profits to influence the machine like the Italians before them. Boonie Black's Royal Family, Larry Hoover's Folks coalition, and Jeff Fort's Main 21 were all pale imitators of the Italian's mafia commission. But Francis Ianni's prediction proved prescient: racism would make it too difficult to effectively negotiate with white elites.[5]

Rather than buy their way to power, black gangs found themselves both locked out and locked up.[6] In fact, the 1970s saw a ferocious war on gangs exemplified by the torturing of more than a hundred black gang members by Chicago police commander Jon Burge. Savage repression, along with catastrophic economic conditions, made it impossible for black gangs to carve out a lasting niche in machine politics like the Italians before them or the Mexicans today. Sal is right: black gangs bought off politicians like every other gang. But he also knows black politicians do not have much clout, and black gangs therefore could not obtain real security or substantial protection.

The inability of black institutionalized gangs to secure positions of influence is an unanticipated result of the exclusion of the black community from real power. Racism is built into machine politics and has inhibited the gangs from successfully practicing what Tilly and Tarrow call "informal politics," or the politics of influence and, yes, corruption.[7] I have concluded from my research that corruption is the sine qua non of gang institutionalization. A successful route for gang members into conventional society requires protection by politicians who can exercise real power. That worked for the Italian Outfit; it may work for Mexicans; but it didn't work for Chicago's black gangs.

The People and Folks coalitions were founded in the prisons and had the dual function of controlling violence and organizing crime. But the promise of broader gang organization would come crashing down. In the 1990s, Gangster Disciples, Black Disciples, and Vice Lords wantonly murdered each other in bloody civil wars. The building of Chicago's "second ghetto," its segregated and overwhelmingly poor housing projects, had provided a social and economic base for the spectacular growth of black gangs in the

1970s. Rather than invest in deteriorating housing projects, in the 1990s the second Mayor Daley ordered them torn down. This eliminated the gangs' strongholds but also scattered them, sowing violence as displaced gang members fought for new territory. The destruction of the projects, battle fatigue by the troops and Chicago residents alike over what seemed to be never ending wars, along with surprising events in the state prison system (detailed below), led to the demise of Chicago's "supergangs."[8]

Blade, the leader of the Insane Deuces, explained how he was locked up for a time in Cook County Jail around 2000 and what he saw:

> I went in for a quick parole violation—it was like in for a month and then out. What I saw was the Folks and People concept, that's all done. I blame Mayor Daley for that. Because he kinda like . . . the blacks were the one who controlled the People and Folks thing because they were the majority in jail. They had your back. They'd say, "What's up, folks," and the Latinos just followed that concept in jail. That's how it went. Now, no more.

Blade saw the demise of public housing and the 1990s internecine gang wars as related: "Mayor Daley started cleaning house, tearing up the projects, Cabrini-Green especially. Robert Taylor Homes. Then the concept started changing. Because you used to have all GDs here, all Vice Lords there [concentrated in neighborhoods]. Now you move guys here and there and you move shit all around." In other words, black communities were plunged into disarray with the forced displacement of thousands of public housing tenants, including gang members. Neighborhoods that had been strongholds of a single gang now had people moving in from the housing projects, some of whom were members of rival gangs. This undermined the local base of the gangs, fanned violence, and encouraged gang splintering.

Incarceration, up until the mid-1990s, had not stopped gang leaders like Larry Hoover or La Tabla from maintaining communication and control over their gangs on the street. An unexpected event jarred the Illinois correctional system in the mid-1990s that would change the prison/gang status quo. A spectacular videotape of mass murderer Richard Speck was shown in which he had sex with another inmate, wore a dress and displayed hormone-enhanced breasts, used drugs, and bragged about his partying life in prison. This lurid video was viewed by legislators, who demanded a crackdown on conditions in prison that coincidentally had allowed incarcerated gang leaders to bribe guards and live a life of relative comfort.[9]

The Illinois House Judiciary Committee in the summer of 1996 heard testimony that gangs "ran" Stateville prison and that the warden consulted with gangs on major decisions. While Speck had already been dead for five years by that time, the gangs bore the brunt of correctional reforms. All of the principal gang leaders were transferred from their Illinois prisons, and the key ones, including Hoover, Gino Colon of the Kings, and Jeff Fort of the P. Stones, were sent to Florence, Colorado, a federal supermax prison where they are in solitary confinement and cut off from regular contact with the streets. Latin Folks leaders, including David Ayala of the 2-6ers and Prince Fernie Zayas of the MLDs, were sent to Illinois' notorious Tamms supermax, which ended their ability to run things from behind the walls and led to mental breakdowns.

As Blade had figured out, SGD was dying along with the People and Folks coalitions. His analysis of the failure of SGD was a combination of the destruction of public housing, Richard Speck, and "hot blood."

> Why they can't get it together? It is the hot blood; the hot blood. That's exactly what it is. Throw a little ignorance in with it and you put poverty in the hood, what ya gonna get? You gonna get trouble. It ain't got nuttin' to do with no job. They hustle no matter what they do. . . . Hey, gangs are going to be here regardless. Right now it's all messed up because there is no leaders, no People and Folks. That concept is done. There is no SGD concept. Finished! No more!

As Francis Ianni had concluded decades before in his black mafia study of New York City, crime would not prove to be a successful route into respectability for Chicago's African American gangs.[10] Ianni went on to argue that this meant black gangs might resemble Hobsbawm's "social bandits" more than organized criminals. While his analogy may be a bit strained, for Chicago his words may prove prophetic.[11]

Chicago's black gangs fractured after the wars of the 1990s and destruction of the housing projects. They no longer have the hierarchical structures of the past and their influence within black neighborhoods is lower than at any time since their formation. With a hint of loss and some anger, Blade says:

BLADE: You see the leaders, they are all in jail. They got long sentences and they ain't never getting out of nowhere. Then you have these new gangs: Breeds, Trays, and Triple As. Why are all these new gangs starting? Nobody ever heard about them. Now there are no more People and Folks, for blacks or us . . .

JMH: But is there a chance that the original concept of SGD and the families could work, that it could come back?

BLADE: No. No one wants to step up. Because [of] the mayor and McCarthy [police superintendent]. This is true. No one wants to step up because they already said: "All right you want to be a gangbanger, we're going to indict the leader. He's going to go down with the RICO act. You do it—we're going to indict the leader." That's what they are saying, so everyone is scared. No one wants to step up. Nobody! Because basically when you step up you go to jail. That's where it is. Even if you are trying to keep the peace.

While there may still be some sort of a comeback by the institutionalized gangs, new gangs are also emerging. Many of these twenty-first-century gangbangers listen more to rappers and follow social media more than they take orders from established leaders of the Vice Lords, Gangster Disciples, and the rest. Today, Chicago's black community is declining in numbers as their neighborhoods are being destabilized by continuing high rates of unemployment, deteriorating vacant homes, a Latino population expanding into traditionally black areas, white gentrifiers, and Mayor Emanuel's dangerous plan to close schools.[12] Black gangs today are less organized than at any time since the 1960s.

What is of concern to me is the possibility that youthful and fractured gangs will angrily resort to spontaneous, nihilistic violence. The real danger for black gangs is that they may follow the pattern Deborah Levenson described when Guatemala City's *maras* were met with brutal state suppression. In her words, Guatemala City gangs transformed from "gangs to live for" to "gangs to die for"—from youth with a rudimentary political consciousness to gangs descending into a culture of barbarism. This is a frightening but real possibility for Chicago's youthful, rebellious, leaderless, and hostile black gangs. Repression, as in Guatemala, will likely make the situation worse.

On the other hand, black gang members can be found among those protesting police brutality, unjust sentences, horrific prison conditions, and other violations of human rights. The blocked conventional opportunities for black youth do not necessarily mean nihilism; rather Chicago activists must understand that black gangs' direction is up for grabs. I think Castells's notion of *resistance identity* well fits today's black gang experience: gangs based on survival but also with an identity of fighters against racist oppression—what Castells cleverly calls "the exclusion of the excluders by the excluded." One gang member summed it up to me: "It's the gang versus the racism."[13]

This presents opportunities for activists and those of us concerned with alienated youth, as Victor Rios argues in his book *Punished*. While it is important to invoke the prosocial path of 1960s black gangs as a positive example for young gang members, today is a very different situation. The old gang leaders' authority is gone forever, and this vacuum in leadership means there is a choice: either our youth will be left on their own to follow a dark path of nihilism or we can intervene and organize them toward a "contentious politics" of protest in the streets. The role of police is necessarily limited. As protectors of property and the powerful, there is a fundamental contradiction between the interests of the police and the interest of the powerless on the streets.

For African American youth to follow a more positive path depends on community activists building trust among youthful gang members and engaging them in protesting mass incarceration and police misconduct, uniting with Latinos against deportations, and demanding jobs and better education. It requires attention to serious racial hostility between black and Latino gangs. Some black gangs may even develop into something akin to Hobsbawm's "social bandits." Given the exclusion of the black community from conventional political power, antimachine and political activism is African American youths' best option for real social change.

LATINOS, SGD, AND THE PROBLEM OF LEADERSHIP

Blade sums up the experience of SGD and points out what he thinks can be one road for Latino gangs today. Organized crime is a real, not imaginary, threat to our youth. "Look at the Mexican mafia over there, that's what it is: they got control, they got a little understanding. Look at the Italians, they got control." *The In$ane Chicago Way* insists that the study of gangs should include the dynamics of politics and corruption, race and ethnic succession, street institutions, prison, and organized crime. Most Latino gang members, like their black cousins, are rebellious corner youth, open to new avenues and a brighter life. But the events of this book exposed a dance of death that went on behind the curtains in the 1990s, orchestrated by gang leaders who were mainly focused on the organization of crime, greed, and their own power. This was the back story of SGD, and this push for broader organization goes on today, and I'm sure not just in Chicago.

What should be apparent is that a Latino path to power in Chicago is different from the politics of a relatively powerless black community. This has enormous implications for Latino gangs, particularly in a city like Chicago, where the state has long been a bricolage of legal and illegal layers overlapping one another. Every major political decision in Chicago is tinged by corrupt influences, the standard meaning of the "Chicago way." Only naive academics, cynical, media-savvy politicians, or sterile bureaucrats call the Windy City's decision-making process "rational." While Chicago may be an extreme example of corruption, every city is marked by it, as Chambliss's work explains. Today's Latino gangs, with ties to fabulously wealthy Mexican drug cartels, can use corruption to become major players in Chicago. I suspect similar opportunities exist for Latino gangs in other cities.

Sal championed SGD within the Outfit because he saw the handwriting on the wall for the old-world Italian organized crime. He saw SGD as new blood, and if they learned the lessons of the mafia, they could flourish.

SAL: *The table, that was what they were trying to create—just like the commission— that's what the registered families were trying to create, or emulate—trying to* *copy. . . . But they're not going to Jose on the corner and telling him, "Jose, you know what, you're part of our organization but we don't want you on the corner of Grand Avenue and Pulaski—we want you to hit the books and get your law degree. So when you're out there and we need you, we're gonna call. We'll pay for your education. Whatever you need, we're gonna pay for your education. But guess what—when we need you to come and represent one of us, there's no hesitation that you come in.*

But the problem is, that they're not doing that. These people (the Outfit) did that. We put our kids through college. We put our kids through law school, medical school, business school . . . they're accountants, you name it, they're doing it. But not the Hispanics.

JMH: Why?

SAL: *Why? You need to know how to hide your money, you need good representation, you need lawyers, you need doctors just in case something happens and you don't wanna go to an emergency room. These are the things these [Outfit] individuals did—they [SGD] didn't know how to do that.*

I asked why SGD didn't behave like the Outfit:

JMH: The more pressing question is why Spanish Growth and Development and Black Growth and Development—you know, what Hoover tried to pull off—they were organized; why didn't it work?

SAL: *My perspective on why it didn't work was there's a lot of bloodshed that has taken place throughout all these years, and they didn't have enough structure; the Outfit has a hierarchy; everything goes according to plan. You have discipline, and discipline is laid out swiftly, and you know what that discipline is. There is no three-minute violation, you're gone. You mess up a hit? You're dead. You better flip or get out of town or whatever, disappear, go to, you know become a Buddhist monk or something. But guess what, you stick around, party's over. They will not only kill you but your family; even the goldfish! The problem with the SGD was that they would not dish out the discipline swiftly.*

I questioned Sal's organizational critique and argued that the Outfit was far from rational, giving the example of the beer wars of the 1920s.

JMH: Yeah, I'm not sure I buy that completely. I mean, I think that's right, but the Outfit had its wars in the twenties as well. The war among the Italians and the Irish was almost as bloody as the nineties . . .

SAL: *Who won that war?*

JMH: Well, Capone and his faction.

SAL: *Who did Capone have on his side? He had the Poles, he had the niggers, he had everybody but the Irish, and at the end, he took them out.*

JMH: But it was also a battle within the Italians.

SAL: *He didn't have everybody under his wing.*

JMH: You know, he had to take the Genna brothers out . . .

SAL: *Absolutely. Those who he didn't take out, he bought 'em. Cash is key. You gotta have a good head and friends. I mean, you know, the mayor was Thompson back then, and Capone owned him. And the one who went against Thompson, like Cermak, what happens?*[14]

JMH: So what you're arguing—I'm trying to sort through your story here—is that you think one of the key factors was clearly leadership, right?

SAL: *Yeah, the Outfit always had leadership. They bought local protection, but they always had problems with the feds . . . but even some of them were in their pocket.*

Sal ends his diatribe on the failings of SGD with implications for what he thinks should be done in the future.

> *That was the problem with the SGD, that's the problem with the blacks, that's the problem with all of them. There is no structure, there is no leader that will do what needs to be done in order to progress or to move forward. There's too much corruption [within the gangs]. There's too many chiefs, not enough Indians. They don't have the savvy or the smarts to deal with the politics because some of them believe they don't need it.*

What Sal was implicitly advocating was the need for a rational, decision-making organizational model to overcome the factional, family-based structure of SGD. Latin Folks leaders did not prove to be good at what DiMaggio and Zucker called the "institutional work" of weaving together the rivalries of their members like Nitti accomplished with Ital-

ians. SGD began in the prisons, and talented gang leadership like Prince
Fernie, David Ayala, and Tuffy C worked together on La Tabla but became isolated from the rank and file as they were moved from prison to
prison. This strongly inhibited communication, strong cross-gang relationships, and the line of command. The Richard Speck incident provided correctional officials with an excuse to crack down, and the gangs
were left with second-rate leaders who couldn't manage organizational
conflict.

To Sal's mind, the emergence of a Mexican Al Capone was the basic answer. Sal saw the need for powerful leaders capable of making intentional,
rational decisions that could embed a Spanish mafia in Chicago politics,
reduce violence, and refine the organization of crime. But rational, bureaucratic organizational models like Sal has in mind have trouble when
internal groups conflict, which is what undid SGD. Organized crime has
a long history of imploding.[15]

I think Sal was correct in his critique that SGD never developed leaders
like Capone or Nitti who could sublimate group conflict into common
purposes. Any future SGD may need a clear victor in a gang war, like Capone. However, there aren't a lot of successful models. The Sinaloa-Zeta
Mexican cartel wars and the unending violence in Colombia are not optimistic signs for peaceful settlements of gang contests for supremacy. The
Italian mafia also sank into family warfare as late as the 1990s. On the
other hand, Chicago's single-family post-Capone Outfit has managed to
maintain a relative peace for eighty years.

Whether after a war or to avoid one, a future farsighted gang leader
must be able to do "institutional work" skillfully enough to get Chicago's
fiercely independent Latino gangs to work together. Drug cartel money
can pave the way for a peaceful solution rooted in corruption, or those
drug dollars can reinforce rivalries and spark even more bloodshed. SGD
will not be the last attempt to organize a Spanish mafia in Chicago, and
while renewed war is likely, it is not inevitable.

The development of a new Spanish mafia, like SGD, is complicated by
the trajectory of Chicago's oldest gang. The Outfit bosses studied the demise of SGD and drew their own conclusions. Contrary to popular opin-
ion, the Outfit isn't going away.

THE OUTFIT AND THEIR ASSOCIATES

Today's Outfit is not the mob of Capone or even Accardo. The organized-crime scholar Robert M. (Mickey) Lombardo, among others, makes a strong case for its apparent demise. Sal would agree that things have changed, but he slyly reminded me of a line from the movie *The Usual Suspects*: "The greatest trick the devil ever pulled was convincing the world he doesn't exist."[16]

This, Sal said, is the Outfit's motto, to trick the public and law enforcement into thinking organized crime is crippled, smashed, or soon to leave the stage. Outfit bosses love it when law enforcement and social scientists pronounce that the Family Secrets trial or some major arrest are signs of the final defeat of organized crime in Chicago.

After the failure of SGD, the Outfit returned to its long-term strategy of surrounding themselves with a web of dispensable associates. This strategy has implications for the future, not only of the Outfit, but for Latino gangs as well.

Who are Outfit associates? There is scant mention in the organized crime literature of them and nowhere is their significance understood. Annelise Graebner Anderson gives a typology of kinds of associates, but they are not central to her analysis.[17] Sal explains who can become an associate and what it means.

Well, because of their ethnic background they are not allowed to be made members of the Outfit. But because of their criminal background and ties to gangs, they bring that criminal expertise that people in the Outfit see as valuable, because their main concern is how can we make money. By utilizing these individuals there are many different avenues of generating revenue. It's like, uh, it ties them together.

I asked him what role the associates play in organized crime.

SAL: *They are the middlemen—the middlemen between the street, the gang-bangers, and organized crime. So most of those associates earned their bones in street gangs.*

Associates do business with a lot of groups, but they will never be presented to the top people; they'll still be middlemen, because they don't really want to associate with—they're too hot. Can you see right now, one of our guys associating with a MLD? I mean all eyes are on them, the cops and the press. So if you can get a middleman in there to do all the legwork, as I stated, it protects us to a certain extent.

JMH: Are there black associates?

SAL: *Yes, there are some. Hispanic associates? Absolutely! Irish, Greek—every ethnic group, every ethnic group. Some of the black guys are tied to the Vice Lords, to the GDs. I mean, they're all tied to these people because most of them are—look, and we talked about this earlier—contracts, minority contracting. When you have these individuals come up and say, "Hey, we need this contract"—they're utilizing these minority-owned businesses—some of those are associates. You gotta have the middleman in there saying, "Hey, we got this bid, we got these people here, let's get this bid and we'll put you there to get it. Oh, you were a veteran, Vietnam? Even better yet"—they put you in there. Not only are you a minority but you're also a veteran. They have so many contracts for these type of businesses that are owned that way, as fronts. They created them, they do all kinds of shit so, I mean, big business, billions, billions of dollars.*[18]

Sal explained to me the process of becoming an associate.

JMH: The status of associate. How do you get that?

SAL: *You're asked. You're introduced. They call on you. If they see you're an earner and they see you're bringing in money, guess what? They know everything that goes on in that neighborhood—they know. And if the money's coming in, they're gonna get their piece. And you know what, you better go to them before they come to you.*

So, when you're conducting business, nothing happens without them finding out. So, if you're pulling off jobs, somebody's gonna know, because they're all related. They're gonna be out and they're gonna be saying, "Hey, so-and-so was out here doing this." Really? So, you know, you get a reputation. Whether you're a brawler, a tough guy, a smart kid—you know, good with numbers. Whatever your creed is, what you're into, if you're good at it, they're gonna know and they're gonna find a way to utilize your services. And they'll exploit you, or whatever you wanna call it, to the fullest, until you are no use anymore. Because everybody's expendable. You know what I mean?

I asked Sal what advantages a gang member or street criminal would have becoming an associate.

SAL: *You're protected and you're making money and everybody else is making money, and if you need a lawyer, you get a lawyer. You get pinched, you get a lawyer. If you're conducting business—if I'm conducting business as an associate, associated to this crew, and I go and, by accident, I step on somebody's toes and someone comes at me, I got muscle, heavy muscle.*

If I'm over here and I'm conducting business, whether it's building or something that needs code, they got the connections to get me that permit or whatever I need with no problem. If I need extra garbage cans or a dumpster they're gonna call and say, "Hey, we need a dumpster over here. Hey, don't mess with this guy." That's the protection that you're seeking or you're getting. Everybody's providing a service for everybody.

Sal and I spent an entire interview session—a couple of hours—discussing associates. He makes some eye-opening claims:

JMH: So, associates—are we talking about hundreds of people in Chicago?
SAL: *Hundreds? More like in the thousands. You have to remember that even those considered associates have their own crews of associates. And even though, like I said, some of them may never get into the fold, there are some that are worth a lot of money, in the millions. With property and all that stuff, they're stacked, and they're not greedy, you know? Because they're hustlers just like the next guy, so they're trying to get their piece, and as long as they get it everything is OK.*[19]

I ask Sal to explain the place of associates in the Outfit hierarchy.

SAL: *Well, it's all a kind of secrecy, a style of organization that is built on layers. You got different layers.*

JMH: You don't want to centralize; you want to decentralize, right?

SAL: *Yes. So it doesn't get back to them [law enforcement]. If you take one out, there's always someone else to take that action, right? There's different layers, the layers of management, that's basically what it is.*

JMH: Right, right. See, my background is in organizational theory, that's what I did my dissertation on. And I recognize this as what is called a loosely coupled system . . .[20]

Sal goes on to explain that this loosely coupled Outfit style of organization was emulated in SGD and within some of the gangs, but too late.

> *And a lot of these street gangs are learning and now are looking at setting up boards. They don't want the one top guy like they used to. Because that's the one that they're going after. Whoever gets singled out—if you're the leader, that's who you're coming after. Nobody wants to be named the leader. But if you have a board, you got—it's spread out, a board of governors. It's diffuse. And what is a board of governors? The [mafia] commission! The commission's the board of governors. Everybody has a purpose, everybody has a job, and you put it to a vote when an issue comes up to the table. But SGD is over and we [the Outfit] had to move on.*

The widespread reliance on associates by the Outfit itself presents some problems for the future of any Spanish mafia or a new SGD.

JMH: But it seems to me one of the reasons why a new SGD will be difficult to build is there exists a structure that already is in place. It is decentralized, but you have an organized crime structure that exists with the associates. What you describe is a structure that's both in and out of the gang world. The associates structure is not going to disappear. The idea of trying to build up a rival like a new SGD probably won't go too far, right?

SAL: *Right.*

JMH: Some of the organized crime experts show me charts of Outfit leaders sent to prison, and say look at how the Outfit is on its last legs. But the charts don't include the associates . . .

SAL: *They are our tentacles. The structure is already there and it's already estab-*

lished, but it's invisible. Do we like it when the organized crime professors and cops make all these comments about our demise? Absolutely!

So that gets back to the SGD and Growth and Development. It didn't work because some of them couldn't learn. We've done business with blacks, with Jews, with Russians, with Japanese, you name it! So we have associates that are Greek, Japanese, blacks, Jews, with the Hispanics. They see it out there and they do business with them because everybody gets a piece. So they [Outfit leaders] visualized the future and the structure that they built is phenomenal. Some of these associates got more balls, more smarts, than even some of the young kids coming up of Italian heritage.

For Sal, the Outfit's associates structure will be, at the very least, a silent partner in any future Spanish mafia. Sal is unambiguous in arguing that his interviews will provide a "rude awakening" to the readers of this book.

To us this is just survival of the fittest. If you thought that we are going to go away, you have another thing coming. Not only will it be a rude awakening to see how entrenched we are in today's society, but also to see who else plays a role. So you think that we are going out of the picture? Hah!

FINAL THOUGHTS

I don't know if the associates will become the main transmission belt between the Outfit and gangs in the coming decades. Nor do I have inside knowledge of the relationship between the Mexican cartels, gangs, the Outfit, and politicians. Whether Mexican gangs will violently compete for dominance or come to agreements to cooperate cannot be known in advance. What the research for this book has taught me, though, is that the rise and fall of SGD is an unfinished story of links between Latino gangs and organized crime. I'm also convinced we should treat organized crime as a barrier to social movements, not any kind of an ally.[21] While Chicago's gang history is unique, this book should encourage others to look more carefully at how street gangs and organized crime intersect and what corrupt roles gangs play in politics. Those who dismiss the SGD story as "it could only happen in Chicago" need to do similar research in their own cities.

What I have done is the product of years of learning the history of Chicago gangs and integrating it with the history of organized crime. I have read books and studied documents but also listened directly to members of both gangs and the Outfit as well as law enforcement. This approach takes patience, determination, and a bit of luck, as well as building relationships over time based on trust. Denying that a link between gangs and organized crime exists in a specific city would mean that someone has looked into this issue and done credible research. I'm not aware of any studies similar to mine, though my methods are standard and replicable.

I have blended the history of gangs in Chicago with the history of the Outfit because this was the only way to make sense of SGD. My story questions the importance scholars have long placed on neighborhood characteristics in understanding the will to power of street gangs and their desire to capture enormous profits. The riches of Mexican cartels and an unquenchable demand for drugs means organized crime is bound to be a persisting tendency among gangs, particularly Latinos.[22]

While organized crime is a proper target for law enforcement, more important for me is the influence of its deadly, instrumental culture. This culture manifests itself in music and the cinema, such as in the idolatry by gang members of Hollywood gangsters like Tony Soprano or Tony Montana. But it can also be seen vividly in Sal's perspective on the failings of SGD.

Sal argued that if only SGD had enforced its laws and discipline more ruthlessly and efficiently, the institution might have survived. He may be right, but here he and I part ways. To me, the instrumental culture of organized crime is a bizarre mirror image of the paramount importance of success in US society and its worship of money and power.

In the case of both SGD and the Outfit, accomplishing these goals often meant murder. Like Robert Merton, I think this success culture is embedded deep within our society, and some—Merton mentions Al Capone—use violence and corruption to get what they want.[23] Public officials condemn this culture in organized crime at the risk of hypocrisy. The world of politics, sports, government, and business are filled with examples of men and women doing whatever it takes to win. As in *A World of Gangs*, I argue our main struggle with gang youth is a cultural one, and the target of our struggle should be mainstream, instrumental, hypermasculine, capitalist culture, not some deviant, vicious gang subculture. For me, there are other cultural values—such as nonviolence and human rights—that are more important than money or power.

The reader must also not forget that while gangs are related to organized crime, they are not synonymous with it. Twenty-five years ago I wrote in my first book: "To label all gangs 'organized crime' because some are, however, is unscientific and wrong."[24] This still holds. In Chicago, the vast majority of Latino gang members were not even aware of their leaders' backroom deals with cops and politicians or cartel drug suppliers. Hundreds of corner boys died solely because of the greed of their power-hungry leaders. Given superprofits from drugs and the current role of the cartels as suppliers, I believe the pressures to organize crime exist for gangs in every city. This tendency to organize crime in gangs must be exposed and opposed. But how?

BRINGING THE STATE BACK IN

I can see the US attorney general or Cook County state's attorney reading this book and citing it as a justification for wider use of RICO conspiracy laws. I know I run this risk, but I firmly believe policy needs to be based on facts, no matter how uncomfortable or politically incorrect. To me this history actually points out how few people were in on the deal, how few were part of the conspiracy, and how few called any hits. As far as RICO prosecutions, this book is an argument for a more selective, not broader, use of this dangerous tool.

Law enforcement's prime directive has seemed to be to lock up as many gang members as possible. Indeed in Illinois, the number of prisoners in 2013 is nearly five times the 10,733 inmates in 1978, when the People and Folks coalitions were organized to control increasing gang tensions in prison. One of the conditions for the organization of crime is the concentration of gang members in our prisons, and today that problem is worse, not better, despite sharply falling crime rates. Any new SGD, like the last one, will likely be prison-based, more similar to La Eme than to the Italian mafia. We have a large pool of inmate recruits produced by our wars on gangs and drugs to thank for this.

I think the impact of our current politics of mass incarceration can be best described with a medical term: *iatrogenic*. This word describes the effects of treatment that instead of making the patient better, does harm—for example, when a surgeon does not properly sterilize an instrument and it causes infection. We need to stop the wars on drugs and gangs that fill our prisons and therefore help crime to organize. But our policy on gangs needs to do more.

The In$ane Chicago Way puts into the spotlight the problem of police and official corruption. Chapters 7 and 8 should have convinced you that corruption is a serious problem in Chicago, but I don't think any city is exempt from corrupt influences or the reach of organized crime—whether of the mafia or the drug cartels. The war on drugs is absolutely corrupting everywhere, and I believe all of us, gang members and police officers included, will benefit by its end. How can the rule of law be supported as legitimate when police officers like the brutal Jon Burge or the corrupt Joseph Miedzianowski and the out-of-control SOS unit are allowed to run wild?[25]

With few exceptions, gang researchers have largely avoided investigating police misconduct and official corruption, and I hope this book helps force this issue onto their research agenda. While not all of us can or should play direct roles working with gangs or young people, we can support police reforms and work to expose and punish corrupt public officials. While it was individual gang members who built SGD, we should never forget that they had help. As the Don said, without the police none of this could happen.

But what about those who have been involved with gangs and violence? What lessons can we draw from this book about them?

WHO ARE THE PEACEMAKERS?

Today in Chicago, the demise of the People and Folks coalitions and SGD means a vacuum in leadership and an unprecedented opportunity for activists to win over gang members to a path of peace and justice. My approach to gangs has always been based on assumptions of social change, not the need for existing authorities to exercise more effective social control. I've always said too few jobs and lousy education fuel an intractable gang problem.

My research from the start has argued that the million or so gang members in the US are necessary allies in movements for equality and social justice. They are alienated and hostile, prime examples of the failure of our economic and political systems. If we are to make meaningful social change, youth in gangs must both benefit from reforms and be part of the process. The 1960s war on poverty, William Julius Wilson taught us, provided some hope for minority middle classes, but left a growing, hostile, black underclass that has festered, not gone away. This book told the story of how Chicago's underclass gangs, rejected and repressed by Daley's war on them, built structures of their own to reduce violence, organize crime, and get their piece of the pie. While they have been part of the problem, I have always believed gang members need to be part of the solution.

Most gang members mature out of their gangs, but as we've seen in these pages, many have participated in violence, and a handful have joined the ranks of organized crime. We should never forget the loss of any life, and no one should get away with murder. However, I have also learned to appreciate the capacity of human beings to change. While I disagree with Sal's instrumental perspective, he has retired from the Outfit and lives a contented family-focused life. I see in the Chicago newspapers pictures of various community leaders who I know to have been gang leaders who were deeply involved in drug deals and violence in the 1990s.

For men and women such as these, I think we need to reject the old answer of punitive incarceration and innovate around the sanctions and healing power of a type of restorative justice. Former gang members who have done wrong and have moved on still need to be held accountable. But accountability need not mean locking them away in places where they cannot contribute their experience in helping win the peace. While some see restorative justice as suitable only for low-level offences, I believe its principles can be our best policy alternative to mass incarceration.[26]

I think about soldiers, who after a war ends with all its killing, come home and try to put their lives together again. I have had students who are former gang members and others who are former US military who have identical symptoms of PTSD. Both need to settle down, but also want to use their experiences to help others. In one of my prior studies, I compared child soldiers to gang members, arguing the need for a supportive, not punitive, society to reintegrate them.[27] Policies of restorative justice and a culture of forgiveness make sense to me for Chicago and beyond.

I recognize that organized crime is bound to be a constant pressure on former gang leaders and remain a tantalizing lure. One way for them to move on is to play the role of peacemaker. Blade kept saying that he thought SGD was all about stopping the violence. The problem of violence is one that former gang members, working as peacemakers in various community organizations, are well suited to play. Their peacemaking history needs to be told, and I think we might find they have had a significant effect on violence in today's ganglands.

Sal might be right: Chicago's violence may be curtailed by new forms of organized crime or Al Capone-like leaders. For my part, I prefer policies that stress a culture of nonviolence advocated by people like Luis Rodriguez to an uncertain peace dictated by La Eme or some new SGD.[28]

Gang peacemakers are important, but I think we, their supporters, should add the slogan "No justice/no peace" to their agenda. *The In$ane Chicago Way* reinforced to me an old insight that the pressing demands of the street need to be included in broader social movements. When I was in Mombasa in 2010 to address a UN gathering of Kenyan police, I showed them a picture of a massive demonstration in Cairo's Tahrir Square during the Arab Spring. I asked them, "Where were the gangs?" The answer, of course, was "In the crowd." Powerful social movements can sweep up nearly everyone, including the gangs.

History tells us that gangs, corruption, and organized crime will probably never go away, no matter what we do, but it does matter what we do. Former gang members can play the role of peacemakers, but for most of you who read this book, there are other crucial tasks. I have singled out as especially important fighting the iatrogenic effects of mass incarceration and targeting police and official corruption. One lesson of this book is that Chicago has always had a serious gang problem because it also has always had a serious problem with corruption and police brutality. In Chicago and elsewhere, history shows the gang *problem* is broader than just a problem of gang *members*.

NOTES

PREFACE: THIS IS NOT A MOVIE

1. The multiple shootings garnered national publicity and were featured in an episode of the sensationalistic TV drama, *Gangland*. The 6:00 p.m. shootings on February 13, 1996, took place on the turf of the Maniac Latin Disciples, called "Monkeyland." The shootings that took place after 6:00 p.m. were spontaneous retaliatory shootings by members of the Spanish Cobras against the MLDs. The 7:20 shooting happened in the same neighborhood. The 8:00 p.m. shooting happened on the main MLD turf at Rockwell and Potomac, called the "Twilight Zone." Some of those shot that night were MLD members as Cobras began retaliation. I'll tell later of the Insane Family's even more lethal response of multiple coordinated shootings.

INTRODUCTION: LIFTING THE VEIL

1. Protecting Sal's identity from disclosure, inadvertent or not, is underscored by the New York City case of Louie Eppolito, the NYPD "Mafia Cop." The book on his life, told to journalist Bob Drury, that included Eppolito bragging about brutality and various on-the-job illegal actions, resulted in his conviction and life imprisonment. Lou Eppolito and Bob Drury, *Mafia Cop: The Story of an Honest Cop Whose Family Was the Mob* (New York: Pocket Star Books, 1992). See also: http://www.nytimes.com/2009/03/07/nyregion/07about.html?_r=0.

2. My first book, *People and Folks*, traced the history of gangs in Milwaukee from their late 1970s origins. *A World of Gangs* included several chapters on Chicago. Its goal was to put what I had learned in Chicago into a global perspective. John M. Hagedorn, *People and Folks: Gangs, Crime, and the Underclass in a Rustbelt City*; Hagedorn, *A World of Gangs: Armed Young Men and Gangsta Culture* (Minneapolis: University of Minnesota Press, 2008).

3. Daniel Bell, *The End of Ideology: On the Exhaustion of Political Ideas in the Fifties* (New York: Free Press, 1960).

4. My views on the inductive method are similar to its practice by the Chicago school. For example, Andrew Abbott and Rainer Egloff, referring to W. I. Thomas's *The Polish Peasant* (*TPP*) say, "In a vague way, this paper prefigures *TPP*. It argues for empirical, comparative, and inductive research. It stresses the utility of documents. It takes social life to be dynamic. It sees the importance of individual psychology even while it considers institutions yoking individual and society and mentions the various social forms of knowledge." Andrew Abbott and Rainer Egloff, "The Polish Peasant in Oberlin and Chicago: The Intellectual Trajectory of W. I. Thomas," *American Sociologist* 39, no. 4 (December 2008): 231. See also Jacqueline Low and Gary Bowden, eds., *The Chicago School Diaspora: Epistemology and Substance* (Canada: McGill-Queens University Press, 2013), 330–31.

5. The significance of Chicago's cross-neighborhood gang organization was under-

scored to me by Alistair Frasier when I was in Glasgow as a visiting professor. Glasgow's gangs have been around as long as Chicago's but apparently have never formed lasting cross-neighborhood organization. See Alistair Frasier, *Urban Legends: Gang Identity in the Post-Industrial City* (London: Oxford University Press, forthcoming); and Andrew Davies, *City of Gangs: Glasgow and the Rise of the British Gangster* (London: Hodder & Stoughton, 2013).

6. The UN Office on Drug Control has estimated worldwide drug trafficking at $320 billion per year. Manuel Castells looks at a range of estimates and makes the point that the global trade in drugs exceeds the trade in oil. See his chapter on the global criminal economy in *The Information Age: Economy, Society and Culture*, vol. 3, *End of Millennium* (Malden, MA: Blackwell, 2000), 196–211. Castells argues that the street gangs in Rio, Cape Town, Chicago, and cities around the world are part of a global criminal economy, a "perverse connection" that includes trafficking in drugs, guns, humans, and stolen goods. Criminal networks span the globe, and connections between Chicago Latino gangs and the Mexican cartels are just one example. In *A World of Gangs* I argued that conditions world-wide were so dire that gangs aren't going away, no matter what we do. I learned from Sal that the amount of money to be made in vice markets means that organized crime will not go away either. See also http://www.unodc.org/unodc/en/data-and-analysis /WDR-2012.html.

7. Angela Me, Enrico Bisogno, and Steven Malby, *Global Study of Homicide: Trends, Context, Data* (Vienna: United Nations Office on Drugs and Crime, 2011). My book concludes that Chicago's gang violence in the twenty-first century is fundamentally different from the organized wars of the 1990s. In the final pages I'll argue that the concern for violence by former gang members makes them ideal candidates as peacemakers, especially when formal gang leadership has been discredited. We have an opportunity for intervention that may close if gangs revert to a more organized state. See my application of this literature to Chicago in John M. Hagedorn, "Chicago, I Do Mind Dying," in *Oxford Textbook of Violence Prevention: Epidemiology, Evidence, and Policy*, ed. Peter Donnelly and Catherine Ward (London: Oxford University Press, 2014), 219–24. For Sal, power and violence are not opposites, as Hannah Arendt asserts; Harrah Arendt, *On Violence* (San Diego: Harcourt & Brace, 1969).

8. I follow Philip Selznick and the institutional school in my analysis of SGD as a social institution: "When we say that the Standard Oil Company or the Department of Agriculture is to be studied as an institution we usually mean we are going to pay some attention to its history and to the way it has been influenced by the social environment. Thus we may be interested in how the organization adapts itself to existing centers of power in the community, often in unconscious ways; from what strata of society its leadership is drawn and how this effects policy; how it justifies its existence ideologically. We may ask what underlying need in the larger community—not necessarily expressed or recognized by the people involved—is filled by the organization or some of its practices. Thus the phrase 'as a social institution' suggests an emphasis on problems and experiences that are not adequately accounted for within the narrower framework of administrative analysis." Selznick, *Leadership in Administration: A Sociological Interpretation* (Berkeley: University

of California Press, 1957), 6. This is a precise statement of one aspect of my book. Gangs are a tiny footnote in organizational theory, and my book suggests that an organizational approach that goes beyond seeing all gangs as "loosely structured peer groups" may be in order. For example, Richard Scott in his influential *Institutions and Organizations* states: "Street gangs may be highly prevalent in urban America, signifying they provide a culturally constituted mode of organizing to achieve specified ends. Although we may readily recognize them, and their structures may be widely reproduced, they often are treated as illegal forms by police and other regulative bodies, and they frequently lack the normative endorsement of established community and societal authorities." W. Richard Scott, *Institutions and Organizations* (Thousand Oaks, CA: Sage, 1995), 47.

9. See the Chief Keef/Lil JoJo tragedy, e.g., http://www.wired.com/underwire /2013/09/gangs-of-social-media/. See also Geoff Harkness, *Chicago Hustle & Flow: Gangs, Gangsta Rap, and Social Class* (Minneapolis: University of Minnesota Press, 2014).

10. However, see the important book by former gang member and scholar Victor Rios, documenting the central role punishment and police repression play in poor communities: *Punished: Policing the Lives of Black and Latino Boys* (New York: New York University Press, 2011). In a different vein, Alice Goffman, *On The Run: Fugitive Life in an American City* (Chicago: University of Chicago Press, 2014).

11. Here is our effort in Chicago: John Hagedorn et al. "Crime, Corruption, and Cover-ups in the Chicago Police Department," MS, University of Illinois–Chicago Political Science Department, January 17, 2013. http://www.uic.edu/depts/pols/ChicagoPolitics /policecorruption.pdf.

12. My methods here have much in common with feminist methodology, e.g., Anne Oakley, "Interviewing Women: A Contradiction in Terms," in *Doing Feminist Research*, ed. Helen Roberts (London: Routledge & Keegan Paul, 1981). I'm also guided by Alvin Gouldner's seminal polemic against Howard Becker, "The Sociologist as Partisan: Sociology and the Welfare State," *American Sociologist* 3 (May 1968): 103–16. Gouldner argues that objectivity requires a struggle against "the need to be loved" and a rigorous commitment to "values not factions." While my methodology requires empathy toward Sal and the gang members I study, empathy does not require that I adopt their values, and Gouldner points out that objectivity requires that I maintain my own. He states incisively, if precariously: "The values we may actually hold may differ from those we must display in order to gain or maintain access to research sites" (113).

13. John M. Hagedorn, *The Business of Drug Dealing in Milwaukee* (Milwaukee: Wisconsin Policy Research Institute, 1998); John M. Hagedorn, "Gangs and the Informal Economy," in *Gangs in America*, ed. Ron Huff (Beverly Hills: Sage, 2001), 101–20.

CHAPTER ONE: THE HIT

1. The shooting, like so many others, had a long history of conflict between rival Latin Folks gangs. For further background on the Latin Lovers/MLD dispute see No. 1-99-2365, *The People of the State of Illinois v. Jose Barajas*, Appeal from the Circuit Court of Cook County, 97 CR 24542. Another example of festering hostility between Insane and

Maniac Family gangs took place September 1, 1994 when William Negron and Roberto Almodovar, both members of the Insane Dragons street gang, had shot and killed Amy Merkes and Jorge Rodriguez of the YLO-Ds, a member of the Maniac Family. The shooting was in retaliation for the YLO-Ds gunning down Carlos Orlon, a Dragon, two days before. Kennelly Saez, a YLO-D member who was present when the shootings occurred, had given police a statement. Negron and Almodovar were convicted, and it was affirmed on appeal. See *People v. Negron*, State of Illinois No. 1-96-0725. The case does not end there, and as this book was being written, the lying of a corrupt gang-squad police officer, Reynaldo Guevera, resulted in the verdict being overturned. See http://www.state.il.us /court/Opinions/AppellateCourt/2013/1stDistrict/1101476.pdf. What this chapter demonstrates is that the cycle of Maniac/Insane retaliation in the 1990s was both more intense and complicated than assumed by outsiders.

2. The MLDs were one of the main beneficiaries of the "Durango Connection." One of Hugo "Juice" Herrera's main partners within the MLDs was Eddie "Evil D" Vasquez. For an overview of law enforcement's attack on the Durango cartel, see Matt Gavin, *Operation Durango Connection: In the War on Drugs, Just Who Are the Good Guys and Who Are the Bad Guys?* (San Jose: Writers Club Press, 2000). For brief law enforcement capsules of the Herrera Family, see http://www.druglibrary.org/schaffer/govpubs/amhab/amhabc3 .htm and especially http://chua2.fiu.edu/faculty/byrnesj/organizedweek6-1.htm.

3. A long string of articles on the Miedzianowski case appeared in both the *Sun-Times* and *Tribune*. In the *Sun-Times* Steve Warmbir provided 2001 coverage of the case as it went to trial. One applicable court document is *United States v. Miedzianowski*, No. 98 CR 923 (N.D.Ill. 02/03/2006). Miedzianowski's illicit dealings with "Baby Face" Nelson Padilla are included in both the legal and newspaper documents. "Joe became my mentor," Padilla said in a recent interview from federal prison in Florida. "I loved Joe." Todd Lighty, "Former Cop Crossed Line, Destroyed it," *Chicago Tribune*, January 19, 2003.

4. Rambo, and his fellow chief, "Godfather," were angered that the MLDs and 2-6ers were still pressing charges. Rambo thought the entire SGD board had become corrupt. Tuffy, the Cobras' representative on La Tabla, had been transferred to a New Jersey prison and wasn't available to help. Rambo knew both Fernie and Ayala were nearly always high, being constantly supplied with drugs behind bars by visitors and even "mules" from their hated rivals, the Latin Kings. See appendix 4 for the SGD formal grievance format from their constitution.

CHAPTER TWO: THE OLD MAN AND THE C-NOTE$

1. Lombardo's classified ad read: "I never took a secret oath, with guns and daggers, pricked my finger, drew blood or burned paper to join a criminal organization. If anyone hears my name used in connection with any criminal activity, please notify the FBI, local police, and my parole officer, Ron Kumke." Reported in John Kass's column: "The Nose Shows Almost Anything Goes under Daley Watch," *Chicago Tribune*, July 27, 1999. For a sketchy outline of Outfit history—and pictures as well—see John J. Binder, *The Chicago Outfit* (Charleston, SC: Arcadia Publishing, 2003). Binder, like nearly all "mafia experts"

argues that the Outfit in Chicago is pretty much finished. A more recent history is Robert M. Lombardo, *Organized Crime in Chicago: Beyond the Mafia* (Urbana: University of Illinois Press, 2013). Sal presents a very different story. To compare Chicago's mafia history with New York City see Selwyn Raab, *Five Families: The Rise, Decline, and Resurgence of America's Most Powerful Mafia Empires* (New York City: St. Martin's Press, 2005).

CHAPTER THREE: THE DON

1. Useni Eugene Perkins, *Explosion of Chicago's Black Street Gangs* (Chicago: Third World Press, 1987). See an online exhibit of the legacy of the Conservative Vice Lords: http://www.uic.edu/jaddams/hull/cvl/index.html#!home/mainPage. For a law enforcement view see the various Chicago Crime Commission reports, such as *Gangs: Public Enemy Number One* (1995); and J. Michael Olivero, *Honor, Violence, and Upward Mobility: A Case Study of Chicago Gangs during the 1970s and 1980s* (Edinburg: University of Texas–Pan American Press, 1991). For a theoretical defense of the resistance identities of gangs, see David Brotherton, "Beyond Social Reproduction: Bringing Resistance Back in Gang Theory," *Theoretical Criminology* 12 (January 2008): 55–77.

2. For Chicago's concentrated poverty and deindustrialization, see William Julius Wilson, *The Declining Significance of Race* (Chicago: University of Chicago Press, 1978); Wilson, *The Truly Disadvantaged* (Chicago: University of Chicago Press, 1987). The Blackstone Rangers' alliance with Jane Byrne against Harold Washington is the most notable example of the disastrous attempts of black gangs to penetrate the machine. See Abdul Alkalimat and Doug Gills, *Harold Washington and the Crisis of Black Power in Chicago* (Chicago: Twenty-First Century Books and Publications, 1989); and Natalie Moore and Lance Williams, *The Almighty Black P. Stone Nation* (Chicago: Lawrence Hill Books, 2010).

3. Quote from Nathan Thompson, *Kings: The True Story of Chicago's Policy Kings and Numbers Racketeers* (Chicago: Bronzeville Press, 2003), 248. Drake and Cayton's *Black Metropolis* gives the best picture on how Policy fit into the black political machine. Their estimates of the payoffs and profits of Policy include a classic diagram of corruption (vol. 2, pp. 481–84). St. Clair Drake and Horace R. Cayton, *Black Metropolis: A Study of Negro life in a Northern City* (New York: Harcourt, Brace, & World, 1970). See also Bell, *The End of Ideology*, 132. Teddy Roe, the last of the black Policy kings, said, "If gambling is to run in the Negro district in Chicago, WE will run it. Not a gang of hoodlums who think they can step in and take control like gangs have done in Negro districts in other cities. We will not tolerate any mob rule." Thompson, *Kings*, 275.

4. "Community institution" is Drake and Cayton's term for Policy in *Black Metropolis*, 484.

5. The heroin story is told in many Outfit histories, and in Alfred W. McCoy, *The Politics of Heroin in Southeast Asia* (New York: Harper & Row, 1972). The quote from Sam Giancana is from Sam Giancana and Chuck Giancana, *Double Cross: The Explosive, Inside Story of the Mobster Who Controlled America* (New York: Warner Books, 1992), 246. In an unpublished manuscript "Policing the Color Line: Race, Power, and Social Change in 20th Century Chicago" from University of Illinois at Chicago, PhD candidate Joey Lipari

details Italian control of heroin sales in the black community in the 1950. The Outfit's Hollywood action is told in Gus Russo, *The Outfit: The Role of Chicago's Underworld in the Shaping of Modern America* (New York: Bloomsbury, 2001); Russo, *Supermob: How Sidney Korshak and His Criminal Associates Became America's Hidden Power Brokers* (New York: Bloomsbury, 2006). A unique Turkish perspective can be found in Frank Bovenkerk and Yücel Yesilgöz, *The Turkish Mafia: A History of the Heroin Godfathers* (Reading, UK: Cox and Wyman, 2007).

6. For more on the Outfit/Rangers connections, see Moore and Williams, *The Almighty Black P. Stone Nation.* They report on p. 141: "It was always believed that Mickey Cogwell had strong connections with the Chicago Mafia. As early as 1970, the *Chicago Tribune* reported that there was a financial alliance between Mafia chiefs and the Blackstone Rangers. The Gang Intelligence Unit of the Chicago Police Department claimed to have had evidence accumulated from months of undercover work and surveillance, which produced the first-ever photographs of a rendezvous between mob emissaries and Blackstone Ranger leaders. According to the police, beginning in 1969, Cogwell and Charles "Reico" Cranshaw were meeting with outfit representatives Joseph "Little Caesar" DiVarco; Joseph "Big Joe" Arnold, who also controlled the North Side lending racket; and Morris Lasky, a gambler who once worked for mob chieftains Jackie "the Lackey" Cerone and James "Monk" Allegretti. The police thought that the Mafia and Blackstone Rangers were collaborating to control the policy racket, clubs, taverns, lounges, and liquor stores in the black community. Cogwell's murder, which coincided with the murder of another union organizer in Las Vegas, may have been mafia hits since both men were organizing unions in mob protected businesses." For the Balestreri/Fort confrontation and the mink coat fiasco, see Henry L. Harris Jr., *Epitome of Courage* (Chicago: 1st Books Library, 2001), 67.

7. Francis Ianni, *Black Mafia* (New York: Simon & Shuster, 1975). No serious studies exist of the ethnic succession in retail vice markets in Chicago from the Outfit to the gangs.

8. An unpublished novel written by former YMCA outreach worker and then Chicago alderman Fred Hubbard gives a realistic, if fictionalized, portrait of the times. This manuscript, provided to me by Jim Short, centers on a story about how black political leaders collaborated with the gangs to use money from dope sales to finance the beginning of a political takeover of city hall. Hubbard's novel has an Outfit leader saying, "And finally, we just gotta face the fact that the niggers ain't easy to handle anymore" (195). This is a paraphrase of the Don's statement that the black gangs "were rough." I was also given an unpublished Gangster Disciple document called "The Chicago Experiment" which told of a conspiracy with the University of Chicago that resulted in an "experiment in the creation of a black Mafia—a new milieu for the conducting of drugs into the U.S." The conspiracy was driven by fear that Hyde Park, the University of Chicago's home, would be swallowed up by the ghetto and that drastic steps had to be taken by Chicago's power brokers.

9. For Daley's war on gangs, see excerpts and commentary from the declaration of war by Daley and his state's attorney, Edward Hanrahan at http://gangresearch.net

/ChicagoGangs/blackstonerangers/Daley.html and a University of Chicago masters thesis. Sherman, Larry W. "Youth Workers, Police, and Gangs 1956–70." (Masters Thesis: University of Chicago, 1971).

10. The history of the 42 Gang is captured in Robert M. Lombardo, "Forty-Two Gang: The Unpublished Landesco Manuscripts," *Journal of Gang Research* 18, no. 1 (2010): 19–38; and amplified in Lombardo's *Organized Crime in Chicago*. John Landesco wrote a life history of a 42 Gang member in "The Life History of a Member of the '42' Gang." *Journal of Criminal Law and Criminology* 23, no. 6 (1931): 964–98.

11. Sal asked me if I knew what the acronyms of the C-Note$, and two other prominent white gangs, the Gaylords and Popes, stood for? I said no, and he chuckled:

C-Note$: Chicago Neighborhood Organization to Eliminate Spics
Popes: Protect Our People, Eliminate Spics
Gaylords: Great American Youth Leading Our Rebellion Destroying Spics

12. Casey Szaflarski was called Chicago's "Slot machine king." See John Kass's description of his role in the Outfit at http://articles.chicagotribune.com/2012-02-09/news/ct-met-kass-0209-20120209_1_motorcycle-gang-chicago-street-gang-sarno. There is one brief mention of the C-Note$ in Robert Lombardo's comprehensive book on the Outfit, *Organized Crime in Chicago* (174).

13. For the student of traditional criminology, this might be seen as simply reflecting Sutherland's differential association theory, as applied by Cloward and Ohlin, and Spergel's notion of "criminal subcultures." Following the text, it will be clear that the C-Note$ were more than just reproductions of the mafia and had characteristics of all the subcultures in the classic gang literature. Edwin H. Sutherland, *Principles of Criminology* (Chicago: J. B. Lippincott , 1934); Richard Cloward and Lloyd Ohlin, *Delinquency and Opportunity* (Glencoe, Ill: Free Press, 1960); and Irving A. Spergel, *Racketville Slumtown Haulberg* (Chicago: University of Chicago Press, 1964).

14. The C-Note$ formed two main factions over the years at Ohio and Leavitt (near the Patch) and Jefferson Park. Each faction formed their own sections, or neighborhood gangs. Each of their twenty-five sections had ten to fifteen soldiers each, but it seemed to outsiders that the C-Note$ were much larger. C-Note$ sections included sets at Superior and Washtenaw, Huron and Campbell, Race and Damen, Huron and Tallman, Ohio and Claremont, Ohio and Noble, Race and Oakley, Rice and Oakley, Ohio and Ashland, Ohio and Hoyne, Erie and Leavitt, Erie and Oakley, Superior and California, Smith Park, Argyle and Lavergne, Cicero and Gunnison, Carmen and Lavergne, Central and Giddings, Elston and Leclaire, Leavitt and Grace, Medill and Oakley, Olcott and Roscoe, Harlem and Addison, Normandy and Belden, and Gompers Park.

15. "Michael Scott" self-published a memoir, *Lords of Lawndale: My Life in a Chicago White Street Gang* (Bloomington, IN: AuthorHouse, 2004). He added on to his stories in a sequel, *Lords of Kilbourn* (Shelbyville, KY: Wasteland Press, 2008). Simon City Royal "Mark Watson," in *Romantic Violence in R-World* (Chicago: Whiteout Press, 2013), explains how he became a white supremacist. This book has sporadic mentions of the C-Note$.

16. Sal, in his usual rational fashion, sums up the problem with the Gaylords and

other defunct white gangs as the failure to adapt and take advantage of continued white ethnic immigration.

> *One of the things that these white gangs failed to do was take advantage of that same situation where you have the Latin Kings and the Two-Six and La Raza that are recruiting guys who just got off the boat. Gangs like the Gaylords and the Simon City Royals should have been doing the same thing with the Polish immigrants coming into this community. Because the majority of their members—that was their descent. They were already second and third generation. And they slowed down on the people that came off the boat.*

17. "Ain't No Pity in Simon City" was the SCR slogan, and although they accommodated Latino members, their home of Kosciuszko Park became targeted territory for a host of some of the strongest Latino gangs, including the Disciples, Kings, and Cobras. I'll later tell the story of the war the SGD board could not stop between the Cobras and Royals over control of Koz Park.

18. Mike James's story and Rising Up Angry is told in Amy Sonnie and James Tracy, *Hillbilly Nationalists, Urban Race Revels, and Black Power: Community Organizing in Radical Times* (Brooklyn, NY: Melville House, 2011).

19. Felix Padilla has written one book about a gang he names the Diamonds, one of the Latin Folks gangs during the period we are describing. He fails to mention either SGD or the families. This level of organization, as Sal said, was kept from most members as well as researchers. Padilla has also written extensively on Puerto Rican Chicago and one unique ethnography on the impact of prison from a woman's perspective. Felix Padilla, *Latino Ethnic Consciousness: The Case of Mexican Americans and Puerto Ricans in Chicago* (Notre Dame, IN: Notre Dame Press, 1985); Padilla, *Puerto Rican Chicago* (Notre Dame, IN: Notre Dame Press, 1987); Padilla, *The Gang as an American Enterprise* (New Brunswick: Rutgers University Press, 1992); and Felix M. Padilla and Lourdes Santiago, *Outside the Wall: A Puerto Rican Woman's Struggle* (New Brunswick, NJ: Rutgers, 1993). See also the interview with Mervin Mendez: http://gangresearch.net/ChicagoGangs/younglords/MervinYLO.pdf.

20. Cha Cha gave an interview to UIC student Erika Rodriguez, who interviewed him for the Chicago Gang History Project. See excerpts of Erika's interview at http://gangresearch.net/ChicagoGangs/younglords/chacha.htm.

21. On June 12, 1966, CPD officer Thomas Munyon was chasing twenty-year-old Aracelis Cruz and his friend through an alley near Damen and Division and shot Cruz in the leg. The community erupted in rioting against the police for three days. On June 4, 1977, a second rebellion on Division erupted after the cops killed two youths, Rafael Cruz and Julio Osorio. In 1978, the Puerto Rican Day Parade was founded to commemorate the uprising. Unfortunately, that parade has been continually marred by fighting between Spanish Cobras and Latin Kings.

22. The Kings role with FALN and Puerto Rican independence is reminiscent of the role of gangs and the "comrades" in the South African liberation struggle. See Clive Glaser, *Bo-Tsotsi: The Youth Gangs of Soweto, 1935–1976* (Portsmouth, NH: Heinemann, 2000). For more on the Latin Kings, see David Brotherton and Luis Barrios, *Between Black and*

Gold: The Street Politics of the Almighty Latin King and Queen Nation (New York: Columbia University Press, 2003); and a polemical treatment of Latin King history, King Mission, *The Official Globalization of the ALKQN* (New York: Lulu, 2008).

23. According to one Insane Family leader, the MLDs were originally called "Maniacs" but "they changed their name because there was a gang called Maniac Destroyers. Their colors were blue and red. Then you had the Latin Disciples. Them two bonded together 'cause they both had the horns, they both had the forks [gang symbols]. They bonded together and made themselves the Maniac Latin Disciples: MLDs. They are all Ds. Destroyers were a little gang and now became big with the Ds. It was just a name."

24. A history of the ISCs, like that of other Chicago street gangs, could be divided into several periods, the first being the peer group era when kids formed gangs, and then when their local gangs affiliated with the Cobras. The 1970s were years of war, particularly between People and Folks, and incarceration. That period saw their main leaders incarcerated, and the Cobras, like nearly all Chicago gangs, were run by their leaders in prison. The Cobras by that time had began to study the mafia experience and model their organization on organized crime.

25. The Medina Family later moved to Milwaukee and formed a chapter of the Spanish Cobras there. I tell their story in my first book, *People and Folks*.

26. Aside from scattered references, there is a nearly complete void in credible research on Chicago's Mexican gangs.

CHAPTER FOUR: SPANISH GROWTH AND DEVELOPMENT

1. All SGD and Latin Folks documents reprinted here were given to me by Sal, who in turn received them from Joey Bags. The organizational chart in figure 4.1 was reproduced from the SGD constitution. Selznick's comments on how to interpret formal constitutions will guide my analysis. Selznick, *Leadership in Administration*, 6–7. A table of key events directly preceding the founding of SGD and major events in their ten-year history can be found in appendixes 1 and 2.

2. Jimmy "the Bomber" Catuara was legendary in Chicago. A south suburb chop-shop (stolen car) operator, he orchestrated the chop-shop wars but was murdered by Outfit hit man Billy Dauber. *Chicago Magazine* wrote about his death in 1978 when he "was found facedown in a pool of blood near his red Cadillac at Hubbard Street and Ogden Avenue." Found online at http://www.chicagomag.com/Chicago-Magazine/March-2005/Devils-Advocate/index.php?cparticle=4&siarticle=3. Note that his death took place two blocks from the Aberdeen Club. Also see Matthew J. Luzi, *The Boys in Chicago Heights* (Charleston, SC: History Press, 2012).

3. "It was a powerful myth of unity" explains SGD as a "rationalized myth." This recalls the institutional classic: John M. Meyer and Brian Rowan, "Institutionalized Organizations: Formal Structure as Myth and Ceremony," *American Journal of Sociology* 83, no. 2 (1977): 340–63. SGD can be classically understood by this essay. "Once institutionalized, rationality becomes a myth with explosive organizing potential" (346). The "mimetic" similarity of the Mafia's commission to SGD can be explained by exploring the concept

of *isomorphism*. Paul J. DiMaggio and Walter W. Powell, "The Iron Cage Revisited: Institutional Isomorphism and Collective Rationality in Organizational Fields," *American Sociological Review* 48, no. 2 (1983):147–60. The popularity of *The Sopranos* and other organized-crime movies and TV series added to the "mimetic" aspect of "institutional isomorphism."

4. Selznick, *Leadership in Administration*, 5. The group-process literature describing the dynamics of relatively unorganized peer groups is founded in Thrasher's classic on gangs and more fully developed by Short and Strodtbeck. Institutional processes are much more complex than "aleatory" or accidental responses or actions. Frederic Thrasher, *The Gang: A Study of 1,313 Gangs in Chicago* (Chicago: University of Chicago Press, 1927); James F. Short and Fred L. Strodtbeck, *Group Process and Gang Delinquency* (Chicago: University of Chicago Press, 1965).

5. For a popular account of the suicidal burglary of Accardo's house, see http://www.ganglandchicagohistory.com/2010/02/feature-article-3-bad-career-move.html.

6. The National Institute of Justice applies up-to-date versions of social disorganization theory to explain variation in homicide during these years in Chicago as reflecting various standard neighborhood variables, which they call "community careers in crime." This is how they explain the rationale of their analysis of variation in homicide: "Drawing on the social disorganization and concentrated disadvantage literature, the focus of this objective will be to assess the degree to which structural characteristics of neighborhoods influence homicide trends, including factors such as poverty, unemployment, single-headed households, immigration, divorce, racial composition, density, and population mobility." Brian J. Stults, "Determinants of Chicago Neighborhood Homicide Trends: 1980–2000" (Washington, DC: United States Department of Justice, 2012), 1–81. For quotes see pages 2 and 3.

What is conspicuously missing in the NIJ report, as well as more sophisticated analyses by Robert Sampson, is that much of the violence in these years was the result of conscious decisions by gangs, such as in the post-1978 the war of the Insanes, and later, as we will see, the 1990s war of the families. Social disorganization theorists, obsessed with the failure of neighborhood controls, simply forget that gangs are social actors and that power and organization, not powerlessness and disorganization, at times are better predictors of violence. They assume that gangs are merely a reflection of their neighborhood, an idea I hope the readers of this book have already questioned.

Further, studies which correlate homicide and social disorganization are helpless in understanding sharp increases and decreases in killings when measures of social disorganization remain relatively constant. Why did homicides triple in Humboldt Park in the 1970s, then level off, then jump up again by a factor of 2 in the 1990s? Were there corresponding tripling and doubling of family disruption, unemployment, or other social disorganization variables, then rapid declines? Hardly. The vagaries of gang warfare, as detailed in this book, make such variation understandable. The UN *Global Study on Homicide* points out that the level of homicide is generally related to underdevelopment and desperation but exceptionally high rates of homicide are related to civil wars between gangs or ethnic groups. Me, Bisogno, and Malby, *Global Study of Homicide*.

The focus in the NIJ study on an "average" Chicago neighborhood, while it might have some statistical uses in trend analysis, simply makes no sense when trying to understand gang decision-making on warfare in specific areas. Immigrant status, a proxy for Latinos (smoothing over variation between Mexicans and Puerto Ricans) was associated with declines in violence, a finding that is not supported in Latino gang neighborhoods like Humboldt Park or Little Village. Gang hits, it should also be pointed out, may not take place on gang turf, but can occur anywhere. Statistical analyses that leave out gangs, in periods such as the 1990s, are at the very least misleading. Robert J. Sampson, *Great American City: Chicago and the Enduring Neighborhood Effect* (Chicago: University of Chicago Press, 2012).

7. See the journalist John Conroy's stirring, comparative treatment of Burge's reign of terror, *Unspeakable Acts, Ordinary People: The Dynamics of Torture* (New York: Knopf, 2000).

8. "The 669th killing of 1984 touched off an unprecedented public outcry for more effective means of curtailing gang violence. The tragedy that struck a vital nerve was the slaying of Benjamin Wilson, a 17-year-old high school basketball star who was being recruited by major colleges across the country. He was shot to death in a sidewalk confrontation with a gang member on the city's South Side on November 20, 1984"; http://www.uic.edu/orgs/kbc/ganghistory/Info%20Era/Washgangs.htm.

9. Sal's perspective clearly reflects a mechanical, or economic, model of organization. My analysis is a standard critique of Weberian models, what Scott calls the regulative pillar of institutions. Scott, *Institutions and Organizations*, 35. My discussion of SGD relies on what Scott calls the "cognitive pillar." For a further comparative discussion, see Charles Perrow, *Complex Organizations: A Critical Essay* (New York: Random House, 1979).

10. I am paraphrasing Selznick's classic analysis of the differences between organizations and institutions and how institutions create identity. Self images, according to Selznick "provide the individual with an ordered approach to his day-to-day problems, a way of responding to the world consistently yet involuntarily, in accordance with approved perspectives yet without continuous reference to explicit and formalized rules" (17–18). Rather than see SGD as merely an expendable tool to perform criminal operations Latin Folks members were encouraged to "to infuse (it) with value beyond the technical requirements of the task at hand" (17). Selznick, *Leadership in Administration*.

11. This can be explained by referring to Weick's concept of "sensemaking" in organizations. People often provide explanations for events or phenomena that both fit what transpired and allow them to represent themselves in the best possible light. In that way, it should be no surprise that the gang leaders I interviewed more than 20 years after the founding of SGD and now leading more or less conventional lives would make sense of those founding events in ways that emphasized peace and education and minimized the seamier sides. Karl Weick, *Sensemaking in Organizations* (Thousand Oaks: Sage, 1995).

12. We will return to the importance of "good violence" to end the "bad violence" of all against all as a necessary act to cement community. René Gerard, *Violence and the Sacred* (Baltimore: Johns Hopkins University Press, 1972). One college-educated Folks leader I

interviewed discussed his gangs' "moral education" and stressed values of minimizing violence. He explained SGD to me with some surprising political allusions and ended with a justification for resorting to violence to stop violence.

> The concept itself was a tool to be used to reeducate members of the union. The executive board wanted members to learn from their past mistakes, and its new vision was to help members of the union better themselves as a people. Their mission was to get members to stop fighting and disrespecting each other and to inform them all that such behavior would not be tolerated. For years they had been fighting each other when the real enemy was the establishment that deprived them all from the basic needs that they were all entitled to under the US Constitution.
>
> Leaders were called upon to come together so that they could combine all their efforts into one. The thought process was that together they could accomplish great things. For years they had been doing things on their own and progress was slow, but with a combined effort things would be better for all of those families who were involved in the process. Ben Franklin said it best: "Life is ten percent what you make it and ninety percent how you take it."
>
> The plan was to unite and start working together so that their members could get a better education, better jobs, and better housing. They were tired of their civil rights being violated on a daily basis by "Chicago's Finest." Working together and adhering to the SGD contract was perceived as the way to accomplish all this.
>
> The new process would now address those individuals who took it upon themselves to either verbally or physically assault a member from another organization. In order to implement such process the union had to assure that they had everyone's buy-in. Those individuals who were allegedly accused of taking the life of one of the union members would be dealt with . . . with extreme prejudice.

13. It might be good to keep roles, identities, and values conceptually distinct. For Castells, identities refer to social actors, e.g., the gang leaders I describe throughout this book. SGD and gangs are prime examples of "resistance identities" as distinct from "legitimizing" and "project" identities. Their identities organize the meaning, while the roles organize the functions, of what they do (6–8). Values, for Castells, appear to coincide with goals and form part of the meaning of an identity. Castells, *The Information Age*, vol. 2, *The Power of Identity*. Selznick says organizations become infused with value as they come to symbolize the community's aspirations, its sense of "identity" (19). "Organizations don't create values as much as embody them" (20). My category "statesman" is modeled on Selznick's definition that a "statesman" or "institutional leader" is "primarily an expert in the promotion and protection of values." Selznick, *Leadership in Administration*, 28.

14. See The *Chicago Tribune*'s article, "Violence Part of the Life for Gang Member," October 3, 1974, for a story about the Deuces' murder of the SCR's Arab. Watson refers to this murder periodically in his book on the Royals, *Romantic Violence in R-World*.

15. Blade explains what his members had to go through once the decision was made to join the Folks Alliance.

Now we have to change all our rules and paperwork, this and that. I did all the foot-work on the streets. So I got a lot of old Deuces from the seventies saying "What the spade mean? What's the dots mean? What the dice mean? What's the shield mean?" I get it all together. I put like "appeals" and everything like in our rules and regulations. I presented it to the meetings. The way they got stuff into the joint was through law-yers back then. They would give the lawyers paperwork. When they got the paper-work in and it came back . . . [shows a three-inch stack of Deuces laws and a six-inch stack of SGD rules].

16. I asked Blade, "Who was more organized, People or Folks?" He made something of an economic comparison:

When we were People they were very organized. But there was no meetings, no orga-nization as far as meetings, but every organization had something going on: This one owned a nightclub; the Unknowns laundered money; PR Stones were about robbery, robbing drug dealers. Somebody had their noses into some niche and it was good. They always had like, the PR Stones owns that bar over there. They own a nightclub. They were organized as far as that concept.

Folks were more organized as far as street talk, put it together on the streets, street unity. When I switched to Folks I said wow, they owned a lot more, they owned car washes, clubs, bigger clubs, they owned a lot more because there are a lot more Latin Folks.

17. See Ianni's detailed discussion of the similarity of unwritten codes of conduct between the Sicilian and American mafias and prison codes between blacks and Puerto Ricans. Ianni, *Black Mafia*, 295–310.

18. This idea was spelled out more clearly by our college-educated Latin Folks leader.

There are many types of contracts used around the world where two or more parties enter with the intentions of creating an obligation of adhering to either a verbal or written agreement. In this particular case the parties involved were entering into a business agreement, and the name of the agreement was called Spanish Growth and Development.

Unlike other contracts such as employment, entertainment or real estate contracts, where the remedy of a breach could lead to compensatory damages and injunctions, the remedy for breaching this contract could result in death to any of the parties involved.

The SGD concept was put together in order for individual families to have a way and a means to communicate, mediate, and resolve conflicts that were taking place on the streets. It was construed with the understanding that all registered families who signed the contract would abide by all the laws set forth by the Executive Board members of the Folks Alliance.

For years disputes pertaining to the actions of members of the Folk Alliance were going on unaddressed either properly or timely, and the result was that of lost broth-ers, young men whose lives could have been saved if there was just a way to democratically address such actions. All the fighting that was taking place in recent years among the families for various reasons was taking its toll as bodies began to pile up in the city morgue. The sad part was, this could have all been avoided had members of these families been offered a means of addressing these issues. And thus La Tabla was formed.

19. This book tells the history of SGD in the same way that social scientists have written about other institutions like the Red Cross, Tennessee Valley Authority, or even the Chicago Police Department. In chapter 6 we will study the rivalry of the subgroups, or families, that ended up shattering the hopes and promises of SGD. I'll show how factionalism is a typical cause of institutional dissolution. Christine Oliver, "The Antecedents of Deinstitutionalization," *Organization Studies* 13, no. 4 (1992): 563–88; Trish Reay and C. R. (Bob) Hinings, "Managing the Rivalry of Competing Institutional Logics," *Organization Studies* 30 (June 2009): 629–52.

CHAPTER FIVE: TWO DAGOS, TWO SPICS, AND A HILLBILLY

1. Lucky's street rep for violence, like Joey Bags's, corresponds to Randol Contreras's vivid description of Pablo in *The Stickup Kids*. The differences between this account and Contreras's is that such brutal methods were seen by Sal and key C-Note$ leaders as crude and lacking the sophistication needed to be an associate or made member of the Outfit. Randol Contreras, *The Stickup Kids: Race, Drugs, Violence, and the American Dream* (London: University of California Press, 2013).

2. Lucky's main business dealings were with Coco from the nearby Harrison Gents, even though he had issues with them. One of the Gents, Tomás, had been sent to prison for the murder of Lucky's brother, Red, though Lucky had decided the real shooter was "Apples" from the Latin Jivers. Lucky had also ripped off 200 pounds of weed from a Gent drug dealer, and his reckless actions almost started a war. But business is business, and his long-term dealings with the Harrison Gents prompted prison-bound Lucky to inquire whether the Gents would sponsor the C-Note$ into membership of the Latin Folks, and thus he would be protected in prison. The Gents had agreed but also began to nibble on C-Note$ turf while Lucky was locked up.

3. For the English hit, e.g., http://americannewspost.com/joseph-fosco/2432 /difronzo-organized-hit-on-chuckie-english/. Adam Salas was arrested in 2012 during a police raid on David Ramirez's burglary operation. According to the newspaper clipping, Salas tried to get rid of "30 grams of heroin and 21 grams of crack cocaine, as well as 'a large quantity' of drugs and equipment used in the drug trade"; http://www.chicago tribune.com/news/local/breaking/chi-cops-parolee-caught-with-more-than-100000 -in-stolen-goods-20121118,0,7214258.story.

4. The Chicago Crime Commission, led by former CPD Superintendent Joey Weis, was embarrassed by the release the 2012 edition of the Gang Book, since several of the gang members pictured in the book had left the gang life decades before. Inaccuracies, like the mislabeling of the LK section at Huron and Hoyne, plagued the book, and Weis soon resigned. This former FBI agent's impact on Chicago was slight and brief.

5. See *The People of the State of Illinois, Plaintiff-Appellee, v. Sotirios Georgakapoulos, Defendant-Appellant*, No. 1-97-2537, March 16, 1999.

CHAPTER SIX: FAMILY FEUDS

1. Paul DiMaggio, "Interest and Agency in Institutional Theory," in *Institutional Patterns and Organizations: Culture and Environment*, ed. Lynne G. Zucker (Cambridge, MA: Ballinger, 1988), 3–21. He says "The institutionalization of an organizational form requires institutional work to justify that form's public theory" (15). I follow Selznick's classic descriptions of institutional processes.

2. "Paseo Boricua, which stretches along Division Street from Western Avenue to Mozart, represents a microcosm of the Puerto Rican historical and cultural experience. The 50 light poles adorned with laser-etched wrought iron banners, representing images of the three cultural experiences that define the Puerto Rican people (the Taino, Spanish and West African), the 16 placitas along the walkway, and the variety of businesses with a Puerto Rican accent, all testify to this reality"; http://www.paseoboricua.com. A major report on the history of Puerto Ricans in Chicago has this to say:

> In recent years, Puerto Rican activism has once again focused on the issue of displacement and gentrification. In 1995, under the leadership of former 26th Alderman Billy Ocasio, Paseo Boricua's two massive steel flags were erected. In the eyes of many community leaders we talked to as part of this research, Paseo Boricua represents an important "logro" (success) for Puerto Ricans in Chicago. It is viewed as evidence of the struggle and desire for community in Chicago. As one community leader put it, "one of our major assets is that we've learned how to do community building and we've done it ourselves." Although our research suggests that many Puerto Ricans have moved away from the area that is commonly identified as the "heart of the community," Paseo, nevertheless, continues to function as a "home." It also functions as a set of rhetorical maneuvers aggressively claiming space against outside developers and gentrifiers who do not wish to build affordable housing for community residents or who do not value Puerto Rican themes. All in all, Paseo and its related initiatives are, indeed, spectacular successes, but underneath the surface there are numerous fragilities and ironies, for it has not been easy for these under-funded activists to shape a politics and economics that fight other visions of what the city and these specific neighborhoods ought to be. In short this report hopes to capture some of this complex story. http://puertorican chicago.org/report.html.

Chicago's Latino neighborhoods were most often the target of gentrifiers rather than African American areas for no reason I can determine except racism. Humboldt Park is home to about 50 percent of all of Chicago's approximately 100,000 Puerto Ricans, half of whom live in poverty. The C-Note$ West Side had seen the entrance of Latinos in large numbers, but significant portions of the Italian population had stubbornly remained. In the 2000s the Patch faced gentrification as well, with a good example the "yuppifica-

tion" of Sal's Aberdeen Club; http://yochicago.com/is-humboldt-park-a-puerto-rican
-community/7108/. A rough timetable of gentrification and resistance follows:

1990s—The Puerto Rican community starts to increase in Logan Square, Belmont
Cragin, and Hermosa, while also decreasing in West Town due to encroaching
gentrification.

1993—After years of struggle with the City of Chicago, the flags of Paseo Boricua are
erected on Division Street. Billy Ocasio is appointed twenty-sixth Ward alderman
by mayor Richard M. Daley to fill the unexpired term of Luis Guitérrez, who was
elected congressman.

1999—Puerto Ricans in Chicago, leaders of the longtime struggle for the release of
Puerto Rican Independence political prisoners, are instrumental in the 1999 release
of eleven prisoners.

2003—Puerto Rican Chicago's own congressman Luis Guitérrez is instrumental in
pressuring the US Navy to finally leave Vieques, Puerto Rico, in 2003 after over
sixty years of military practices that included the use of toxic chemicals.

http://puertoricanchicago.org/pdf/01_History_and_activism.pdf.

3. The New York Latin Kings' transformation into a community organization is documented in Brotherton and Barrios, *Between Black and Gold*. At least two movies have
been produced on the LK experience, including a sensitive HBO exposé, *The Latin Kings:
A Street Gang Story*. See the trailer at http://www.youtube.com/watch?v=PneRfRYysPA.
An uncritical movie, made with the participation of LK leaders was *Black & Gold*. You can
watch it online at http://www.snagfilms.com/films/title/black_and_gold.

4. Both Timothy "Bimbo" Gilfillan and Jeff "Tuffy" Gilfillan, early SCR leaders, were
among those killed in clashes with Hispanic gangs. The Gaylord/Royal wars are reported
from the Gaylord perspective by "Michael Scott" in *Lords of Lawndale* and *Lords of Kilbourn*. Read further tales of Royals "sex and violence" in Watson, *Romantic Violence in
R-World*.

5. The GD/SCR alliance was discovered by police in 1980, but how it fit into the Folks
coalition was unknown. Jerry Thornton, "91 Arrested in Raid," *Chicago Tribune*, August 19,
1980.

6. See *The People of the State of Illinois, Plaintiff-Appellee v. Sotirios Georgakapoulos,
Defendant-Appellant*.

7. The Cobras were also the beneficiary of an SGD decision as La Tabla was getting
started. In 1989, as SGD was being established, two members of the Latin Eagles, who
became an Almighty gang, testified in a murder trial against two Spanish Cobras, Big
Juan Johnson and his brother Henry. The Cobras grieved this violation of SGD laws to
La Tabla, who ruled in their favor. One of the investigating detectives, Ernesto Guevera,
had a long history of eliciting false confessions and perjured testimony. When many years
later, the Latin Eagles witnesses who had broken SGD rules recanted, Big Juan won the
largest settlement in Chicago history, $21 million. After his release Big Juan worked for the
gang peace group CeaseFire and was arrested in Operation Snake Charmer. Johnson was
arrested as he discussed a crack sale on his cell phone. Indigo, the former street leader of

the Cobras, insisted to me that Big Juan was set up because police were "out to get him" after he won his big settlement. Others I interviewed were not so charitable about Big Juan's capacity to make sound decisions. See appendix 6 for the text of the SGD grievance on Big Juan's case. See http://www.chicagotribune.com/news/local/chi-federal-police -lawsuitjun23,0,3802704.story, and http://www.law.umich.edu/special/exoneration /Pages/casedetail.aspx?caseid=3331 and http://articles.chicagotribune.com/2008-10-16 /news/0810150865_1_gang-violence-anti-violence-undercover.

8. For the famous raid by the FBI on the Apalachin Commission meeting and a list of those attending, see http://www.thechicagosyndicate.com/2007/11/mobsters-at -apalachin-mob-meeting.html. Chicago Outfit representatives had yet to arrive when the retreat was raided.

9. For more on the Montañez case, see http:jacquelinemontanez.com.

10. Scott explains a cognitive view of institutionalized action as composing "social scripts, routines, and performance programs." Scott, *Institutions and Organizations*, 13.

11. The Herrera Family was skilled in the art of corruption in Durango, Mexico, con- trolling police and government officials. See http://esp.mexico.org/lapalabra/una/18397 /the-herrera-family-in-durango. For a discussion of the disputable FBI tactics, see Gavin, *Operation Durango Connection*. For the facts concerning Manuel Herrera's March 28, 1984, arrest, see http://law.justia.com/cases/federal/appellate-courts/F2/757/144/426040/. The Herrera Family purported to avoid dealing directly with Outfit wise guys, preferring their direct connections with gangs. Gavin, 81. The conviction of Angel Herrera was put in jeopardy by the murder of a confidential informant, Jose Martinez, who wore a wire that led to Angel's conviction. Murder charges were not pressed on Herrera when it was learned that Martinez had also worn a wire on nine cops who were running a related protection racket. Martinez was not murdered by the cartel drug czar, but by an officer named Lafavor, one of the nine dirty cops. The tale of Officer Lafavor and the cops' protection racket is reported in Gavin, 289. Angel Herrera, the "hero" of Gavin's book— Gavin was his lawyer—settled on West 26th Street in the heart of Mexican Little Village and cemented Herrera Family connections to Mexican gangs there. Gavin, 27.

12. Among the reasons Juan "mellowed" was my expert witness testimony in the case of another Cobra charged with murder. Trust is earned and always takes time.

13. In appendix 7, I reprint the Insane Family by-laws. Take note of the "Triple 8s" at the top of the page.

CHAPTER SEVEN: ENVELOPES AND ETHNIC POLITICS

1. Ianni, *Black Mafia*, 327. Ianni speculates why Italians and Hispanics get along, in- cluding common Catholic religion and emphasis on family (319). Ianni also forecast that the drug business would be the ticket to both blacks and Hispanics in building organized crime enterprises. He comments, "Finally, there is the possibility of using drug monies to corrupt police and other government officials without whose protection no form of orga- nized crime could long endure" (318). He finds Hobsbawm's analysis of social bandits to be applicable to conditions in the black ghetto: "Mafias tend to develop in societies where

there is not an effective social order and where Mafia provides a parallel machine of law and organized power. . . . Each of these conditions exists in black ghettoes today" (326). He points out that "black militancy in crime draws at least some of its value orientation from the same sources as more legitimate protests among blacks" (84). He concludes: "The new black Mafioso, will, in fact, be an urban social bandit" (326). See also Eric Hobsbawm, *Bandits* (New York City: Pantheon, 1969).

2. Sal goes on to puncture stereotypes about Latinos, as well as, in a way, contradict himself.

> You have people bad-mouth Latinos and say things about Latinos, but they're not as dumb as some think they are. They're making a lot of money—heart, sweat, and tears—and it's gonna continue, and they're getting smarter because they're putting their people and educating their people, they're putting them into the law schools, they're putting them into the medical field, they're putting them into political science. I mean, it's just evolving and evolving and it's goin'—it's going fast.

3. Thrasher spends a few pages on Prohibition and the $1 million a year the syndicate paid to politicians. He says at one point, "While the power of the gangs to corrupt public officials has been due in part to their ability to deliver votes, it has been greatly augmented by the enormous profits which they have derived in recent years from the manufacture and sale of illicit alcoholic beverages—profits which have undoubtedly amounted to millions of dollars. . . . These huge profits have in some cases enabled gang leaders to purchase protection from interference." Frederic Thrasher, *The Gang: A Study of 1,313 Gangs in Chicago* (Chicago: University of Chicago, 1927), 480. But Thrasher fails to understand the dynamics of the consolidation of gangs violently brought about by Capone and how his mob used its "enormous profits" to institutionalize. In fact, Thrasher dismisses as a media "crime wave" the record homicide totals of the 1920s (448). His gang stories are long on the Irish and short on Italians. His most prominent Italian example is Sam Cardinelli, a Black Hand mobster who was executed on April 15, 1921 (it happened while he was sitting in a chair: he refused to get up out of it). Cardinelli was the model for the famous movie *Little Caesar*. Neither Capone, nor his mentor, Johnny Torrio, merit mention in *The Gang*. See also Luzi, *The Boys in Chicago Heights* (Charleston, SC: History Press, 2012).

4. Daley's history was one of unbridled opportunism. As state's attorney he had given Jon Burge an award and failed to investigate claims of torture. His main accomplishment, aside from getting ready to run for mayor, was a focus on "juvenile gangs." Bernard Epton, a Hyde Park liberal Republican, embraced racism while the machine was being lectured by the national Democratic Party to support Washington, with their eyes on the black vote in the 1984 presidential election against President Reagan. Jane Byrne threatened a write-in race, and Daley quietly endorsed Washington, though his Bridgeport base went overwhelmingly for Epton. Epton, intoxicated with the potential of a Republican winning city hall, simply ignored Latino issues, and it cost him. "The single most important aspect of the nationality vote was the dramatic shift in support among Latinos for Harold Washington." Abdul Alkalimat and Doug Gills, *Harold Washington and the Crisis of Black Power in Chicago* (Chicago: Twenty First Century Books, 1989), 104. Larry

Bennett presents an alternative perspective. In praise of Richard M. Daley as a "Builder" and reform mayor, he argues that HDO was an example of the inability of the regular machine to deliver. Why it was collapsed back into the machine after multiple scandals is not addressed. In Bennett's survey of the accomplishments of Mayor Daley II, little is said about the police or Daley's praise of Jon Burge and refusal to prosecute him or embark on any meaningful reform of the CPD. See chapter 3, "The Mayor Among his Peers," in Bennett, *The Third City: Chicago and American Urbanism* (Chicago: University of Chicago Press, 2010). For a perspective that suggests, like Sal, that the machine may not be dead after all, see William J. Grimshaw, *Bitter Fruit: Black Politics and the Chicago Machine, 1931–1991* (Chicago: University of Chicago Press, 1992), 213.

5. By 2010, Latinos had nearly reached parity with whites and African Americans, each having about a third of Chicago residents. According to a Loyola University report on population trends, Hispanics accounted for all of the growth population in the city of Chicago since 2000; http://www.luc.edu/media/lucedu/sociology/pdfs/johnson/Chicago_Report.pdf. For a more political analysis see http://news.medill.northwestern.edu/chicago/news.aspx?id=182511. See the analytical treatment of Hispanics and the Washington administration in Maria de los Angeles Torres, "The Commission on Latino Affairs: A Case Study of Community Empowerment," in *Harold Washington and the Neighborhoods*, ed. Pierre Clavel and Wim Wiewel (New Brunswick, NJ: Rutgers University Press, 1991), 165–87. The final two sentences in Dick W. Simpson's important book on Chicago politics say: "As the fastest growing population, Latinos will inevitably play a more important role in Chicago's politics. They may not be willing to continue as junior partner, as they have in the reign of Mayors Washington and Daley." Simpson, *Rogues, Rebels, and Rubber Stamps: The Politics of the Chicago City Council from 1863 to the Present* (Boulder: Westview Press, 2001), 290.

6. Andrew Martin and Laurie Cohen, "Ex-Mell Worker Tie to Gang Told: Links Come Out in Murder Trial," *Chicago Tribune*, November 10, 1996.

7. Court documents on the Lozano/Latin King connection can be found at http://il.findacase.com/research/wfrmDocViewer.aspx/xq/fac.19880310_0000341.IL.htm/qx.

8. The poverty rates in 2010 were three times higher for blacks than whites at 32.2 percent, with Hispanics at 23.7 percent and whites at 10 percent. http://quickfacts.census.gov/qfd/states/17/1714000.html. http://www.chicagonow.com/chicago-muckrakers/2011/02/second-city-or-dead-last-chicagos-sky-high-minority-poverty-rate/.

9. Sara Paretsky, *Total Recall* (New York: Random House, 2001), 243.

10. Pierre Clavel and Wim Wiewel, introduction to Clavel and Wiewel, eds., *Harold Washington and the Neighborhoods*, 24.

11. For example, in 1999, Daley spent $3.41 million on the mayoral primary, more than two-thirds of it for consultants and promotional material. Still there was a tidy sum left over for getting out the vote. Richard C. Longworth, "The Political City," in *Global Chicago*, ed. Charles Madigan (Champaign: University of Illinois Press, 2003), 79. Some reformers argue that "bossism" and its corruption have gotten worse under the new Daley administration, e.g., James L. Merriner, *Grafters and Goo Goos: Corruption and Reform in Chicago, 1833–2003* (Carbondale: Southern Illinois University Press, 2004), 249. Simpson

relates how Daley II's support now comes more from "wealthy lawyers, lobbyists, bankers, stock traders and the construction firms and unions that depend on contracts from city hall" than from the grunt force of the machine. Dick W. Simpson, *Rogues, Rebels, and Rubber Stamps: The Politics of the Chicago City Council from 1863 to the Present* (Boulder: Westview Press, 2001), 289. The Shakman Decree abolished much of the job patronage the machine wielded and was replaced by contracts called "pin stripe patronage."

CHAPTER EIGHT: POLICE CORRUPTION
FROM THE SUITES TO THE STREETS

1. This is the standard social disorganization model for criminology. In gangs, this perspective is best presented by Irving Spergel's "Comprehensive Model," adopted by the Justice Department. Spergel advocated a mix of police suppression with opportunities provision, social intervention, community mobilization, and organization change and development. See Irving A. Spergel, *The Youth Gang Problem: A Community Approach* (New York: Oxford University Press, 1995). For an online description of the comprehensive model: http://www.nationalgangcenter.gov/Comprehensive-Gang-Model/About. Spergel himself was a dedicated adherent of opportunities provision as the key factor and an early advocate of working with former gang members in outreach. Not publicized by the DOJ, Spergel's model program in the Little Village neighborhood of Chicago, home of both Latin Folks 2-6ers as well as the Mexican branch of the Latin Kings, was sabotaged by the Chicago Police Department and denied funding. Just browse through any major gang research text, like Howell's or Klein's, and you will look in vain for more than isolated and unremarkable examples of police corruption or brutality. While gang hostility to police is noted in most (but not all) studies, no major gang study treats police corruption as a central variable in understanding gangs. For example: James C. Howell, *Gangs in America's Communities* (Los Angeles: Sage, 2012); Malcolm W. Klein and Cheryl L. Maxsen, *Street Gang Patterns and Policies* (New York: Oxford, 2006); and Malcolm W. Klein, *The American Street Gang: Its Nature, Prevalence, and Control* (New York: Oxford University Press, 1995).

2. At a press conference announcing the release of a report on police corruption in Chicago (for which I served as principle investigator), I began my remarks by arguing that Chicago's histories of corruption and gangs are related. To tackle corruption, I argued, is one way to weaken the influence of gangs. This is one of the conclusions of this book as well. For the complete report on Chicago police corruption: Hagedorn, et al., http://www.uic.edu/depts/pols/ChicagoPolitics/policecorruption.pdf.

3. For example, Almir Maljević, Darko Datzer, Elmedin Muratbegović, and Muhamed Budimlić, "Overtly about Police and Corruption" (Sarajevo: Association of Criminalists in Bosnia and Herzegovina, 2006). In the introduction, they state, referencing the World Bank, "Corruption in Bosnia and Herzegovina is characterised by the insufficiency of public administration which is reflected in widespread bribery in public offices; distorted business environment and a significant burden on poor households, exacerbating poverty and inequality" (10). See also Rasma Karklins, *The System Made Me Do It* (London:

M. E. Sharp, 2005). For a discussion of state takeover, see Jean-François Bayart, Stephen Ellis, and Béatrice Hibou, *The Criminalization of the State in Africa* (Oxford: International African Institute, 1999). Samuel Huntington provides the definitive explanation of the negative correlation between modernization and corruption that I contest by spotlighting Chicago, hardly a "weak state." Samuel P. Huntington, "Modernization and Corruption," in *Political Corruption: A Handbook*, ed. Arnold J. Heidenheimer, Michael Johnston, and Victor T. Levine (New Brunswick, NJ: Transaction Books, 1989).

4. William J. Chambliss, *On the Take: From Petty Crooks to Presidents* (Bloomington: Indiana University Press, 1978), 154, 6.

5. "According to this theory, which bordered on official Department doctrine, any policeman found to be corrupt must promptly be denounced as a rotten apple in an otherwise clean barrel. It must never be admitted that his individual corruption may be symptomatic of underlying disease." Knapp Commission, *Report of the Commission to Investigate Alleged Police Corruption* (New York: George Braziller, 1972), 6, 7. Murphy's statement can be found in Tim Newburn, "Understanding and Preventing Police Corruption," in *Police Research Series*, ed. Development and Statistics Directorate Research (London: Policing and Reducing Crime Unit, 1999), 15.

6. Susan Rose-Ackerman, "Corruption: Greed, Culture, and the State," *Yale Law Journal Online* 120 (2010): 125–40. See also Richard C. Scott, "Corruption, Machine Politics and Social Change," *American Political Science Review* 63, no. 4 (1969): 1142–50. Transparency International is an international anticorruption organization: http://www.transparency .org/. Rose-Ackerman is critical of the ethnographic approach and argues in a convincing manner: "The state is here to stay, whatever romantics on the libertarian right or on the cultural-studies left might wish. We had better stop bemoaning that fact and instead seek realistic reforms that balance state capacity with political will." The Chicago police anticorruption report is an example of this hard-nosed approach. It has been ignored by both the CPD and city machine.

7. Richard C. Lindberg, *To Serve and Collect: Chicago Politics and Police Corruption from the Lager Beer Riot to the Summerdale Scandal: 1855–1960* (Carbondale: Southern Illinois University Press, 1998), 317. See also Chicago Crime Commission, *Report on Organized Crime* (Chicago: Chicago Crime Commission, 1971), 2. For more background on Chicago corruption see John Landesco, *Organized Crime in Chicago* (Chicago: University of Chicago Press, 1968 [1929]); and Karen Abbott, *Sin in the Second City: Madams, Ministers, Playboys, and the Battle for America's Soul* (New York: Random House, 2007).

8. See Lindberg, *To Serve and Collect*, 215 and 265. For a newspaper report on the sergeants' union scam: http://articles.chicagotribune.com/2012-06-06/news/ct-met -police-officer-prison-20120606_1_sergeants-dues-john-pallohusky.

9. Arthur J. Bilek, *The First Vice Lord: Big Jim Colosimo and the Ladies of the Levee* (Nashville: Cumberland House, 2008); and Mars Eghigian, Jr., *After Capone: The Life and World of Chicago Mob Boss Frank "the Enforcer" Nitti* (Nashville: Cumberland House, 2006).

10. Hanhardt's tale is more amazing than I can fit in. This is from a story in the *New York Daily News*: "In 1986, while still on the job, he acted as a defense witness in the Ne-

vada conspiracy trial of Anthony Spilotro, the Chicago Outfit's man in Las Vegas. Hanhardt's testimony helped discredit one of the mobster's key accusers." See http://www.nydailynews.com/news/crime/chicago-crooked-article-1.291259#ixzz2S8tLKG1Q. On Hanhardt's release from prison, see John Kass's story: http://articles.chicago tribune.com/2011–07–20/news/ct-met-kass-0720–20110720_1_bill-hanhardt -hanhardt-friend-federal-prison. In it Kass also describes Hanhardt's ties to Outfit boss Joey Lombardo.

11. Contained in Roti's indictment were charges that he attempted to fix a murder trial for an El Rukn gang member. The El Rukns, formerly known as the Blackstone Rangers, ordered its soldiers at times to work as hit men for hire in the prisons, including contract murders for the Outfit. Both Harris and Outfit hit man Frank Culotta describe the actions of a Blackstone Ranger leader, "General Thunder." Henry L. Harris Jr., *Epitome of Courage* (Chicago: 1st Books Library, 2001), 123. Dennis N. Griffin and Frank Culotta, *Culotta: The Life of a Chicago Criminal, Las Vegas Mobster, and Government Witness* (Las Vegas, NV: Huntington Press, 2007), 100.

12. Cooley said this about the First Ward: "Like Capone, Accardo saw politics as crucial in keeping his stranglehold on criminal activities in Chicago, and the key to that power was the First Ward. The city had fifty wards but none compared to the First. In terms of power and prestige, it contained both the city's central business district, known as the Loop, and the mansions on the Gold Coast. It had the factories and packing plants on the South Side, and equally important, the slums around them, where the Mob could run its rackets and recruit its soldiers." Robert Cooley and Hillel Levin, *When Corruption Was King: How I Helped the Mob Rule Chicago, Then Brought the Outfit Down* (New York: Carroll and Graf, 2004), 108. In another place, Cooley says about Hanhardt's indictment: "No way was Bill Hanhardt just one bad apple. To this date, no one has ever taken a second look at all the officers he promoted and supervised in his last years as chief of detectives" (318).

13. On Rodriguez and Milito: http://www.ipsn.org/milito.html. You can read the whole complicated story in a six-part series by David Jackson, *Chicago Tribune*, October 2000. "The vast majority of Chicago officers perform their duty with unnoticed valor. But Zonis is one of at least a dozen Chicago officers who have come under FBI or internal police scrutiny because of suspected crime syndicate ties since 1985, a *Tribune* examination of law enforcement records shows. His law enforcement career exposes disturbing flaws in Chicago police procedures for vetting recruits and investigating officers suspected of wrongdoing." Rodriguez was caught on a secret videotape visiting a mob hangout tailor shop. But he was not alone. Jackson reports:

> The surveillance reports show that the parade of Saturday morning regulars ranged from then-Deputy Supt. George Ruckrich, the department's third in command, to Charles V. Gentile, a former Chicago police sergeant who had been forced to resign in 1987 after he was convicted of using a false name, a misdemeanor, while being questioned by federal agents. U.S. Drug Enforcement Administration officials had stopped Gentile after he allegedly tried to pick up a cocaine-packed suitcase at O'Hare International Airport.

Police Internal Affairs Division reports list several crime figures known to hang out with police brass at the tailor shop over the years. Among them were insurance swindler Allen Dorfman, who was gunned down in a 1983 mob hit, and former police officer Anthony Chiavola, now deceased, who was convicted in the storied Chicago mob case that exposed crime syndicate skimming at the Tropicana casino in Las Vegas.

Another tailor shop regular, former detective Fred Pascente, said reputed book-maker Matt Raimondi also frequented the shop during the 1990s. "I was in there with him a number of times," said Pascente, who resigned from the department in 1993 and later pleaded guilty to committing insurance fraud with a group of criminals. . . .

Days after Rodriguez walked into the tailor shop, the Internal Affairs Division surveillance was shut down.

Then-internal affairs chief Raymond Risley said in an interview that he cut short the investigation because he felt it would be ethically questionable for him to conduct a secret probe of the superintendent to whom he reported.

Cooley reports on two more CPD officers who were made members of the Outfit: Blackie Pesoli and Ricky Borelli. Cooley and Levin, *When Corruption Was King*, 118. http://www.ipsn.org/zonis.html

14. On Zonis: http://www.ipsn.org/zonis.html.

15. Merriam's grandfather, Charles E. Merriam, was a University of Chicago political science professor, former Hyde Park alderman, and unsuccessful reform candidate for mayor in 1911. His nephew, former Fifth Ward Ald. Robert Merriam, was a decorated World War II captain who ran as a Republican against Mayor Richard J. Daley in 1955, then served on president Dwight Eisenhower's staff. As an alderman and later as a public figure, Robert Merriam was a fierce critic of the way Chicago's political patronage system had clouded the integrity of its police department. In one speech, he demanded that Daley reform the police department after the Summerdale District police burglary scandal broke in 1960. David Jackson, *Chicago Tribune*, October 23, 2000, 1.

16. Merriner, *Grafters and Goo Goos*, 253.

17. See Jackson's series on police corruption, *Chicago Tribune*, October 24, 2000.

18. The Marquette Ten were in a way transition figures of corruption. They included two cops with some shady Outfit ties. One of the Ten, Thomas Ambrose, died in prison after his conviction and his son, John, was shepherded through life by William Guide, a fa-ther figure who also was the brother of fellow Marquette Ten convict, Joe Guide. Ambrose, who became a deputy US marshal, was sentenced to prison in 2009 in the mob-busting Family Secrets trial. Ambrose had used his job as US marshal to gather information to give to the Outfit on hit man turned informant Nick Calabrese. John Ambrose siphoned infor-mation to Joe Guide on Calabrese's whereabouts and what he might say; Joe Guide then passed the information on to his buddies in the Outfit. For the Family Secrets trial see John Kass's column at http://articles.chicagotribune.com/2009-10-28/news/0910270444_1 _ex-cop-chicago-outfit-witness-protection-program. James Tuohy and Rob Warden, *Greylord: Justice, Chicago Style* (New York: Putnam, 1989). For Cline's controversial role, see http://articles.chicagotribune.com/2003-09-28/news/0309280045_1_chicago-police -officer-search-warrants-deputy-commissioner.

19. In my field notes, I wrote that this officer told me, "We made lots of arrests and that upset the big boys." What did that mean, I asked him? "We cut into their pocketbook and they went after us." He explained that his unit arrested so many people that some of them were kicking back to other cops, including higher-ups who became angry at them, and thus their indictment. Compare this to Ianni's informant in *Black Mafia*: "If a small time cop on the beat tries to fuck with one of the big men, though, it could mean a lot of money and he will be interfering with the sergeant's or the lieutenant's take and so when the sergeant gets wind of it, probably from the operator himself who will call and ask what the hell is going on here, the sergeant must get the cop out of the way, transfer him or talk to him" (287). Or if that doesn't work, maybe get him indicted? Other stories of police corruption lend some support to my officer's contention. The *Chicago Tribune*'s Annie Sweeney reported on November 2, 2012, about supervisory collusion with two officers, Sgt. Ronald Watts and officer Kallatt Mohammed, who were shaking down drug dealers. Two other officers, Shannon Spalding and Daniel Echeverria, reported to their superiors their suspicions of the shakedowns. According to Sweeney, "But when they told their supervisors, they were ordered to 'disregard' the wrongdoing. And when, as a last resort, they went to the FBI with their claims, high-ranking police officials labeled them 'rats' and retaliated against them by putting them in do-nothing jobs." Commanders told the officers, "Sometimes you have to turn a blind eye" to wrongdoing, according to a lawsuit filed against the CPD.

20. Peter K. Manning, *Policing Contingencies* (Chicago: University of Chicago Press, 2003).

21. Tim Newburn's review of the police corruption literature contains many key findings which apply to Chicago and the war on drugs. For example:

- police corruption is pervasive, continuing and not bounded by rank;
- any definition of corruption should cover both "financial" and "process" corruption, and should acknowledge the varying means, ends and motives of corrupt activities;
- the boundary between "corrupt" and "non-corrupt" activities is difficult to define, primarily because this is at heart an ethical problem;
- police corruption cannot simply be explained as the product of a few "bad apples";
- the "causes" of corruption include: factors that are intrinsic to policing as a job; the nature of police organisations; the nature of "police culture"; the opportunities for corruption presented by the "political" and "task" environments; and, the nature and extent of the effort put in to controlling corruption;
- some areas of policing are more prone to corruption than others;
- although there are many barriers to successful corruption control, there is evidence that police agencies can be reformed;
- reform needs to go beyond the immediately identified problem;
- reform must look at the political and task environments as well as the organisation itself;
- reform tends not to be durable; and
- continued vigilance and scepticism is vital.

Newburn, "Understanding and Preventing Police Corruption." See also David A. Carter, "Drug-Related Corruption of Police Officers: A Contemporary Typology," *Journal of Criminal Justice* 18 (1990): 85–98.

22. Steve Warmbir, *Chicago Tribune*, January 19, 2003. All quotes from Miedzianowski at his trial were taken from the series of stories written by Warmbir. This sentence was taken from taped conversation with a fellow police officer.

23. Steve Warmbir, *Chicago Sun-Times*, February 8, 2007.

24. See *US v. Joseph Miedzianowski, Alina Lis, and Omar Feliciano Defendants*, Case No. 98 Cr 923 in the United States District Court for the Northern District of Illinois, Eastern Division. Alina Lis returned to court and eventually had her sentence cut to twenty years even though she steadfastly refused to testify against Miedzianowski. Todd Lighty, "Cop's Mistress Has Sentence Cut," *Chicago Tribune*, October 4, 2006.

25. Ray Risley, head of Internal Affairs at the time and who conducted the investigation of Miedzianowski's alleged misconduct with ATF, insisted to me that IAD received no information at all on Miedzianowski's drug dealing before 1997 and implied that the ATF case by the US attorney Brian Netols was a frame-up.

26. Yes, there were more police officers than just Joe and his partner, John Galligan, involved in the drug conspiracy. For example, from the *Chicago Tribune*: "Chicago police Detective Jon Woodall and officer James Benson, along with fellow Grand Central District officer Peter Matich—who did not work on any pending drug cases—are charged with stealing 11 pounds of cocaine from an impounded car in 1998. Each plotted to receive $12,000 from the sale of the drugs, said the federal indictment unveiled Monday. Gang specialist Joseph Miedzianowski, sentenced to life in prison last week for rampant corruption, referred the officers to a drug dealer who could sell the coke for them, prosecutors said." Frank Main, "Cops, Prosecutors Looking into '98 Drug-Related Slaying," *Chicago Sun-Times*, January 30, 2003.

27. For more evidence that Miedzianowski was a not a sole bad apple who practiced these techniques, here is a court document of a more recent case of CPD corruption that illustrates the way it works.

Mike Shamah and Richard Doroniuk were corrupt Chicago police officers. They worked as partners in the 22nd District on a tactical unit and would often patrol high-crime gang areas. In 2004, they began discussing the idea of keeping money they seized from suspected drug dealers during traffic stops and searches of premises.

From 2005 through October 2006, the partners put their scheme into action. If a suspect was unsure about the exact amount of cash he had on his person, Shamah and Doroniuk would inventory some of the cash and pocket the rest. They would take the money on the spot or withhold a portion of the money during the booking and inventory process back at the station. The officers also took drugs so they could plant them on people if a future stop or search did not establish probable cause for an arrest.

In May 2006, Shamah and Doroniuk began to work with drug dealer Larry Cross. Cross became their personal informant and guide to drug dealers who could be counted on to have large amounts of cash or drugs. Cross also became their go-to

"John Doe" informant for the purposes of obtaining search warrants from state judges, meaning that he provided the basis for a warrant without being named. Several warrant searches were based on false information provided by Cross. During vehicle stops and premises searches, Shamah and Doroniuk used guns, handcuffs, and other police powers to break down doors and restrain suspects. The partners evenly split any proceeds once they determined if and in what amount Cross should be paid.

United States of America, Plaintiff-Appellee, v. Mahmoud Shamah, Defendant-Appellant, No. 09-2767, argued May 28, 2010–October 12, 2010.

28. Editorial Board, "A Matter of Trust," *Chicago Sun-Times*, December 21, 1998.

29. The ten officers were Jerome Finnigan, Keith Herrera, Carl Suchocki, Thomas Sherry, Bart Maka, Brian Pratscher, Donovan Markiewicz, Guadalupe Salinas, Stephen DelBosque and Eric Olsen. Officers Thomas Sherry and Carl Suchocki had their charges dropped in February 2009 because they could not be placed at the scene of the crimes. Officers Stephen DelBosque and Eric Olsen pleaded guilty in April 2011 to conducting illegal searches and lying about it, in court or before a grand jury. Officers Bart Maka, Brian Pratscher, and Guadalupe Salinas pleaded guilty to charges of felony theft; and officer Donovan Markiewicz pleaded guilty to charges of official misconduct in September 2009. Herrera was charged in April 2011 along with officer Jerome Finnigan on charges of tax evasion and conspiracy to violate the civil rights of individuals. Finnigan also pleaded guilty in April 2011 to conspiracy to commit murder for hire and hiring a former hit man to kill former SOS member Keith Herrera; http://articles.chicagotribune .com/2012-05-05/news/ct-met-sos-officer-0506-20120505_1_light-sentences-police -officer-officer-keith-herrera. See also Hillel Levin, "Officer Finnigan," *Playboy*, April 2012; and Katie Couric's interview with Keith Herrera at http://www.cbsnews.com /video/watch/?id=4143148n.

30. For these and many more reports of convicted Chicago police officers, see Hagedorn et al., "Crime, Corruption, and Cover-ups in the Chicago Police Department," MS, University of Illinois–Chicago Political Science Department, January 17, 2013.

31. *United States of America v. Saul Rodriguez et al.*, United States District Court, Northern District of Illinois Eastern Division, No. 09 Cr 332, Government's Evidentiary Proffer Supporting the Admissibility of Co-Conspirator Statements, 17. The proffer also states: "Glenn Lewellen served the Rodriguez Enterprise and the Rodriguez DTO by, among other things, directing and participating in the illegal activities of the Enterprise, including, but not limited to, obstruction of justice, kidnapping, robbery, and narcotics trafficking. Lewellen drew on his experience as a Chicago police officer and provided certain members and associates of the Enterprise with information concerning the fact of, and extent of, ongoing federal criminal investigations into the Enterprise's illegal activities" (10). Rodriguez was later asked by Jesús Vicente Zambada Niebla, or Vicentillo, a high-ranking Sinaloa cartel official, to assassinate the Flores brothers, cartel operatives who were turning state's witness on Vicentillo and El Chapo's organization. ("El Chapo" was named in 2013 as Public Enemy Number 1 by the Chicago Crime Commission; http:// www.cnn.com/2013/02/14/justice/chicago-public-enemy.)

CHAPTER NINE: THE ECSTASY AND THE AGONY

1. Donald Black, "Crime as Social Control," *American Sociological Review* 48 (February 1983): 34–45.

2. The C-Note$ were living a good life:

One of the Note$' associates owned his own business, and every year he would throw a customer appreciation party for his patrons. He would get top-shelf liquor cases and keep them in storage just for the party. Did he buy them retail? What do you think? His employees never had a clue that the liquor had fell off a truck. All I know is that they loved the guy and thought he was the best boss ever. He did throw some kick-ass parties—he just was not the big spender everybody thought he was. All I could say is no one could ever say that they went hungry or thirsty at one of his shindigs.

3. This kind of deadly verbal duel eventually became commonplace in Chicago. See Geoff Harkness, *Chicago Hustle & Flow: Gangs, Gangsta Rap, and Social Class* (Minneapolis: University of Minnesota Press, 2014).

Some other terms of gang disrespect commonly in use among Latin Folks:

Gang Vocabulary 101
Amhoes or Animals—Disrespect toward the Ambrose
Rashes—Disrespect toward the La Raza
Rolaids—Disrespect toward the Royals
Duche Bags—Disrespect toward the Deuces
Gayrods—Disrespect toward the Gaylords
Paper Bags—Disrespect toward the Playboys
Gumballs—Disrespect toward the Imperial Gangsters
Bananas or Platanos—Disrespect toward Latin Kings
Tweety-Birds or Bird Shit—Disrespect toward Latin Eagles
Vicky Lous—Disrespect toward Vice Lords
Hoebras—Disrespect toward Spanish Cobras
Cunts—Disrespect toward Latin Counts
Two-Shits—Disrespect toward Two-Six

4. This even applied to the bitterest enemy of the C-Note$, the Latin Kings. For example, in 1994 three Latin Kings, David Oakley, Chet Hateway, and Jesse Navarro, saw a C-Note in a northwest side parking lot and jumped him. They did not know that a bar across the street was a hangout for the C-Note$ and Outfit guys, who poured out and put a severe beating on the three Kings. Despite being against Latin King laws to testify in court, the three guys were headed for the witness stand against the C-Note$. With their newfound respect as I-Team members, the Note$ set up a meeting in Menard Prison with the Latin King Corona, Lord Gino. The LK leader requested a $10,000 payout to assure that the individuals would not show up in court. The payment was to take place on the court date. But it was quickly apparent that "the code of the streets ain't what it used to be." The Latin Kings showed up and testified anyway. The $10,000 was never paid. One of the three Kings, David Oakley, ended up "flipping" Satan Disciples,

meaning he quit the Kings and joined the SDs in order to avoid any discipline from Lord Gino for testifying.

5. At Sal's urging, Mo Mo made sure he gave respect to the older, sometimes retired members and Outfit associates. Even if these guys were no longer active on the streets, he would make sure he would "pick up their tabs" at restaurants and bars when he dropped in. Sal heartily approved and took advantage of Mo Mo's largesse himself on more than one occasion. Mo Mo accepted that street taxes of 10 percent on various scams and illegal businesses on C-Note turf was "acknowledging that everyone has to eat." But some of the guys were getting greedy, and Mo Mo opposed as "disrespectful" the practice of a few who imposed street taxes of up to 20 percent. This added to his "rep" among older guys.

CHAPTER TEN: THE WAR OF THE FAMILIES

1. E.g., A press release from Homies Unidos, the LA gang intervention agency, stated:

March 9th 2013 marks the one-year anniversary of the truce between El Salvador's two major gangs, MS-13 and Barrio 18. The peace agreement can be credited with saving thousands of lives and dropping El Salvador for the first time off the list of countries with the highest homicide rates for 2012. Despite much public skepticism about the reliability and durability of the truce, the benefits of the truce continue to grow. It is important to recognize what an enormous and historic achievement this peace represents, and to credit the small group of individuals and groups that have worked tirelessly to make this peace a reality—in particular the leadership of MS-13 and Barrio 18, the facilitators of the truce, Raul Mijango and Monsignor Fabio Collindres and their team, and those within the Salvadoran government who supported this process. The Organization of American States (OAS) deserves special mention for its courageous stand as guarantor of the truce and the leadership it has taken in the international community.

It is imperative that this process, which has established greater public safety in El Salvador than years of expensive and harsh law enforcement, be supported by all stakeholders. The benefits of a safer and more peaceful society accrue and belong to all of Salvadorans, not only the participants of the truce. The introduction of the second phase, the violence free municipalities, is a welcome opportunity to share the peace dividend from the truce to some of the communities most affected by violence in El Salvador. The formation of the Fundacion Humanitario and the addition of three other gangs (Mao Mao, La Máquina y la Mirada Locos); Father Antonio Rodriguez and mayors from both major political parties to the ranks of those supporting the truce and actively working for peace gives strength and additional legitimacy to the process.

However despite the success of the peace process and additional supporters, there is much more support required to ensure the peace lasts and cycle of violence that has afflicted El Salvador for over thirty years ends. For this reason it is imperative that all of Salvadoran society be part of this process in order for it to succeed.

Gang truces are documented in many places, including Tom Hayden, *Street Wars: Gangs and the Future of Violence* (New York: New Press, 2004); and Carl Upchurch, *Convicted in the Womb: One Man's Journey from Prisoner to Peacemaker* (New York: Bantam Books, 1996).

2. Don't believe El Paso's numbers? Http://www.kvia.com/news/2010-Murder -Rate-Not-Seen-Since-1965/-/391068/542418/-/g4u08e/-/index.html. Similarly, in 2010 Tijuana had 818 homicides, and San Diego, separated by only a border crossing, had just 29.

3. Http://www2.sacurrent.com/news/story.asp?id=71176.

4. Angela Me, Enrico Bisogno, and Steven Malby, *Global Study on Homicide*.

5. For a cogent presentation of the neighborhood variable argument, see Andrew V. Papachristos, David M. Hureaub, and Anthony A. Bragab, "The Corner and the Crew: The Influence of Geography and Social Networks on Gang Violence," *American Sociological Review* 78, no. 3 (2013): 417–47. The data for Papachristos's study was drawn from police reports taken during the twenty-four-month period between January 2008 and December 2009, a time period *after* the conclusion of the war of the families and a more lethal war between the Gangster Disciples and Black Disciples. Thus what is being measured is violence after a war ends, something quite different as Chicago's gangs fractured and violence became more atomized and spontaneous. Most gang studies on violence suffer from the threat to validity of *history*, of not understanding how gangs and their use of violence can change over time. Gangs are treated as if they are always the same, and conditions of war are ahistorically treated as constant. The elevated levels of violence in Chicago of the wars of the 1990s dropped by 2008 to a low point not seen in Chicago since 1967. This was not a result of law enforcement as much as the exhaustion of a war. See, e.g., Joan W. Moore, "Gangs, Drugs, and Violence," in *Gangs*, ed. Scott Cummings and Daniel J. Monti (Albany: State University of New York, 1993), 27–48. How "social networks" (e.g., gangs and organized crime organizations) intersect with neighborhood characteristics is only beginning to be investigated.

6. Zucker defines entropy as "a tendency toward disorganization in the social system"; Lynne G. Zucker, "Where Do Institutional Patterns Come From? Organizations as Actors in Social Systems," in *Institutional Patterns and Organizations*, ed. Zucker, 23–49. Zucker (26–27) casts entropy as opposed to "homeostasis," relative stability of institutions: "In the normal course of events, however, we should expect to see institutions gradually erode by their own imperfect transmission and more dramatically subverted by other forces such as power that reassert self-interest." The homeostasis perspective is represented by Paul DiMaggio, "Interest and Agency in Institutional Theory," in *Institutional Patterns and Organizations: Culture and Environment*, ed. Lynne G. Zucker (Cambridge, MA: Ballinger, 1988), 3–21. DiMaggio does admit that "institutional theory tells us even less about deinstitutionalization: why and how institutionalized forms and practices fall into disuse" (12). See also Oliver, "The Antecedents of Deinstitutionalization."

7. Oliver, "The Antecedents of Deinstitutionalization," 564 and 569. There is also a literature on identity and institutions: Peter J. Burke and Donald C. Reitzes, "An Identity Theory Approach to Commitment," *Social Psychology Quarterly* 54 (1991): 239–51. See also

Peter J. Burke and Donald C. Reitzes. "The Link between Identity and Role Performance," *Social Psychology Quarterly* 44 (1981): 83–92.

8. An especially relevant study of the nature of violence is René Girard, *Violence and the Sacred* (Baltimore: John Hopkins University Press, 1972). He states: "Medea, like Ajax, reminds us of a fundamental truth about violence; if left unappeased, violence will accumulate until it overflows its confines and floods the surrounding areas. The role of sacrifice is to stem this rising tide of indiscriminate substitutions and redirect violence into 'proper' channels" (10).

9. Girard, *Violence and the Sacred*, 14.

10. The Cobras were also having their own internal problems, with Tuffy in prison in New Jersey and Rabbit, the number 2 guy also off the streets. They had consolidated their factions in the early 1990s, bringing all their sections for the first time under universal laws. But the process was uneven and violence at times broke out between governors, or section leaders. Bradley, Chiefy, and Indigo were among the main street leaders. Bradley had his own substance abuse problem and Chiefy did not have same kind of "street cred" and respect as other leaders from the Cobra membership.

11. Blade, from the Insane Deuces, a strong supporter of SGD, sums up regretfully what was beginning to happen within the MLDs.

> Back then, when they had the SGD concept and they had David Ayala [2-6ers] and Fernie [MLDs] leading it, everything was peaceful, everything was good, no wars. But what happened is that some of the guys in MLD wanted to take over. They said, "We can make more money over here if we have that corner. So they had a couple of guys who say yeah, fuck them. So that's what they do—they start making power plays, that's what they do. Fuck leadership.
>
> Fernie at that time was so powerful the Bum brothers figured the only way they're gonna be able to do that is get him high, get him stuck, strung out on his own shit. So that's what they did. Because, you see, you're in jail, whatta you got to lose? He got eighty years. He's never getting out. He's doing his appeals, but what's going on? Nothin'. So now his own boys are "feeding" him. It goes to a point he's got a habit. It's to the point that Fernie can't make no decisions in SGD; he's out of control. He can't understand what is going on anymore. It's all a game. Now Fernie's gotta get violated. His own boys beat him so he's no more in play. . . .
>
> His own boys did that. The Bum Brothers wanted to be in control of the gang, so they wanted to make a move. "We're gonna to do it this way," the Bums said. Fernie and Rick Dog said, "No let's keep it the way it is." The Bums said, "No we're gonna do it that way." At that time there were a lot of Ds who had been Cobras and Cobras who had been Ds. They were family. [Once it started], it was like a virus that eats itself. You got all these gangs together but they couldn't get it right—like the Mexicans.

12. Http://articles.chicagotribune.com/1996-07-28/news/9607280306_1_gang-members-public-campaign-witnesses.

13. Annelise Graebner Anderson, *The Business of Organized Crime* (Stanford, CA: Hoover Institution Press, 1979), 22.

CHAPTER ELEVEN: THE FUTURE OF GANGS IN CHICAGO

1. For Lupo, one meaning of *polygenesis* was the transforming of a criminal into an "honored member of society." Lupo knew that soldiers of the mafia, like the gang members I've studied, are not one thing. Polygenesis should be differentiated from the more narrow "group process" playgroup-to-gang human development model of Thrasher and the Chicago School. Salvatore Lupo, *History of the Mafia* (New York: Columbia University Press, 2009).

2. Eric Hobsbawm, *On History* (New York: New Press, 1997), 59. He also states: "It is important to remind ourselves from time to time that we don't know all the answers about society and that the process of discovering them is not simple" (216). One set of facts left out, some of you may have noticed, pertains to female gang members. Recall, this is a history of *gang leaders*, and I pushed Sal and others to talk to me about the roles of women. They had little to say. Hobsbawm lists three basic roles for women: (1) As lovers, wives, or conquests of male bandits; (2) as links to the outside world; and, finally, less frequently (3) as armed bandits themselves who sometimes turn to violence, often as a consequence of rape. We see all of these roles in this book.

The landscape of organized crime and gang leadership is almost completely devoid of women, though I reported on Ala's and Tina's important roles in chapter 7. The Lady D's Jackie Montañez is perhaps a better example, of a young girl raised to leadership and then abandoned as she proved her loyalty through a horrific act of violence. Joey Bags's womanizing lifestyle ended up with him dead in a jail cell, while Mo Mo's more stable relationship with a woman led him away from "the life." For organized crime figures like Sal, stable, traditionally gendered relationships are preferable. Because of security concerns, I was reluctant to interview the women in gang leader's lives who were not fully aware of their men's secret activities. Female leaders are few and often do not last long.

My interviews with Sal and other Latin Folks leaders were largely "men's talk." Still, women make up perhaps a third of all rank-and-file gang members, and as Joan Moore reminds us, girls and women play indispensable roles in neighborhood life. We have very few studies of women as gang leaders and need more attention to this as does Joan W. Moore, *Going Down to the Barrio: Homeboys and Homegirls in Change* (Philadelphia: Temple University Press, 1991).

3. James C. Howell and John P. Moore, "History of Street Gangs in the United States," ed. Office of Juvenile Justice and Delinquency Prevention (Washington, DC: National Gang Center Bulletin, 2010). The concept of bringing the state back in was a seminal text in political history; Peter B. Evans, Dietrich Rueschemeyer, and Theda Skocpol, *Bringing the State Back In* (Cambridge: Cambridge University Press, 1985). There are too few social scientists who bravely explore how a punitive state criminalizes youth, and these variables were never central to "ecological" analyses of gangs; but see Rios, *Punished*.

4. Joan W. Moore, *Homeboys: Gangs, Drugs, and Prison in the Barrios of Los Angeles* (Philadelphia: Temple University Press, 1978); Moore, *Going Down to the Barrio*; Carl Taylor, *Dangerous Society* (East Lansing: Michigan State University Press, 1989); Diego Vigil, *A Rainbow of Gangs: Street Cultures in the Mega-City* (Austin: University of Texas, 2002); Deb-

orah Levenson, *Adios Niño: The Gangs of Guatemala City and the Politics of Death* (Durham: Duke University Press, 2013); and Susan A. Phillips, *Operation Fly Trap: L.A. Gangs, Drugs, and the Law* (Chicago: University of Chicago Press, 2012).

5. For example, an unpublished 1970s novel by African American Chicago alderman Fred Hubbard details several black gangs' plan to buy politicians and control the drug market in both cooperation and conflict with the Outfit. The novel fictionalizes real events and transparently describes prominent gang leaders and politicians of the day, including Jesse Jackson, assassinated West Side alderman Ben Lewis, and several Italian organized crime figures and machine politicians. Hubbard surely knew corruption when he saw it. He joined a long line of Chicago aldermen to spend time in prison after he embezzled $98,000 in city antipoverty funds.

6. Black gang members have also run for office and have been fiercely—and successfully—opposed by the machine. The focus of most gang politics has been on entering the machine, not overthrowing it, as if African Americans were just another ethnic group. As Jim Jacobs observed long ago, "Insofar as the gangs had a model of development it was the Daley model," not following in the more activist footsteps of the Panthers or militant organizations. The Daley model assumes ethnic succession into political power, and that hasn't happened for African Americans. As we saw in chapter 7, the Daley administration served notice that there would be no more Harold Washingtons as whites allied with Latinos to cripple black political power. James Jacobs, *Stateville: The Penitentiary in Mass Society* (Chicago: University of Chicago Press, 1977), 145.

7. Charles Tilly and Sidney G. Tarrow, *Contentious Politics* (Boulder: Paradigm Publishers, 2007).

8. Arnold R. Hirsch, *Making the Second Ghetto: Race and Housing in Chicago 1940–1960* (Cambridge: Cambridge University Press, 1983); Sudhir Alladi Venkatesh, *American Project: The Rise and Fall of a Modern Ghetto* (Cambridge, MA: Harvard University Press, 2000); John M. Hagedorn and Brigid Rauch, "Housing, Gangs, and Homicide: What We can Learn from Chicago," *Urban Affairs Review* 42, no. 4, 2007): 435–56.

9. For background on the Speck case, see http://www.chicagotribune.com/news/politics/chi-chicagodays-richardspeck-story,0,4911196.story. For the video, Google it. I have not been able to confirm sources who told me the videotape was handed over to attorneys by a Gangster Disciple who used it as payment for attorney fees.

10. Ianni's fascinating conclusion to *Black Mafia* asks a fundamental question that also applies to my study of Chicago gangs. He asked: "Blacks and Hispanics must face the same basic dilemma that confronted earlier generations of Irish, Jews, and Italians: *How do you escape poverty through socially approved routes when such routes are closed off from the ghetto?* Crime resolves the dilemma because it provides a quick if perilous route out" (328).

11. Social bandits were peasant rebels. "A man becomes a bandit," Hobsbawm says, "because he does something which is not regarded as criminal by his local conventions, but is so regarded by the state or his local rulers." Thus Ianni (ibid., 326) argues that the qualified support for drug dealers in the black community is analogous to rural "social bandits." E. J. Hobsbawm, *Primitive Rebels: Studies in Archaic Forms of Social Movements in the 19th and 20th Centuries* (New York: Norton, 1959), 15.

12. John M. Hagedorn, "Gang Violence and School Closings," Report for *Swan v. Chicago Board of Education*, Chicago, US District Court for Northern Illinois, July 2013.

13. John M. Hagedorn, "Race Not Space: A Revisionist History of Gangs in Chicago," *Journal of African America History* 91, no. 2 (2006): 205. Resistance identity of gang members was also central to my *A World of Gangs*. Manuel Castells, *The Information Age: Economy, Society and Culture*, vol. 2, *The Power of Identity* (Malden, MA: Blackwell, 2004), 9.

14. The shooting of Mayor Cermak is seen by most as the result of an attempt to assassinate President Roosevelt that missed and killed the Chicago mayor. Other sources stress that Cermak's shooting happened directly after he attempted to kill Outfit boss Frank Nitti. See Eghigian, *After Capone*.

15. DiMaggio, *Interest and Agency*, 13–14. *Institutional work* is defined as "the socialization of new participants, which is undertaken most conscientiously by members with the greatest stake in the existing institutional order." See also the comprehensive discussion of the decision-making literature and how conflict is resolved in Charles Perrow, *Complex Organizations: A Critical Essay* (New York: Random House, 1986), 119–56: "Elimination of conflict is always the goal, even if it is seen as constructive in the short run" (132).

16. Robert M. Lombardo, *Organized Crime in Chicago: Beyond the Mafia* (Urbana: University of Illinois Press, 2013). The original quote is from Baudelaire.

17. Anderson lists associates as category A, B, C, and D. Category A are Italians who are not made but do the work of the mob. They may or may not be invited to membership or have been rejected in the past; category B may or may not be Italians and run or are part of crews doing vice work. Category C manage illegally funded businesses: "He is basically a businessman, not a gangster"; category D are lawyers and professionals or businessmen who take part in mob schemes. *The Business of Organized Crime*, 39–40. A true-crime website displays the 2010 Outfit hierarchy and details more numerous associates of four crews. Judging by their last names, these associates appear to be nearly all Italian, consistent with Anderson's concept but not Sal's; http://www.swfcabin.com/swf-files/1324779271.swf.

18. Associates are also political middlemen. Sal explains a key factor of the Outfit's reach into the machine.

I could put somebody in office right now in the next election if I wanted to. I can round up the troops and put him in and he'd be a puppet alderman just like the rest of them. You know who is the backbone of all those people? precinct captains—very powerful individuals. And some of those precinct captains are associates—believe it or not. They're associates; they are middlemen from this group to this group [Outfit to machine].

19. Sal goes on to explain the complex, continuing relationship of the Outfit to street gangs.

You know, we know hundreds of Folks street gang members, but I'm not gonna go and conduct business with these people, because half of 'em I can't trust them as far as I can throw 'em. But, there are other individuals—even the ones that have never been in a gang but are associates or grew up with us; they call 'em neutrons—that hang around, that come to you and conduct business. You'd rather do business with those individuals, because you know their whole family structure from kindergarten on up. They're less likely to become informants on you, because they know your family and your mother knows his mother and this one knows their aunt and how you going to be seen if, "Oh, little Johnny, he cooperated with the police"—What? You better move. You know what I mean? So the likelihood of them cooperating with law enforcement is so minimal. Could it happen? Absolutely, depending on the circumstances.

20. Karl E. Weick, "Educational Organizations as Loosely Coupled Systems," *Administrative Science Quarterly* 21 (1976): 1–19; John M. Hagedorn, *Forsaking Our Children: Bureaucracy and Reform in the Child Welfare System* (Chicago: Lakeview Press, 1995).

21. Can organized crime be progressive? While crime has been utilized in the past to finance revolutionary movements—e.g., the Tupamaros in Uruguay or the IRA in Ireland—a study of history finds organized crime itself is more likely to be a reactionary than a progressive force. Hobsbawm says banditry "does not constitute a social movement. It may be a surrogate for it . . . or may even be a substitute for it"; *Primitive Rebels*, 26. Criminal organizations, he believes, are dangerous and by nature violent. In trying to win youth over to a contentious politics of the streets, organized crime is part of the problem, not an ally.

22. There are wildly varying estimates of illegal business activity and how much is controlled by gangs and organized crime. The UN Office on Drugs and Crime in 2009 estimated that transnational organized crime generated $870 billion a year, or more than six times the total amount of official development assistance. This represents nearly 7 percent of the total world exports of all merchandise. UNDOC http://www.unodc.org /toc/en/crimes/organized-crime.html.

23. Robert K. Merton, "Social Structure and Anomie," *American Sociological Review* 3 (1938): 672–82. "Capone represents the triumph of amoral intelligence over morally prescribed 'failure'" (679).

24. Hagedorn, *People and Folks*, 174.

25. Gary LaFree, *Losing Legitimacy: Street Crime and the Decline of Social Institutions in America* (Boulder: Westview Press, 1998).

26. Http://www.justicepartyusa.org/restorative_justice_issue_call. For a public health approach to violence that endorses restorative justice, see Ernest Drucker, *A Plague of Prisons: The Epidemiology of Mass Incarceration in America* (New York: New Press, 2011).

27. John M. Hagedorn, "Institutionalised Gangs and Violence in Chicago," in *Neither War nor Peace: International Comparisons of Children and Youth in Organised Armed Violence*, ed. Luke Dowdney (Rio de Janeiro: 7Letras, 2005), 312–30.

28. See powerful efforts being made to build peacemaking models, as in http://weare peace.org.

APPENDIX I: MAJOR EVENTS IN CHICAGO GANG HISTORY PRIOR TO SGD

Neighborhood Gang Formation

1952   C-Note$ are formed in the West Town neighborhood known as "The Patch"

1952   Ted Roe is gunned down by Outfit hit men, completing take-over of black vice king Policy rackets

1954   Gaylords form on corners of Grand and Noble

1957   Tony Accardo steps down as formal boss of Outfit, but maintains real power

1960   Summerdale Police Scandal—CPD officers run burglary ring

1963   Simon City formed in Simons Park; renamed Simon City Royals in 1968

1963   Latin Kings formed at Kedzie and Ohio

1965   Cha Cha Jimenez elected leader of Young Lords

1966   Sam Giancana leaves Chicago for Mexico, but solidifies Outfit heroin connections

1966   Latin Disciples formed by Albert "Hitler" Hernandez from an older gang called the Latin Scorpions

Multi-Neighborhood Gang Organization

1966   Puerto Rican Day Parade erupts in violence after police shooting of Aracelis Cruz

1968   Bull Hairston convicted of solicitation to murder; his incarceration allows Jeff Fort to negotiate deal with Outfit for black control of retail vice businesses

1970   Assassination of Latin Disciples' Hitler Hernandez by Latin Kings

1972   UFO formed of Gaylords, C-Note$, Playboys, and Ventures

Uncontrolled Violence and Incarceration

1972   Gustavo "Lord Gino" Colon, leader of the Latin Kings, gets life for murder

1974   Young Lords leader Cha Cha Jimenez runs for alderman of 46th ward and gets 39% of the vote

1975   FALN bombing of Chicago buildings; Latin Kings and many Humboldt Park activists have ties to Puerto Rican independence groups

1975   Sam Giancana assassinated in his home a day before he was to testify in US Senate organized crime hearings; Joey "Doves" Aiuppa serves as top Outfit boss

1976   Young Latino Organization (YLO) formed from Spanish Cobras and Latin Disciples; YLO later splits as YLO-D and YLO-C

1976   Simon City Royals assassinate Insane Unknowns' leader Capone after luring him to a "peace conference"

1977   Puerto Rican Day Parade erupts with Latin King and Cobra violence

1977   Murder of Earl Abercrombie, one of dozens killed by the Outfit in the "chop shop wars" taking control of the profitable stolen auto parts business

1978   UFO III is formed of Playboys, Ventures, Rice Boys, C-Note$, Gaylords, Hells Devils, and Jousters

1978   United Latino Organization (ULO) is formed to combat the UFO; It consist of Latin Disciples, Spanish Cobras, Imperial Gangsters and Latin Eagles

People and Folks

1978   Tony Accardo's home burglarized and in the coming months 6 professional burglars are murdered in retaliation; Burglaries remain a major source of Outfit earnings

1978   People and Folks coalitions formed in Stateville, organized by Gangster Disciple leader Larry Hoover; ULO members vote to join Folks

1979   Richard "KC" Medina is killed by members of the Insane Unknowns and sparks off "The War of the Insanes"

1980   DEA/CPD drug sting busts 46 MLDs including chief Jose "Freckles" Cedeno

1981   Tuffy C, leader of the ISC arrested for intent to murder; Will be sentenced to 70 years; David Ayala, jefe of the 2-6ers, orders hits of two Latin Kings; Two bystanders are killed instead; In 1983 he gets a life sentence

1981   UFO III breaks up when the Gaylords support the Jousters in a dispute with the C-Note$

1983   MLD Prince Fernie Zayas sentenced to life for triple homicide of Insane Unknowns; Unknowns would be nearly obliterated after wars against the MLDs, Royals, and Cobras

1983   Gaylords, Freaks, Jousters, and Playboys join People Alliance; C-Note$ become independent; Will vote to turn Folks in the 1990s

1983   In congressional primary election, Dan "Rosti" Rostenkowski, backed by declining Polish gangs, Playboys, Ventures, Pulaski Parkers, Jousters, and Chi-West defeats Puerto Rican challenger Luis "El Gallito" Gutiérrez, backed by MLDs and Cobras; Gutiérrez, alderman of the 26th ward, would finally win election to Congress in 1993

1984   Manuel Herrera, leader of Chicago's branch of the Herrera Family, indicted for distribution of cocaine

1985   Indictments of 135 people in Chicago for drug trafficking tied to Herrera Family closely tied to Maniac Latin Disciples

1987   Jeff Fort convicted of terrorism for plot to buy LAW rocket from Libya; Beginning of the end of the power of the El Rukns, or Blackstone Rangers

Spanish Growth and Development

1989   Call to 43 Latin Folks gangs to register as Spanish Growth and Development; 17 accepted as members of the Latin Folks Union

APPENDIX 2: TEN YEARS OF SGD, SIGNIFICANT EVENTS

1989	Call to 43 Latin Folks gangs to register as Spanish Growth and Development; 17 accepted as members of the Latin Folks Union
1990	After being a part of the People Alliance for 10 years the Insane Deuces went to war with the Latin Kings over the Lathrop Homes Projects; Eventually this led them to turn Folks by 1992
1990	Alderman Fred Roti indicted for extortion and trying to fix a murder trial; FBI labels Roti as a "made member" of the mafia; Roti's co-defendant Pat Marcy, was a Democratic Party leader and " a fixer for the Outfit"; Roti was instrumental in getting Outfit associate William Hanhardt appointed as CPD chief of detectives
1992	Gang loitering ordinance adopted
1992	Murder of two Latin King soldiers by Jacqueline Montañez and two other MLD women
1992	The Jefferson Park and Ohio St. factions of C-Note$ unite
1992	United in Peace: Black Gang Peace Summit; First of several held by gang members and their supporters
1992	Tony Accardo, "Joe Batters," dies of natural causes; He is eventually succeeded by Joey "the Clown" Lombardo from the Grand Avenue Crew
1993	The flags of Paseo Boricua are erected on Division Street; Billy Ocasio is appointed 26th Ward alderman by Mayor Daley to fill the unexpired term of Luis Gutiérrez, who was elected congressman
1993	C-Note$ make formal decision to seek membership in SGD
1994	Ecstasy and GHB becomes major drugs; C-Note$ begin to take over the market
1995	The Latin Lovers and the C-Note$ join the Insane Family
1996	Hi Lo, an enforcer for the Maniac Latin Disciples street gang, is shot in the mouth by members of the Insane Spanish Cobras in February
1996	February 13 *Godfather* style simultaneous hits by Maniac Family
1996	March: Insane retaliation begins with shootings all over Chicago area
1996	April 3 assassination of MLD leader Enrique "Rick Dog" Garcia
1996	Satan Disciples vs. C-Note$ war begins with the murder of Armando "Mando" Rodriguez
1997	C-Note$ control Chicago's ecstasy market as #1 supplier
1998	Gang Squad officer Joseph Miedzianowski indicted for corruption
1999	Operation Devils Head against the MLD; 17 are charged, including Thomas "Outlaw" Ross who would be the shooter in Carlito's assassination
1999	C-Note$ voted in as members of SGD by La Tabla
1999	Carlito is assassinated on the steps of a peace conference, ending the SGD experiment; The Outfit washes its hands of Latin Folks

APPENDIX 3: FACTUAL CHARGES OF AMBROSE ON LA RAZA TO SGD BOARD

FACTUAL LIST OF CHARGES

(PLEASE NOTE): The following is a list of charges that bare substance and facts, that we are certain that our respectful S.G.D. BOARD along with it's members will comprehend our reasons for eradication. We are also confident that the Board will rule in our favor after reviewing and weighing all facts from both Families, their's (RAZA'S) as well as ours. We THEE ALMIGHTY AMBROSE FAMILIA, will respect and honor any and all final decisions made by our S.G.D. BOARD and BOARD MEMBERS.

(1.) RESPECT FOR AMBROSE RIGHTFUL BOUNDARIES AND TERRITORIES:

From the very beginning, during the process of the Raza registration into our S.G.D. UNION, it was mentioned, stipulated, as well as agreed upon by the Raza's, that all territories and boundaries of both Familias Raza's and ours as well, would be defined and respected at all tines, Although we AMBROSE have till this day, respected and enforced to all our various sections and their responsible coordinators in charge, that no matter what, no one is to violate our agreement with the Raza Familia, and we will at all times respect their territories, and boundaries. We kept our word to them but they broke their agreement by slowly moving into our territories and in time setting up and claiming sections in our territories. We had a tragic down fall a couple of years ago on 18th. and Throop, we were raided by a sting operation and lost at least 40 of our members from 18th St., the Raza Familia found it appropriate to take advantage of our situation and gradually started to claim several of our Sections. By the loss of the majority of the membership in different sections, the Raza's began to bully the only members left out ther alone, and those left were all youngbloods. Those youngbloods of ours were subjected to several violent attacks by the Raza's, some of them were injured by gun fire. The situation has only been getting larger as time passes. There is no reason or justification for any of our Brother's to be abused or gunned down in our own territory, especially by any Familia who claims to be a part of the same Union that we are a part of. We will present any facts and proof to varrify our claim.

(2.) RAZA'S COOPERATING AND ASSISTING THE LAW IN PUTTING AWAY AMBROSE.

It is a sad but proven fact that because of the Raza's, there are several of our members incarcerated, some for crimes that they had nothing to do with. Nothing or no one can ever justify why certain members of the Raza Familia wold take the stand in court and testify against our brothers, sad but true. Even the Raza's can testify to this charge, They can't deny this accusation. This is a serious matter, that has been costing our brothers to be subjected to be put away for most of their lives. There is no way that anyone can justify why our brothers are being incarcerated, merely by the testimonies of Raza's. We are sure that the Board can and will agree with us.

(3.) ANTI-AMBROSE GRAFFITI AND DISRESPECT IN OUR HOODS:

The Raza Familia have continually been putting up various <u>ANTI-AMBROSE</u> graffiti and disrespect all through our hoods and we will submit recent proof of this. Being a part of this <u>S.G.D. UNION</u> the Raza should have the common respect to recognize that these are our neighborhoods and that we fought for those hoods, sometimes costing us great sacrifices.

These are only a few issues that we feel we need to address to the Board, what more needs to be said? We will answer all questions, and we will be available for any sort of explanations required by our <u>S.G.D. BOARD</u>. We respectfully close this document, with plenty much <u>LOVE</u>, <u>RESPECT</u> and <u>HONOR</u>, to all of our <u>S.G.D. BOARD</u> and its Board Members. <u>AMOR A LA LUCHA</u>!!!!

RESPECTFULLY SUBMITTED,

THEE ALMIGHTY AMBROSE
LEADERSHIP

APPENDIX 4: SGD GRIEVANCE FORMAT

GRIEVANCE FORMAT

To: <u>Central Committee Members</u>

From: _____

Sub: _____

Date: _____

Dear Coordinator,

I, _____, have cause to file the following complaint against (Personnel, Union), afforded me by the Constitution and Leyes.

<u>STATEMENT OF FACTS/</u>

NATURE OF GRIEVANCE/

RELIEF SOUGHT/

APPENDIX 5: INDEPENDENCE OF THE SGD WITHIN THE ORGANIZATION

INDEPENDENCE OF THE SGD WITHIN THE ORGANIZATION

PURPOSE: First, i.e., see union Preamble, and also to provide a higher level of understanding that will enable our Union to grow into diversified businesses which will allow us to reach our COMMON COLLECTIVE GOALS AS A UNION. *GOALS DESIGNED BY IDEAS OF OUR PERSONNEL.*

DEFINITION: The S.G.D. Union does not imply, nor does it mean for anyone to abandon their original Faction. We as Hispanics are merged in that we can accomplish COMMON COLLECTIVE OBJECTIVES set forth by our delegated committees, and ideas given to our leadership by all our personnel who are able to propose and manifest said ideas. The leadership cannot do anything without the aid of its membership.

LAWS: Our laws are universal laws which do not conflict with the laws of others and that enables the S.G.D. to maintain Unity and Strength within. The S.G.D. will honor and respect the laws and policies of the One People Concept. The One People Concept being the SGD, BGD, and BD under one concept of unification.

V's: For the personnel's concern, and for the firmness in discipline of the S.G.D.'s, we shall punish our own, unless otherwise instructed by the S.G.D ranks.

FINES: Whenever an S.G.D. is fined, the Viceroy is to be informed of the fining. All fines by a BGD or BD staff member will be forwarded to the S.G.D. box. Any fines by the SGD staff members will be forwarded to the BGD or BD box.

ALLIES: As the One People Concept, the SGD, BGD, and BD's under the Six-Pointed Star, join within a common enterprise and bid Love, Life, and Loyalty. We recognize how we have been oppressed but we must further cultivate our Education, maintain a Politically oriented awareness, and we must establish Economical Resources within our Hispanic Societies. Such a task will require the full cooperation of all of our personnel and Unity as One.

SINCERELY, YOURS

EXECUTIVE CHAIRMAN
AND
BOARD OF DIRECTORS

APPENDIX 6: GRIEVANCE OF THE ISC AGAINST THE LATIN EAGLES

To: The leadership of the Almighty Latin Eagles
and the SGD Board and Union
From: The Insane Spanish Cobra Organization's Leadership
Re: ALE members tricking on members of the ISC members

We ask all the members of the board as well as the union to accept our bid of love loyalty and devotion to the Spanish Growth and Development Concept. We would like to bring to the attention of the ALE's as well as the SGD Board the nature of this grievance. We currently have a Board member, a Governor, and a respected member incarcerated now for a few years. These individuals are serving time due to the fact that the member of the Almighty Latin Eagles testified as witnesses against these brothers.

In the past Board Members of the SGD in the outside world gathered to address and resolve issues at the Logan Square Y.M.C.A . . . I the writer (Stoney) was present at one of these meeting, when the issue of these brothers who are incarcerated was brought up. The leadership of the Eagles was present at this meeting (one of these individuals was known to have testified against two of the incarcerated). I the writer know this to be a fact for I also was charged by the state by providing false evidence to convict. Our Leadership questioned the individual known as Peanuts aka Juanche as to why he and other members did what they did. He stated in front of everybody that he was told by his fellow leaders. At that time they offered to correct the wrong they had committed in front of those that were present at this meeting. As of this date they have yet to correct the wrong they have committed.

Due to this serious mater we rightfully ask that those who committed this wrong be dealt with according to the SGD Laws. That the leadership not be allowed to participate in any of the Unions functions, that they have no say so as to the Union until they have there house in order. That their registration be reviewed since they have not participated in any decision making on the Board due to the fact that they have been imposed previous sanctions. In closing we would like to request that if anyone has information pertaining to any of our members cooperating with the government that they provide us with the information because we do not tolerate any of our members doing so and will deal with them immediately in order to make sure that no member of the Union is incarcerated due to our members.

AMOR Y PAZ

Leaders of the Insane Spanish Cobra Organization

APPENDIX 7: BY-LAWS OF THE INSANE FAMILY

Every Family is obligated to have their Families issues on paper, before each meeting and given to the Chairman and/or Secretary before each meeting is to begin.

After a "prayer" is said to open a union meeting, The Chairman and/or Secretary will read out loud every issue that is to be discussed in today's meeting.

After all issues to be discussed have been read out loud, The Coordinator will read the name of the Family whose issues will be discussed first. The order of all Families issues will be discussed in the order sheets were given to the Coordinator.

Then, the coordinator will name the first topic on that families issue sheet. Then that Family will be allowed "10 minutes" to address that specific topic. If more time is needed, we "The Board" will take into consideration the emergency of the issue, and all other issues not discussed and come to a decision on how much time extra will be given to that Family.

If any other Family has a rebuttal, comment, question, or suggestion on the issue at hand, they must raise their hand and make sure the Coordinator acknowledges that he raise his hand. Then the Coordinator will write his name down, and after the man with the floor completes his talk on the issue, The Coordinator will call out everyone's name who raised their hand in the order they raised their hand that that Family will be allowed "5 minutes" to rebut, suggest, give a comment, and/or ask question on the issue just talked about and only that issue and after every Family has finished giving their rebuttal, comments, question and suggestion, and all questions have been answered, The Coordinator will write down the issue discussed and the conclusion that case came about in the discussion and then the Coordinator will read the next issue to be discussed.

While a Family is addressing an issue on their time they are to have everyone's utmost attention, with no interruptions what so ever. If anyone is caught in violation of interrupting without raising their hand or is involved in a different conversation and not paying attention, That person will be fined $25.00 which will be due at the next meeting held and if anyone has to be excused for whatever reason that person must raise his hand and ask to be excused while a meeting is in session.

There will be between 1 and 3 Representatives from each Family in the "united Contract" to attend all union meeting when they are called. At least one member from each Family in must be present order for meetings to be held accountable for major decisions. But at the same time a "Majority Vote" rules over all.

Three alternatives are accepted in case 1 or 3 main Representatives cannot make it to a union meeting. But there must be at least one alternate member from each Family that is able to make major decisions for their entire Family, and be acknowledged accountable for their Family in case any type of "vote" may occur. The 3 main Representatives and 3 Alternatives from each Family listed in the "United Contract" will be the only ones that will be able to attend union meeting (As well as Security). Security will not have "Hearsay" on any issues discussed at union meetings.

Each meeting held must be known at least 2 days in advance to all other Families that are registered in the "United Contract" as well as probational Families. So that all leading Representatives from each Family will be able to attend or at least send one or between 3 of their Alternatives. If no 2 day notices is "acknowledged" to all other Families, Then that Family in charge of holding that Demonstration will be subject to a fine of $50.00.

Meetings will start no later than 7:00pm. Any Family entering after 7:05pm will be subject to a $50.00 due to the fact of Tardiness, which will be due at the next meeting. Meetings will be held and sponsored by the Family next in line by this order: AV, SC, OA, LL, C$N, DRS, ID.

All future Families that are registered with this "Concept" (The United Contract) will follow the chain accordingly. There will be a time limit of 2 hours on each meeting held. In case more time is necessary, that will be decided by The Board, depending on how crucial the meeting and the issues are

APPENDIX 8: APPLICATION OF THE C-NOTE$
FOR SGD MEMBERSHIP

Date: October 30, 1995
To: The S.G.D. Executive Board
From: The Insane C-Note$ Family

We the leadership of Thee Insane C-Note$ Family would like to open up this letter with respect to show forth a true commitment to the ideology and concept of the S.G.D. Union. We clearly understand that at the present time our family is not a registered family, yet we currently have strong ties and open lines of communication with various families that are registered and in good standings.

The intentions of this letter is to inform all member of this Union that the Insane C-Note$ Family have applied for registration into the Folks Alliance which is governed by the S.G.D. Concept. For this to happen as you know the voting process must be implemented and your vote on this issue is required. A vote of "YES" would be in favor of this family be granted registration; a vote of "NO" would be against this family being registered. You may "Refrain" from voting if you do not wish to take part in the process of this decision. You are however, required to submit a response on this matter, for the purpose of everyone being assured that your family has been notified of the decision process taking place and for the purpose of insuring that you, the representatives of your family, have submitted your decision and that one family will not (Can Not) speak for another family.

We would like to bring to everyone's attention of where we stand in society. Our membership is currently made up of mixed ethnic cultures. In our present time our enemy is every registered family's common enemy. Those who choose to oppress us from attaining the fruits of the land and those who attempt to dictate and mislead. We have our goals and objectives which are all positive and similar to some of the current registered families. These are all available upon request.

In the past we've had conflicts with some families that deem themselves to be Folks. Those conflicts have either been resolved or are in the process of being resolved. Our intentions and commitments to this Union is serious. We simply like to state that we will continue to build our ties and communications with those who have accepted us and will continue to be readily available in the struggle against those who oppose the common goals and objectives of this Union. For we truly believe that our family has much to offer this Union. We fully understand and are ready to comply with the policies and concepts which govern all families deemed to be Folks. We eagerly await the results of this vote.

In conclusion, we say to you that as leaders we are all responsible for the success of this union as a whole. If accepted we will work together to insure fairness and equality among all families of this Union. Together we can assist in making all the right decisions for all the right reasons at every level of this Union. Your decision on this matter is due no later than November 30, 1995. You may contact in writing your vote to the selected officials. Failure to register your vote by this date will result in your having excluded yourself from voting on the issue of the I-C-N-$ registration.

In closing, we bid you all love, honor and respect from the C-Note$ Family.

APPENDIX 9: LEYES OF THE SGD UNION

LEYES

1. All personnel of the union must respect and participate in maintaining a Code of Silence within the Union. Those going beyond the limits of this code will be subjected to the consequences.

2. All personnel of the union must respect one another and at no time conduct themselves in a disrespectful manner. Respect the moral feelings of all of our family members, Moms, Pops, sisters, & brothers etc. . . . At no time will any personnel dishonor the women of our Union.

3. All personnel of the union in transgression will experience and undergo the same penalty imposed upon any personnel who breaks or goes beyond the limits of our constitutional leyes.

4. All personnel of this Union must acknowledge the authoritative commands handed down to them by their superiors. Insubordination will not be tolerated.

5. There is to be no changing from faction to faction. Any personnel who wishes to leave his original faction has to be released by his superior. Any personnel released from his faction in good standings will remain as an SGD until he regains his freedom. Then it is optional for the personnel as to what faction he wants to register with.

6. Any personnel of this Union with allegations to his membership in question will undergo a screening investigation and the outcome will be determined by his superior. Therefore, anyone found making false accusations without legal documentation containing evidence of a participant shown to be a witness, informant, or collaborator toward another person, will be held accountable.

7. Upon release, no personnel of this Union will retaliate against any personnel of this Union who has participated in any actions taken while within any institution.

8. Eradication of a member that is in a particular faction rest soely upon the superior of said faction.

9. All disputes or arguments among our personnel must be taken through the proper chain of command in place before any action is taken. Anyone acting on their own accord will be subjected to discipline.

10. Any personnel of this Union caught creating dissention or treasonary acts will be expelled from the Union.

11. At no time shall we disrespect any person of another Union. All grudged within you about a non-personnel of this Union will be put aside until your return to the streets. Meaningless struggles will only prolong your stay.

12. All personnel are to acknowledge and respect our allied B-D and B.G.D. Unions and will aid them in any difficulty be it mentally or physically. Yet, we are an independent Union with superior of own to adhere to.

13. At no time will any personnel of this Union use or encourage the use and consumption of addictive drugs such as: T's and Blues, Herion, Valiums, Crack, or the act of free-basing. This Union will not tolerate any personnel indulging in such acts.

14. Any personnel who habitually uses any hallucinogenic drugs intoxicants, or mind altering substances causing incidents that are detrimental and jeopardize the Union or himself, will be restricted from such use for a minimum of 6 months, and a maximum time period of one year or longer in order to control such acts, addictions, or abuse.

15. Personnel of the Union are not permitted to rape or take part in a conspiracy to commit rape, nor will the personnel of this Union indulge in any kinds of homosexual activities.

16. Personnel of the Union are not allowed to play with any officers. They are off limits unless they are beneficial to the individual or to the Union. Meaningless arguments are not beneficial or consistent with our leyes.

17. Stealing from another individual or from another organization will not be tolerated within the Union. Lying will not be tolerated within the Union or among the personnel.

18. Within every institution there will exist a bank system for the personnel. Those who are able are required to contribute to help others of the Union who are not as fortunate.

19. There is no excuse for the ignorance or our set leyes. All personnel of the union must take the initiative to perceive and understand the full

meaning of our Union leyes and are required to apply themselves to our leyes and to the entire SGD concept. This does not imply the abandonment of your original faction.

20. Upon the suspension of an Ex. Director from the Ex. Board—for reasons of sanction—The suspended Ex. Director wills still have his title or position within his original faction. By honoring the Ex. Board and its decision of sanction, the suspended Director will not stagnate the SGD Union and the suspended Director's faction will adhere to and abide by the laws and policies prescribed in the Union's Constitution.

21. When the Ex. Chairman sets forth a directive of which an Ex Director deems the directive to be prejudicial toward the Ex. Director and his faction, the Ex. Director can appeal the directive by making available a memorandum to show purpose of veto and thus allowing the entire Ex. Board a vote.

22. Anyone who backs up or withdraws terminating his membership in this Union shall be considered to be a non-affiliate. Furthermore, association with these particular types of individuals will not exist unless otherwise sanctioned by the Ex. Board.

23. Any personnel who has served in this Union with Years (Minimum of 10) of love, dedication, and loyalty, and that for legitimate reasons seeks status as Retiree of this Union, shall be entitled to this sanction only with the sole approval of the Ex. Board. Retiree status will only be considered once a year.

24. The Ex Board will maintain total jurisdiction over a personnel of this Union when he is in violation of the following acts

A) When an individual is positively known to be an informant;

B) When an individual is positively known to be a homosexual;

C) When an individual commits an assault upon another personnel of this Union;

D) When a personnel of the Union is positively known to have lived or been there, under protective means;

E) When a personnel of this Union abandons or is positively known to of abandoned another personnel of this Union in a situation where potential bodily harm has inflicted to a personnel of this Union.

25. The Ex. Coordinators maintain Veto powers over the Ex. Board. However, each Ex. Coordinator must be in conjunction with one another for Veto to stand affirmed. In the event of a disagreement between the Ex. Coordinator, the Veto power becomes void immediately.

26. Personnel of the Union who have held the position of a Coordinator and/or Asst. Coordinator throughout the other inter-locations will be acknowledged and recognized by the overall Union as being a Hierarchy in this Union. Individuals in this category will have access to both the Executive Board and to the Central Committee or said committee in place at a particular inter-location.

27. A sanction of exemption and/or participation of various activities within any inter-location may be granted by the Ex. Board to any Ex. Director requesting same for authoritative personnel of the Director's faction.

28. All personnel of the Union will ordain and abide by the set concept or our Constitution.

INDEX

The letter *f*, *t*, or *d* following a page number denotes a figure, table, or document, respectively.

Weick, Karl, 241n11
Weis, Joey, 244n4
white ethnic immigration, 139, 238n16
white gangs, 40, 42–47, 49–50, 52–53, 62–63, 81, 237n11, 238n16
white greaser street gangs, 110–11
White House. *See* Stateville penitentiary
white power, 40
white supremacy, 237n15
Williams, Lance, 236n6
will to power, 18, 33, 123, 225
Wilson, Ben, 61, 241n8
Wilson, William Julius, 6, 228
wire, 114, 145, 158, 194, 198, 247n11
Wire, The, 11–12
women, roles in gangs, 93, 261n2
Woodall, Jon, 255n26
work, legitimate, 94, 102
World Bank, 250n1

X. *See* ecstasy
X-men, 174–75
XTC (club), 176

YMCA, 61, 205–7
Yonkers, John Dollar Bill, 112
Young Latin Organization (YLO, YLO-Ds), 49, 63, 234n1, 265
Young Lords Organization, 32, 45–47, 49, 109, 265
Young Notes, 97–98, 106, 182
youth, and gangs, 4, 8, 116, 226

Zayas, Fernie (Prince Fernie), 22, 50–51, 62, 116–20, 200–202, 204, 213, 219, 234n4, 266
Zero Gravity (club), 176
Zonis, Pierre, 145, 252n13
Zucker, Lynne, 193, 218, 259n6